Surveying for Archaeologists and Other Fieldworkers

CROOM HELM STUDIES IN ARCHAEOLOGY
General Editor: Leslie Alcock, University of Glasgow

CELTIC CRAFTSMANSHIP IN BRONZE
H. E. Kilbride-Jones

EARLY MAN IN BRITAIN AND IRELAND
Alex Morrison

SURVEYING FOR ARCHAEOLOGISTS AND OTHER FIELDWORKERS

A. H. A. Hogg

"There is a marvel in the region which is called Ercing. There is in that place a sepulchre . . . And men come to measure the tumulus. In length it has sometimes seven feet, sometimes fifteen, sometimes twelve, sometimes nine. In whatsoever measure you measure it once, you will not find the same measurement a second time; and I have tested it myself." — from *The Marvels of Britain*, attributed to Nennius (ninth century)

Croom Helm London

© 1980 A. H. A. Hogg
Croom Helm Ltd, 2-10 St John's Road, London SW11

British Library Cataloguing in Publication Data

Hogg, Alexander Hubert Arthur
    Surveying for archaeologists and other
    fieldworkers.
    1. Archaeological surveying
    I. Title
    526.9'02'493   CC76.3

    ISBN 0-85664-767-5 ✓
    ISBN 0-7099-0185-2 Pbk

To my former colleagues of RCAM Wales

Printed and bound in Great Britain
Redwood Burn Limited
Trowbridge & Esher

Contents

Part I: Introduction

1. General Discussion 5

2. The Basic Principles 13

Part II: Chain Surveying

3. Equipment 21

4. The Elements of Chain Survey 27

Tables

Figures

General Editor's Introduction

The original intention of the Croom Helm Studies in Archaeology was to provide a comprehensive survey of the archaeology of Britain and Ireland, at a level that would be of use and interest both to university students and to informed laymen. A series of period studies was therefore commissioned, and the first volumes are now well advanced.

It was soon realised, however, that there are a number of topics, of equal interest and importance to archaeologists working in these islands, which transcend the conventional period boundaries. These might include ancient technology, archaeological techniques, and the ancillary sciences. As opportunity arises, therefore, the period series will be supplemented by other studies.

I am glad to welcome A. H. A. Hogg's *Surveying for Archaeologists* as the first of these supplementary volumes. As the author rightly stresses, the making of plans to an appropriate level of accuracy is the central discipline of field archaeology. But it is a discipline which is often sadly neglected by practising field workers, and no wholly satisfactory manual of survey principles and practice has previously appeared.

No one could be better fitted than Dr Hogg to write such a manual. He brought the skills of a trained civil engineer, as well as the enthusiasm of an archaeological amateur, to the post of Secretary of the Royal Commission on Ancient Monuments in Wales. The fruits of the practices set out in this book are to be seen in the Commission's three *Inventory* volumes for Caernarvonshire, and in the first volume for Glamorgan.

What Dr Hogg preaches here, on the basis of a quarter of a century of practice, is not free from controversy. Some experienced field workers may consider, for instance, that he undervalues the plane table. But they will find that he always presents a reasoned case for his preferred methods, as well as a sufficient account of the techniques of which he disapproves.

Above all, Dr Hogg gives fully worked-out and illustrated examples of the widest possible range of techniques, from the simplest sketch-plan to surveys demanding costly equipment and mathematical calculations. It would be difficult to find a problem in field surveying for which his book does not furnish a solution.

Leslie Alcock

Preface

The study of Archaeology is addictive, but many of those affected cannot hope to get a paid appointment in the subject of their choice. After twenty years as a professional civil engineer and an amateur archaeologist, I had the good fortune to obtain such a post.

Part of my earlier work had involved surveying, either practically or as a lecturer, and it had always seemed to me self-evident that an *accurate* plan was an essential part of any definitive description of a field monument. I was therefore rather shocked to discover that many professional archaeologists had a less than rudimentary understanding of the basic principles of surveying; but my new colleagues proved anxious, and fully competent, to learn the necessary and essentially simple techniques.

The object of this book is to enable any archaeologist, whether amateur or professional, to attain any desired degree of competence so far as necessary for his work, without any instruction beyond that given here. Obviously practical tuition is desirable, but it cannot always be obtained. To attain this object I have had to give verbal descriptions of techniques which can be demonstrated far better and more quickly in the field (for example, Para. 7.3), and to include much material which is essential for reference in case of need but which many archaeologists may never require, such as Part V on numerical work.

You may consider that I have placed excessive emphasis on accuracy. There are several reasons for this. First, that the moderate degree of accuracy aimed at here does not add in any way to the work involved. Second, that errors may accumulate, so that a collection of careless measurements, each only slightly wrong, can build up to cause an appreciable distortion of the final plan.

1

And third, that even if for some reason you decide that rough work is acceptable you ought to understand what its effects will be.

No attempt has been made to cover the whole field of surveying. Precise geodetic work is not discussed, and at the other extreme important practical matters such as curve ranging are omitted, for they are not relevant to archaeology. Nevertheless, surveyors concerned with other disciplines may well find much that is useful in this work.

Part I
INTRODUCTION

1 General Discussion

1.1 *Surveying and Archaeology.* Field Archaeology and Excavation are the foundations upon which the whole structure of archaeological knowledge is built, and of the various techniques which make up these methods of investigation surveying is probably the most important. The need for *accurate* plans is surely self-evident, whether to accompany an excavation report or as part of the definitive description of any field monument.

Nevertheless, of these techniques surveying is also the most neglected. There is an illusion that it is difficult, and as a result works which are otherwise excellent describe idiosyncratic methods which are both unduly laborious and potentially inaccurate; the difficulties which these methods try to avoid are mostly imaginary. In fact, many thousands of field monuments can be surveyed accurately without using any more abstruse mathematical knowledge than the recognition of a triangle combined with the ability to make and record measurements correctly and systematically. This latter requirement is not as easy as it sounds, but anyone who is really incapable of fulfilling it, and not merely too lazy to do so, should be diverted to some other field of research; for if he (or she) *cannot* observe and record accurately, how can any of his results be trusted, especially in far more difficult problems such as disentangling complex stratification?

One point of view, which arises out of this neglect of surveying, must be most strongly condemned. Some archaeologists consider that the preparation of plans can be safely entrusted to technicians with no archaeological knowledge; the 'experts' will then sketch in archaeological detail which the technicians have missed, and will interpret the results. My own experience, supported by that of others, leaves no doubt at all that for even a moderately complex structure actual participation in the detailed work of measurement

5

is essential if the full harvest of potential information is to be gathered.

1.2 *The Purpose of the Book.* Like most techniques, surveying is best learnt by a prolonged practical apprenticeship, but few practising field archaeologists can spare the time to give the necessary instruction, and moreover they have all too often been wrongly taught themselves. Even in those University Departments which do arrange for instruction in surveying, the course is usually provided by lecturers from some other department, and though extremely valuable it is not directed primarily towards archaeology, and seldom discusses the difficulties which are likely to arise in the field.

In writing this book my aim has been to describe all surveying techniques likely to be needed by any archaeologist working on land, and to explain them in such detail that anyone can apply them competently, even if no experienced adviser is available. I have paid particular regard to the needs of the full-time archaeologist, but I have also kept in mind my own difficulties as a beginner, strongly addicted to field archaeology as a part-time activity but handicapped by the lack of advice on recording. The last chapter (28) is dedicated to those who find themselves similarly placed.

I have taken as the upper limit of sophistication the type of equipment which might reasonably be hoped for in an adequately equipped School of Archaeology, or at least might be lent without too great reluctance by another Department: that is, a dumpy level and a theodolite capable of reading to one minute of arc. These are amply accurate enough for the sort of work envisaged and more precise instruments, besides being more expensive, can in some circumstances actually add to the surveyor's difficulties.

The only important restraint imposed by this limitation is that reliable astronomical observations are not possible.

1.3 *The Functions of Surveying.* In an archaeological context, the functions of surveying can best be defined in relation to an ideal scheme of research; 'ideal' is here used in its primary sense; the scheme, though strictly logical, would require several lifetimes to complete, apart from various other objections. Nevertheless, it provides a useful background against which to organise one's ideas. For convenience, to avoid abstractions, the scheme will be outlined in relation to 'hill-forts', but with slight modifications it is applicable to any type of structure.

Logically then, the first step is the recognition of a distinct class of defended enclosure. These enclosures need to be placed in their topographical context by locating them on the map. One aspect of surveying, therefore, is the accurate location of sites.

The individual members of the general class of hill-forts will be found to differ from each other in many details. Clearly some form of typological analysis is desirable, so an accurate objective plan and description of each hill-fort is needed. The distribution-map will assist typological classification by allowing the separation of the 3,000 or so hill-forts of Britain into groups of manageable size. This problem, of typological classification, is discussed further below.

Finally, so far as this particular class of structure is concerned, excavation of apparently representative types should provide material which may or may not support the supposed typology and which may relate the type to other structures and place it in its correct chronological context. Surveying is necessary to provide an accurate description of the site and of any features revealed during the excavation, and to assist in analysing and recording the stratification.

In practice, all those stages of investigation are in progress at the same time and generally without relation to each other. On an excavation, accurate surveying is of primary importance, more so than the correct identification of the objects found; for the latter will normally be preserved for future study, whereas structural features are inevitably destroyed. Nevertheless, it is probably by the detailed recording of surface features that surveying can make its most valuable contribution.

The study of hill-forts can again be taken as an example. Until the last decade or so, with a few honourable exceptions, archaeologists could attain far-reaching conclusions from the examination of a brooch or of the decoration on a potsherd but regarded hill-forts as a single type, whether they enclosed 0·5 or 50 ha and whatever the details of their plan (hut groups were approached with similar insensitivity). Yet hill-forts are just as much artifacts as potsherds, and even though some may have taken a millennium to reach their present form they should, at least in principle, be equally open to typological analysis. Since adequate excavation of a hill-fort may take up to a decade, only a few of our 3,000 or so examples can be examined, and the information so obtained can only be extended to other sites on the evidence of their typology. Similar reasoning applies to most types of field monument.

Most archaeologists who have tried, with some success, to classify such remains have been compelled to rely on subjective criteria, but recently attempts have been made to develop objective methods; the chief problem seems to be that the techniques used have been designed for items which may have fifty or more recognisable and distinct characteristics, whereas few field monuments have as many as ten. It would be inappropriate to discuss methods of classification in detail, but the subject has been mentioned in order to emphasise the need for reliable plans, from which the characteristics can be determined with certainty.

1.4 *The Arrangement of the Book.* Advice as to how to use this book is given in the next section, but some account of the principles governing its arrangement may be helpful. It is divided into several parts, the first two being mostly essential information for anyone intending to make a survey; the remainder are for reference if needed.

Part I forms an introduction. The current chapter (1) explains the general scheme of the work, and Chapter 2 deals with basic principles which are common to almost all aspects of surveying.

Part II covers chain surveying. It is, appropriately, the longest part, for this is the method of choice for practically all archaeological survey work. More than nine sites out of ten require no additional apparatus, and even on those where the survey network can be more easily fixed by a theodolite or other instrument chaining still remains the best and simplest way of measuring detail in almost every case.

The technique is of great antiquity. Something very similar is shown in Egyptian tomb-paintings, and it had been fully developed in Britain by the seventeenth century, primarily for the survey of estates, which requires accuracy similar to that needed for archaeological plans. As a result of this long evolution, the equipment needed has been reduced to a fairly compact and standardised form, while probable difficulties and sources of mistakes have been recognised and ways found to overcome them. As indicated earlier, the belief that the technique is 'difficult' is mistaken, and attempts to evade the imagined difficulties are misdirected.

Chapter 3, the first of this section, describes the equipment needed, Chapter 4 explains the elementary principles on which the technique is based, and Chapter 5 shows how these principles would apply in practice by a detailed account of a simple (imaginary) survey. Chapter 6 deals with plotting the survey and preparing the plan for publication.

So far, the discussion has assumed, for simplicity, that no problems arise, and no mistakes are likely to be made. Chapter 7 gives fairly simple ways of overcoming the defects of the real world, so far as they affect surveying. It also describes how to set out a rectangle when a chain only is available, and explains the modifications of technique necessary when dealing with buildings. The title of Chapter 8 is self-explanatory.

Part III (Chapters 9, 10 and 11) discusses the use of the level, which is the most commonly available instrument, and Part IV (Chapters 12 to 15) treats similarly of the theodolite or tacheometer.

Part V (Chapters 16 to 20) describes methods of numerical calculation. Some readers will turn away from this in horror. They will not find themselves intolerably handicapped if they do, for as indicated earlier most sites can be surveyed using nothing more than the simplest and most elementary geometry. Nevertheless, they will find it worth while to try to overcome their distaste, for just as a theodolite is sometimes useful, so occasionally a calculation will greatly simplify a difficult piece of surveying, and improve its accuracy. To understand a numerical method it is essential to work through a representative example, and the resulting blocks of arithmetic are admittedly heavy and repulsive; but anyone who is capable of looking up a number in a telephone directory and dialling the result will find himself numerate enough to work through them. Perhaps at this point an apology should be offered to those other readers who may feel insulted at being given an explicit definition of a cosine or of a 3–4–5 triangle; but it is hoped that they will understand the reasons for so doing.

In Part V, therefore, I have included an example of what I believe to be the simplest method of solving any problem likely to arise in archaeological surveying. Problems are mostly solved by the laborious use of logarithms, for that approach is necessary in order to understand what is being done; but since electronic hand-calculators are now widely available and save an enormous amount of work duplicate methods of solution using these are also given.

Among the Miscellaneous Techniques (Part VI), Chapter 21 describes various methods, none requiring a computer, for plotting from oblique aerial photographs. Chapter 22 deals with other uses of photography, including the use (but not the preparation) of photogrammetric surveys, and a simple emergency method of following a feature such as a ditch exposed in the face of a working quarry. Chapter 23, included reluctantly for reasons there given, deals with the plane-table. Chapter 24, alone among the contents of this book, is derivative, for I have had the good fortune never to have been involved in underground surveying. Nevertheless, I think that I have gleaned from various sources enough useful items to justify its inclusion. That would not be true about underwater surveying, which is why I have excluded it.

Much fieldwork is only concerned with locating a site on a map. On occasion, also, circumstances may prevent preparation of anything more than a sketch plan. In Part VII, Chapters 25 and 26 are relevant to this type of work. They have been left to the end of the book because the work involved is usually rather rough and accuracy should be sacrificed only if you know what you are doing. The contents of Chapters 27 and 28 have all been covered earlier, but are recapitulated here for convenience, with the relevant cross-references. Chapter 27 deals with excavation, which for many archaeologists is the main application they are likely to make of survey techniques. Chapter 28 is intended for those who are deeply interested in archaeology and who would like to make their own contribution to the subject but whose available time is restricted.

Finally, there are four appendices. The first concerns the use of units. Throughout this book, I have used metric linear measurements and the Babylonian system of degrees, minutes and seconds for angles, not because I like them but because they are now official. Nevertheless, the accuracy of a survey does not depend on the units used, and you may find that you have or wish to use equipment differently graduated.

Appendix I therefore lists other common systems of measurement. Appendix II lists the approximate (1978) prices of items of equipment, arranged by chapters, with the names of some suppliers. Appendix III assembles the data used in the numerical examples in Part V, and Appendix IV contains short tables of some useful quantities.

1.5 *How to Use the Book.* My object has been to give all the information needed even if you cannot get other instruction, but obviously if you can manage to do so you should attend a course in surveying and especially get some practice in using the equipment, working with an experienced surveyor. At the same time though, you should work through the relevant sections of this book, for most courses of instruction are not directed primarily towards archaeological fieldwork, and a really experienced man may well rashly take the risk of scamping precautions which you, as a beginner, should follow slavishly.

If you are trying to learn surveying by yourself, without any experienced guide, the best procedure will be to choose a fairly small and easily accessible site for which a published plan exists. Then, without further reference to that published plan, survey the site yourself, and draw out your own draft plan quite independently. After you have done that, compare your draft in detail with the published plan, measuring identifiable distances. If the two plans agree, you can reasonably feel confident that your technique is fairly reliable. What, though, if they do not agree? You are not necessarily the one who is wrong, so select one or two easily identifiable and appreciably different measurements, preferably *not* actually part of your network and check them in the field; and if you find that you are at fault, try to work out what went wrong.

I have been concerned throughout with the needs of a fieldworker. If though, your primary objective is to pass an examination, you will probably find some of the material unnecessary, as for example Chapter 7; you should check your requirements by a study of papers set in the past.

For actual fieldwork, Parts I and II are essential reading. The others are for reference, depending on the work which you are undertaking. If you wish to supplement and extend your knowledge by additional reading, there are many text books of varying quality. Those originally written by David Clark, and by R. E. Middleton and O. Chadwick, have passed through several editions, any of which would be of value; but all contain much more material than is necessary for archaeological work. Similarly, the *Manual of Topographical Surveying* (HMSO, latest edition 1965, anonymous; earlier editions by Sir Charles Close) is concerned with the type of accuracy needed for national maps; but it includes incidentally comments and other material of interest to a field archaeologist.

1.6 *Sources.* This book is based for the most part on surveying practice that has been current for a century or more, which I have slightly modified where appropriate as a result of experience in the field. A few items are original, and others have been assimilated from colleagues and from reading during half a century, mostly more than 25 years ago. I have therefore included no formal references, but occasionally the source is indicated in parenthesis. Should anyone feel that I have used their work without giving due credit, I offer my apologies for this oversight.

2 The Basic Principles

2.1 Accuracy; 2.2 Choice of Network; 2.3 Booking; 2.4 General Remarks.

2.1 *Accuracy.* There is one essential difference between a trained and an untrained surveyor. The former recognises that all measurements inevitably contain errors, and plans his survey so that these tend, so far as possible, to cancel out, not to accumulate. The sort of overall accuracy which may be expected using the methods described in this book is generally about one part in five hundred or a thousand, perhaps rising to one part in two thousand if special care is taken. Having regard to the nature of archaeological sites, this degree of accuracy is acceptable. Greater precision requires a quite disproportionately greater amount of work.

In this context, it is useful to have some idea of the sort of precision obtainable by different methods of measurement, assuming even ground, good visibility, and little wind. These are tabulated below; the figures are of course only rough indications, and are very dependent on circumstances.

Linear Measurements:

Steel band, in catenary	1 in 10,000
Steel band, on specially prepared ground	1 in 2,500
Chaining	1 in 800
'Linen' tape	1 in 200
Tacheometry (rapidly diminished by bad conditions, and limited to about 150 m)	1 in 100
Pacing between known points	1 in 50
Pacing only	1 in 20

Angular Measurement:

Theodolite (simple type, reading to one minute)	02' = 1 in 1,700 approx.
Prismatic Compass	1° = 1 in 60 approx.

In a survey which aims at accuracy, therefore, the prismatic compass is only useful for fixing the approximate north point, though it can provide a check on possible mistakes.

The point has been made that the trained surveyor recognises that 'errors' will occur in his measurements, but he also recognises that he will sometimes make 'mistakes'. It is useful to distinguish between these two types of inaccuracy. An 'error' is small and unavoidable; for example two measurements of the same length might differ by 0·03 m, or of the same angle by half a minute. A 'mistake', on the other hand, is an actual misreading; perhaps of 9 m on a chain instead of 11 m, or of 1° in an angle.

2.2 *Choice of Network.* Surveying a site falls into two main parts. The first is to establish a network of lines covering the whole area. Detail is then recorded by measurement from those lines, or sometimes from the stations at which they meet. This section is concerned with the arrangement of the network. The traverse, which is an alternative way of fixing a system of lines, is described in Chapter 19.

The network must obviously be 'rigid', that is, the measurements which are taken must fix the shape of the network exactly and unambiguously. The simplest arrangement of this kind is the triangle, the shape of which is (theoretically) determined exactly by measuring all three sides, two sides and the included angle, or one side and two angles. Most accurate surveys, therefore, are based on networks built up of triangles.

At first glance, it would seem that nothing more is needed than to add one triangle to another until the whole site is covered; but in practice some precautions have to be observed, for unfortunately all measurements contain errors, even if mistakes are avoided. Single triangles should be 'well-conditioned', that is, their angles should not be very different from 60°. The effect of using an ill-conditioned triangle is shown, exaggerated, in Figure 2.1. The radii of the arcs drawn from two known points are supposed to differ from the correct distances by errors e; the diagram shows how the displacement of the point of intersection from the correct point becomes appreciably greater than e for triangles of this shape. An ill-conditioned triangle is never desirable, but may sometimes be tolerated if you are measuring angles as well as distances.

The cumulative effect of errors in a network of triangles can be envisaged if you imagine it to be built up of Meccano-like strips,

2.1 Ill-conditioned Triangles

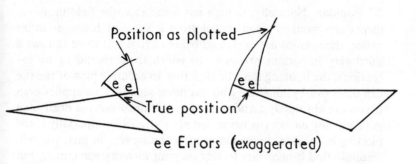

Position as plotted

True position

e e Errors (exaggerated)

with a little slackness at every joint, corresponding to the error. You will appreciate that the relative movement of two widely separated points in the network is likely to be much greater than the movement at each separate joint, and that it will also increase as the number of intermediate joints increases. Your object, therefore, should be to enclose the site with a large rigid network comprising relatively few triangles, which is then subdivided as necessary. In brief, you work from large to small. The detailed arrangement will depend on the nature of the site, but will usually consist of several triangles forming a polygon, or of two, three, or more polygons interlocking (see Chapters 4, 5 and 20).

As a basic principle in designing a network, the inevitable presence of errors must always be allowed for; but the near certainty of an occasional mistake must also be kept in mind. Some apparently unnecessary lines should always be included, so that except in the rare event of two mistakes balancing each other the network becomes geometrically impossible to draw unless all the lengths have been correctly recorded. The errors may introduce *small* discrepancies in the drawing, but these will normally be evened out by eye. Thus a quadrilateral can be drawn, though incorrectly, if the four sides and one diagonal have been measured, even if one measurement is wrong; but if the other diagonal is also recorded the presence of a mistake will become obvious as soon as you try to draw the outline.

If a mistake is present, you will have to check measurements on the site. For that reason, a small-scale plot of all measured lines, without detail, should if possible be made before leaving the district. The location of the mistake will be simplified if magnetic bearings have been taken along all measured lines.

2.3 *Booking.* Normally, though not invariably, the field measurements are 'booked', and the plotting is done at home or in an office; the reasons are explained below. From this there follows a third very important principle, to which there should be no exceptions: the booking must be such that an accurate plan of the site can be drawn by someone who has never seen it. This applies even if you are absolutely certain that you will draw out the draft plan yourself, for memory is never completely reliable, especially if the plotting is not done immediately after the survey. In fact, you will certainly find it necessary to rely on your memory sometimes, but whenever you do you should mentally count a small black mark against your technical competence.

One of the main indications of the poor standards of much archaeological field survey is the widely held belief that before a plan is accepted as finished it must be 'taken out into the field for checking'. If your field notes are such that this so-called 'checking' really seems necessary, your technique is very defective indeed, and the final plan cannot be accepted as fully reliable. It is surely self-evident that detailed point by point measurements of visible features will give a more reliable plan than if the same features are sketched in by eye; but this does not preclude sketching natural detail which is not structurally significant, where this will give a better impression of the nature of the ground.

A less obvious danger is that the archaeologist 'checking' the plan will 'correct' it to fit his preconceived, and possibly mistaken, interpretation of the site. This is not a hypothetical risk; I have come across at least half a dozen examples, but it would probably be libellous and certainly unkind to specify them.

This is not to say that all subjective interpretation must be rigidly excluded from your field notes. The first aim should be always to make a record which is so far as possible completely objective, but subjective comment can be included in your notes, and even added to the finished plan. For example, it would be perfectly legitimate to mark two overlapping ramparts 'Period I?' and 'Period II?'; but archaeologically it would be a mortal sin to disregard your field measurements and 'correct' your plan to make this interpretation look more probable.

2.4 *General Remarks.* As noted earlier, measurements and other details are normally booked in the field as more or less rough notes, and the final plan is plotted in the office (which does not exclude work at home). The main reasons for this are economy and convenience. The time available for work out of doors is limited; to make a survey after dark is difficult, and over much of Britain bracken or other vegetation inhibits fieldwork from June to November. Moreover, even an unpaid amateur will probably have extra expenses when in the field, while a professional's work will be costing his employer some subsistence payments. Whenever possible, therefore, work should be done in the office merely for reasons of economy. Further, conditions out of doors are seldom ideal for accurate drawing, especially if the plan is large.

Apart from these considerations, it does not matter whether a plan is drawn out in the field or office. On an excavation, the needs of the work almost always compel the surveyor to plot in the field, despite the accompanying inconveniences; for there is usually a lot of close-set detail which could not easily be booked by conventional methods, and which often has to be recorded as quickly as possible so that further levels can be uncovered.

One further point needs to be emphasised. The suggestion is sometimes made that a learner gains by seeing the plan develop in front of him as he works on the site. This is a mistaken approach. If a student learns to work in this way he will probably be completely at a loss when weather conditions are unsuitable, or when he has to deal with a large site, where the framework has to be 'balanced' (that is, the errors have to be distributed fairly evenly) before plotting can start.

One other general rule remains to be noted. Calculations, however simple, are more likely to be done incorrectly in the field than in the office. The actual observations, therefore, should always be booked. Examples appear in Paras. 5.6 and 13.2.

Finally, mention should be made of the 'rituals' which form part of surveying technique, such as the repetition of a reading which has been given to you. At first, some of these seem meaningless, but they are all directed towards reducing the risk of mistakes. They should therefore be performed with special care whenever fatigue and foul weather tempt you to scamp them, for it is under those conditions that mistakes are most likely to occur.

Part II
Chain Surveying

Part II
Chain Surveying

3 Equipment

3.1 *Basic Requirements*. Chain surveying is a technique of considerable age (see Para. 1.4). It is the most useful method of recording detail, even when the main network has been established in some other way; and for the majority of sites a straightforward chain survey is all that is needed. The principle is very simple. A network of interlocking triangles is marked out by 'ranging-rods' or 'poles' at their vertices ('stations') and the sides ('chain-lines') are measured; details are fixed by measurement from these chain-lines.

The equipment is equally simple. It comprises poles, the chain, 'arrows' used as temporary markers during measurement, and a tape for measuring distances from the chain. These are the essentials. A means of measuring the slope of chain lines and one for fixing the north point are very desirable. On a survey which will last more than one day you will need pegs (which are expendable), a hammer to drive them in and preferably a saw to make them. 'Wands', also expendable, are sometimes useful. Material for pegs and wands can almost always be found near the site.

You will also need a field book ('chain book' Para. 4.6), an 'HB' or 'H' pencil and probably a good eraser.

3.2 *Detailed list* (Figure 3.1.) The *chain* is of steel, with main links nearly 0·2 m long, joined by two or three smaller links. The reason for using this, rather than a tape, is that it will lie in position and thus forms in effect a graduated ruled line on the ground, from which measurements can be made; save under quite exceptionally favourable conditions a tape will blow about.

A 20 m chain is to be preferred. Do not get a 30 m one, under the impression that because you will not have to move it so often you will save work. It is very inconvenient indeed to fold up and to handle when folded, and measurements can easily be misread.

3.1 Equipment for Chain Survey

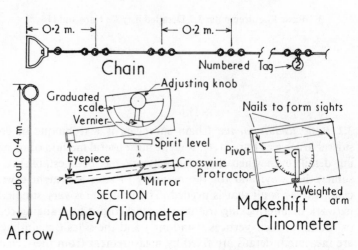

A linen or plastic *tape* (in case) 20 m or 30 m long; in this case, 30 m is preferable.

'*Arrows*' in a set of five or ten. These are narrow steel rods, 30 to 40 cm long pointed at one end and formed into a loop at the other. They should each be fitted with a tag of broad bright-coloured tape, preferably four red and one yellow or five of each. You will almost certainly have to buy a set of ten, but five is enough for most fieldwork. Since they are easily lost, keep the other five in reserve; and they may often be useful as anchorages for chain or tape.

Six (at least) 2 m *poles* or *ranging-rods*. These may be of wood or metal. They have a steel-shod point at one end, and are painted alternately red and white (or sometimes red, black and white) in 0·5 m or 0·2 m lengths. The latter are preferable; they are more clearly visible at a distance, and can be used for measurement.

By far the most useful type of pole, very well worth the extra expense, is the sectional type, of metre lengths with screwed ends. They are very much easier to carry (in a suitable shoulder-bag) than the full 2 metres (which are often too long to fit in a car), and can be screwed together to build up longer poles, which are often invaluable.

A set of six poles is the minimum requirement, but if you have only that number you will often be inconvenienced, so if at all possible get a dozen or more.

Simple ranging-rods and arrows could be made at home, but in general the saving by using 'home-made' equipment is so small, in proportion to the total cost, that the work involved is not worth while, especially since the result is seldom very satisfactory.

In addition to the above essentials, it is an advantage to have:

A Prismatic Compass (for description see Para. 25.5). In chain surveying, this is only needed to get the approximate north point; but it is almost indispensable for rough reconnaissance fieldwork.

An Abney Clinometer (or substitute) (Figure 3.1). This is essentially a sighting-tube (not usually telescopic) pivoted to a protractor with a spirit-level. A small opening with a mirror at 45° halfway along the tube allows the bubble to be observed at the same time as the line of sight, so that the spirit-level can be brought horizontal, and thus the slope of the line of sight measured. In chain surveying it is useful for correcting the measured length of a line to allow for slope; but rougher methods (Para. 4.5) may be adequate. It is also useful for measuring profiles of earthworks, if a level is not available (Para. 26.8).

If you intend to use the clinometer for slope-corrections *and for no other purpose*, an inexpensive makeshift can be good enough (Figure 3.1). In its crudest form two nails driven into a roughly shaped board form the line of sight. A school 180° protractor is then fixed to the board with its base parallel to the line joining the nails (this order of work is easier than trying to get the nails on the sight line after fixing the protractor). A weighted arm, recessed as shown, is pivoted at the centre of the protractor. In use, the nails are sighted along the correct slope and the arm is gripped in position with the thumb. Two or three readings should be averaged. With care, this device could also be used to measure a profile provided no great accuracy is required.

Pegs can almost always be made on or near the site, by sawing through a 3 to 5 cm diameter branch and pointing one end. The length required depends on the nature of the ground; 10 to 20 cm is usually adequate. It is hardly ever necessary or even desirable to get commercially cut pegs of squared timber. Invariably, though, the pegs should be sawn, not broken. A sawn end can always be recognised as artificial, whereas a broken end can easily be mistaken for a natural object.

Wands are merely straight twigs, used as temporary marks and treated as expendable. They can be made more recognisable by peeling off the bark. Given an adequate supply of poles, they are not often needed on ordinary chain survey.

3.3 *Care and Use.* For most of the equipment, the main hazard is loss rather than damage. Sectional poles should have their joints kept lightly oiled, and should not be left screwed together for a long time as they can seize up. Poles should *never* be used as javelins, despite the temptation, for this loosens the attachment of the shoes and may bend or even break the pole.

The *chain* (see also Para. 4.4) must *always* be unfolded and folded according to a strict ritual. **Never** take the two handles and pull them apart, since this will certainly strain the links and may cause breakage. The correct procedure is as follows: one of the party, A, keeps hold of both handles and throws the rest of the chain away from him as hard as possible. The other, B, finds the 10 m tag and moves away, A still holding *both* handles, until the doubled chain lies straight. A then releases one handle, and B backs away running the chain through his hands until it is fully extended; if folded properly, it will slide over itself without getting tangled. It is then inspected to get rid of any kinks or interlocked links. The chain should be left extended until the end of the day's work, and transported merely by pulling the leading end.

If you are working single-handed, after throwing out the chain anchor one handle firmly and the other lightly, so that when you have straightened out the doubled chain you can easily release one end by pulling harder.

To fold up the chain, take the 10 m mark and walk away with it until the chain is nearly doubled. Then hold together the first pair of links (that is, those which meet at 10 m) and fold the second pair against them. Then fold the third pair in the opposite direction, and so on folding the pairs backwards and forwards alternately until the handles are reached, and tie firmly with a cord or strap passing through the handles.

If the chain is wet or dirty it should be dried and wiped fairly clean, but unless it is to be left unused for a very long time there is no need to oil it; a day's work in grass or heather will remove most rust.

Although a chain is very durable it is liable to stretch slightly over years of use. If you are only concerned with small sites, the necessary correction is likely to be negligible. If you survey large sites or require special accuracy, or indeed if you just want the satisfaction of knowing that your chain really is right, you should check it occasionally, perhaps once a year, or at the beginning of any major survey. You may have access to some institution which owns a steel band or other sufficiently reliable standard of length; a University Geographical or Civil Engineering Department may well have something suitable. Lacking this, soon after you have bought the chain you can chisel marks on a concrete path, or drive two very substantial pegs (preferably of oak and set in concrete) which you can mark with brass nails. Your new chain can be used as standard. For choice, this 'standard length' should be in an area under your own control, since there is always a risk that a bit of kerbing by a public road, which might otherwise be suitable, may be disturbed. The marks need not be exactly 20 m apart; you could, for example, keep a record that '20 m = standard plus 122 mm', the extra 12·2 cm being measured by a tape or scale.

There are three ways of dealing with a stretched chain. The most rational is to keep a log-book, in which the actual length of the chain is recorded at regular intervals, say a fixed date every year, plus any time the chain has suffered an accident, such as being run over by a lorry. This method has the advantage that the correction at every given date can be estimated with fair accuracy. If for example, the chain was 12 mm too long on 1 September 1976 and 18 mm too long a year later, then to apply a correction of 16 mm for a survey done in May 1977 would not be far wrong. Take care not to forget, when applying such a correction, that if the chain is too long the true length of a line will be *greater* than the apparent length as measured.

The second method, which can be very laborious and is therefore seldom used, is to shorten a number of the small oval links by hammering, until the stretch is eliminated. This has the merit that no correction is needed and that the strength of the chain is little affected.

The third, most widely used, method is to remove the necessary number of small oval links. It is essential that those removed should be distributed evenly along the chain. This method also removes the need for any correction, but has the disadvantage that the chain is weakened.

It is good practice to keep a record of the history of the chain, for you may sometimes need to estimate a correction when no check has been possible. In an organisation owning several chains, these can be numbered by file-cuts on the handles.

4 The Elements of Chain Survey

4.1 *General.* This chapter discusses the principles on which chain surveying is based. An imaginary survey, illustrating the practical applications of those principles, is described in the next chapter. Both these assume ideal conditions; the ways of overcoming various practical difficulties are explained in Chapter 6.

4.2 *Choice of Network.* The principles which should govern the arrangement of a network have been described in Para. 2.2, but its actual form must depend on the site. Various types which are widely applicable are illustrated in Figure 4.1.

The simplest of all is the quadrilateral (a). The diagonals may well pick up no detail, but one must be measured to make the network rigid. One diagonal alone, though, provides no way of balancing errors or of detecting mistakes, so both diagonals should always be measured. There is no need to book the chainages at their intersection.

This emphasises an important point: *To measure a chain line without booking any detail does not take very long, so it is often worth while to include lines simply to secure a rigid network.* Detail is picked up from subsidiary lines.

Most common, perhaps, are oval enclosures. Networks such as (b) are suitable for these, but are greatly improved if two radial lines can be collinear (c) or better still several (d). When the enclosure has substantial ramparts, it may be useful to have a double ring of chain lines, one set following the inside of the defences, the other the outside (e). This is also a very good rigid network.

Large sites may require networks of two or more interlocking polygons (f, g). An effort should be made to get one or more continuous alignments running right across the site, or at least to note the intersection points of some lines produced (as x, x in f, g).

4.1 Networks for Chain Survey

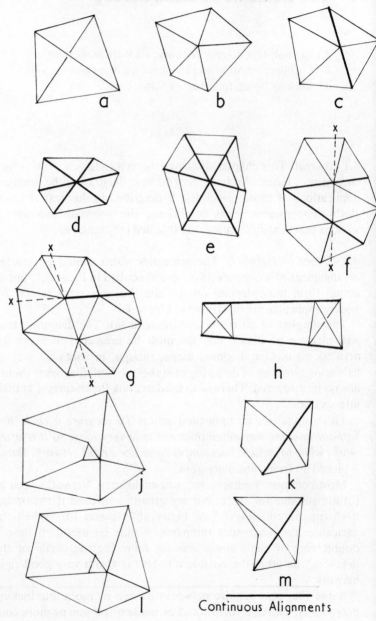

Continuous Alignments

Sometimes the feature to be surveyed may be itself an obstacle to accurate measurement. A possible example of a suitable network (appropriate to a long cairn) is given in (h).

Finally, beware of traps. For example, (j) and (k) look at first glance like quite good networks; but they are not in fact rigid, for the same measurements can give the shapes (l) and (m).

It may be worth while to emphasise again that these are all merely examples of the main network. Additional subsidiary lines can be inserted as desired to pick up detail.

If you have no compass available, you should preferably aim at least one of your chain lines towards some landmark identifiable on the OS map, so as to establish the north point.

Unless it is absolutely certain that the work can be finished in one day the stations must be marked by pegs; but the actual stations are at the poles, which should therefore be replaced in the same holes each day. In fact, for chain surveying, the difference in positions between pole and peg will be insignificant, but it can affect your calculations in theodolite work.

4.3 *Preliminary Booking.* Before starting the detailed survey, a sketch of the framework must be drawn in your fieldbook, each station being designated by a letter (or number, Arabic or Roman). Usually, in practice, you will also record each station's position (Para. 7.2).

It is an advantage, also, to take any necessary compass bearings, and where relevant to note the slope of the ground. You are less likely to forget these things if you do them at this stage.

It is also very good practice simply to measure all chain lines once without booking detail (which of course requires a repetition of that measurement). The risk of a mistake is almost eliminated. Whether you in fact follow this good practice often involves a difficult choice (see Para. 5.5).

4.4 *Chaining.* Measurement of the chain lines follows a ritual which has developed over many years; it should be adhered to, as it is the most efficient method. The ideal team comprises three people, a leader, L and a follower, F, who handles the chain, and the surveyor who books the records. The third man is a luxury, and usually F is also the surveyor. The party is assumed to have a chain, five arrows, and one or two poles (optional), and to be measuring from A to B.

The first step is, rather obviously, to unfold the chain (Para. 3.3). When that has been done, if you are using one for the first time, you should make yourself familiar with its graduation. It is made up of 100 major links each nearly 0·2 m long, connected by smaller links. The system of numbering on metric chains is not rigidly standardised, but usually every metre is marked by a yellow tag, with red tags, numbered 5 or 10 as appropriate, at the 5-metre points; the distance given is always from the *nearer* end, and zero is the outer face of the handle. You will be wise to practise a little by taking points at random, noting their chainage (to 0·01 m) and then checking it with the tape.

For measurement, L has initially the five arrows and a pole. F holds the end of the chain at A, and 'lines in' L's pole so that it is on the line AB, about 20 m from A. L stands to one side of the line facing towards it, and is directed by F who may say, for example, 'To you half a metre; from you 10 centimetres; to you in the head', (the top of the pole is leaning away from L); 'to you two centimetres; right!' L fixes the pole in the ground, and having established the right directions he then pulls the chain *tight*, applying a fairly strong tension; it can be brought to the required straight line by a flick of the wrist. F is holding the handle against the pole at A, and L puts a red-tagged arrow firmly in the ground against the outer face of the handle at his end.

Leaving the arrow in the ground, L and F both move on for 20 m along line AB, L pulling the leading handle of the chain. Time will be saved if F gives a count-down as his end of the chain moves past the arrow. 'Five' ('metres' implied), 'four, three, two, one, STOP'.

The procedure is then repeated, F at the arrow lining in L's pole, and L then putting in a second 'red' arrow, 40 m from A.

When they move on to the third 20 m section, F lifts the first arrow and carries it with him (and similarly at each successive stage), so the number of red arrows which he is carrying shows how many multiples of 20 m he has moved. At the 100 m point, L puts in the yellow-tagged arrow, and F hands back to him the stock of four 'red' arrows. The same ritual continues, F returning the 'yellow' arrow to L when convenient. F then knows that if he is carrying a 'yellow' arrow he has moved some multiple of 100 m, if he is carrying (say) 3 'red' arrows he has moved some multiple of 100 m plus 60 m.

An alternative, perhaps preferable, is for L to start with six arrows; their colours do not matter. When measuring the 100 to

120 m length, F has five arrows, which he transfers to L, and the sixth arrow is marking 120 m, and similarly on passing each multiple of 100 m.

The follower F will find a pole helpful for 'lining in' L, but it often proves a tiresome extra burden especially if F is taking notes, and it is not essential.

The last 20 m or so of the line can, if desired, be taped.

4.5 *Allowance for Slope.* A plan represents a projection on to a horizontal plane at sea level. For our type of work, the effect of height is negligible, but chain lines are often far from horizontal and a correction is needed. The corrected distance is always less than the measured distance. As a rough guide, if the slope is less than 1 in 20 no correction is needed, and if more than 1 in 10 measurement 'by steps' is best. The standard method of dealing with this problem is to work out the correction for each 20 m length, and then to insert the arrow not at the end of the chain but the appropriate distance beyond it. The objection to this is that numerous calculations have to be made in the field, with consequent delay and increased risk of mistake. It is preferable, except on very steep slopes, to measure along the ground, record the relevant slope, and correct in the office. The corrections are almost always small, so the work can be a bit rough. Three methods are available.

(a) *With Clinometer.* The slope is measured and recorded, either during the chaining or as a preliminary. The latter is preferable, as having too many jobs to do at once leads to confusion and thus to mistakes. Generally, the slope from one station to another is uniform enough for a single measurement to be adequate. If there is a marked break in the ground, it can be recorded as, for example, 'Line AB, fall 5° 10' for 63 paces, 2° 20' for the remaining 92 paces'; as the correction is small, controlled pacing between fixed points is accurate enough.

If theodolite observations are being made slopes can be measured with that instrument.

(b) *With Dumpy Level.* If a level is available, probably the quickest way of correcting for slope is to take the necessary spot levels. At a break in slope between stations, a mark must be left where the level was taken. The level book will contain the note 'between A and B; see chain book', and the chain book will record, against the appropriate chainage 'see level book'.

(c) *'By Eye'.* This is a very rough method for use in an emergency, but as the correction is usually small it is often adequate. All measurements are along the chain line.

Lay down a pole or some other obvious mark on the ground. Walk about 30 paces downhill. Turn round and hold your arm out horizontally to give a (very roughly) level line of sight. Walk uphill until that line of sight passes through the mark. Then pace the remaining distance.

Tables relevant to methods (a) and (c) are given in Appendix IV.

If the slope is steep, it is always less trouble, and compared to method (c) more accurate, to measure in steps (Para. 5.4). When this is done the actual measurements should be recorded, not merely the total chainages. This reduces the risk of mistakes associated with arithmetical calculations in the field.

4.6 *Allowance for Sag.* The chain line has sometimes to be carried across a deep hollow. For choice, a tape should be used to measure the unsupported distance, for it can be pulled tight so little or no error will be introduced. The measurement should be made between marks where ordinary chaining is interrupted. Sometimes, as for example in a high wind, a chain may be more convenient. In that case, sufficient accuracy can be obtained by estimating the sag by eye, and deducting the correction for sag, as given in Appendix IV.

4.7 *Booking Detail, Introductory Notes.* When detail is to be recorded near a chain line, measurements along the line are made as above, but after F has lifted the arrow at his end the chain, and of course the other arrow, are left in position until all the features near that 20 m length of chain line have been recorded. This is usually done by measurement of 'offsets', horizontal distances taken perpendicular to the line of the chain; a fuller description is given below.

For the tape, 30 m rather than 20 m is to be preferred. The case is held by L, who usually remains at the chain and reads off chainage and offset or other measurements. F holds the free end of the tape, and does the booking. Two general points should be noted. First, F should *always* repeat L's statements of distance and L will correct him if he is wrong. It may seem absurd to do this when L and F are only separated by a few metres, but even at that short distance mistakes can occur, and in rough weather and perhaps 20 m apart the risk is considerable. For the same reason in 'fi*v*e' and 'ni*n*e' the *v* or *n* must be overemphasised, and 'oh' or 'zero' is preferable to

4.2 Conventions for Booking Detail

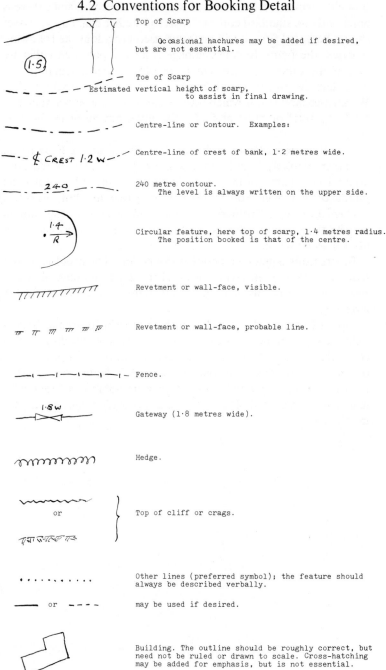

Top of Scarp

Occasional hachures may be added if desired, but are not essential.

Toe of Scarp
Estimated vertical height of scarp, to assist in final drawing.

Centre-line or Contour. Examples:

Centre-line of crest of bank, 1·2 metres wide.

240 metre contour.
The level is always written on the upper side.

Circular feature, here top of scarp, 1·4 metres radius.
The position booked is that of the centre.

Revetment or wall-face, visible.

Revetment or wall-face, probable line.

Fence.

Gateway (1·8 metres wide).

Hedge.

or

Top of cliff or crags.

Other lines (preferred symbol); the feature should always be described verbally.

or   may be used if desired.

Building. The outline should be roughly correct, but need not be ruled or drawn to scale. Cross-hatching may be added for emphasis, but is not essential.

'nought', which can be confused with 'four'. Second, since there is apparently no standard convention as to whether chainage or offset should be stated first, it will be found useful to adopt the following practice: the figure for the chainage is always preceded either by 'at', if the other measurement is an offset perpendicular to the chain line, or 'to', if the other measurement is not at right angles. Which measurement is which then remains clear, whether stated as 'at 5·25, 4·91' or '4·91 at 5·25'. Examples are given in the next section.

Details are recorded in a 'chain book'. This is about 20 × 10 cm or larger, strongly bound along a short side. A pair of red lines about 1 cm apart run perpendicular to the short sides, along the middle of each page. Some types have only one line, but this is less convenient to use. Ordinary note books are seldom strong enough for the rigours of fieldwork, so the extra cost of a proper chain book is worthwhile.

Before using a new chain book it will be found helpful to give it a (consecutive) reference letter or number, and to number alternate pages. A page or two should be left blank at the beginning for indexing.

Most of the detail which has to be recorded in archaeological field survey can be classified under a very few headings. It is convenient to use standardised conventions for these. A possible set of such conventions is set out in Figure 4.2. Note, though, that these are merely suggested as useful; they are not in fact 'standard', and to use other symbols is not 'wrong', provided your colleagues use the same.

5 An Imaginary Survey

5.1 Conditions Assumed; 5.2 Choice of Network; 5.3 Measuring and Booking, Preliminary Remarks; 5.4 Booking Detail; 5.5 Completing the Survey; 5.6 Supplementary Notes on Accuracy, Booking, and Squaring Off.

5.1 *Conditions Assumed.* The procedure for an actual survey can best be followed by describing in some detail how the work would be approached in practice. To introduce all the difficulties which may sometimes be encountered would be confusing at this stage, so they are discussed in Chapter 7; but to emphasise the advantage of having plenty of poles, even on such a small site, we will assume that you only have a set of six 2 m sectional ranging-rods.

The site to be surveyed is a small enclosure, roughly semi-circular in plan, on slightly sloping ground at the edge of a steep natural scarp (Figure 5.1). On the north and east is a modern wall, too high to measure or to see across, with a gateway at the north-east corner. The party comprises L (the leader) and F (the follower) who is organising the work.

5.2 *Choice of Network.* After obtaining the tenant's permission, the first step is to fix the stations. There are two good clear lines: from the scarp edge through the gateway, and along the east side of the modern wall; so stations A and B are fairly easy to select. You find, to your relief, that a 4 m pole (that is, four sections screwed together) at C is visible from A and B (though not conversely) so after a little to-ing and fro-ing you decide on that station. You will obviously need a line on the north side of the wall, so you line in stations D (on AC) and E (on AB). Given a set of six poles, you will only have 1 m sections available for these. If possible, you would also have fixed the line from E through the entrance by another station on line AC, but you have run out of poles. It is by now obvious that you will not finish the job in a day, so L goes round driving pegs at A, B, C, D and E while F makes a freehand sketch of the site and network (Figure 5.2) (including stations which will obviously be needed but are not yet marked), and takes magnetic

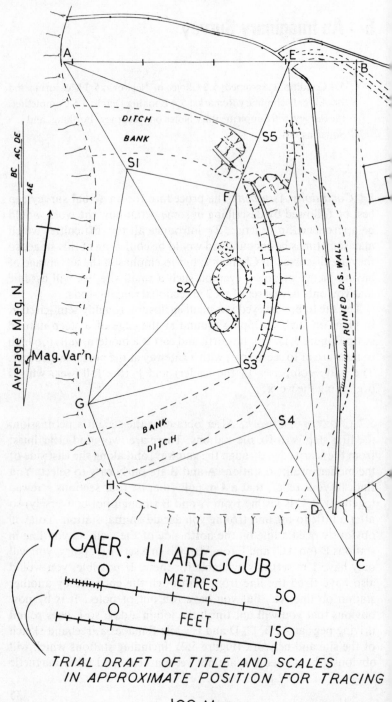

Y GAER. LLAREGGUB

METRES

0   50

FEET

0   150

TRIAL DRAFT OF TITLE AND SCALES
IN APPROXIMATE POSITION FOR TRACING

100 Metres

REFERENCE SCALE USED DURING PLOTTING

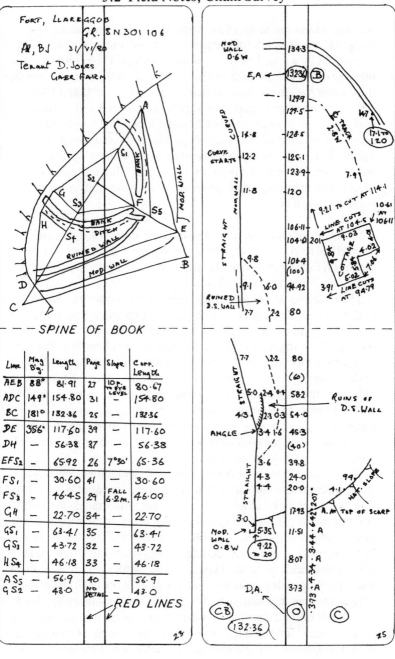

FORT, LLAREGGOB

GR. SN 301 106

AH, BJ   31/VI/80

Tenant D. Jones
Gaer Farm

SPINE OF BOOK

Line	Mag B'g.	Length	Page	Slope	Corr. Length
AEB	88°	81.91	27	10 p. TO EYE LEVEL	80.67
ADC	149°	154.80	31	—	154.80
BC	181°	132.36	25	—	132.36
DE	356°	117.60	39	—	117.60
DH	—	56.38	37	—	56.38
EFS₂	—	65.92	26	7°30'	65.36
FS₁	—	30.60	41	—	30.60
FS₃	—	46.45	29	FALL 6.2m.	46.00
GH	—	22.70	34	—	22.70
GS₁	—	63.41	35	—	63.41
GS₃	—	43.72	32	—	43.72
HS₄	—	46.18	33	—	46.18
AS₅	—	56.9	40	—	56.9
GS₂	—	43.0	—	NO DETAIL	43.0

RED LINES

23

MOD WALL 0.6 W   1343

E,A   1323 ⓑ

1299
CURVED   129.5   G TRACK 2.6 W   447
14.8   128.5   17.1 TO 120
CURVE STARTS   12.2   125.1
123.9   7.9?
11.8   120
9.21 TO CUT AT 114.1
LINE CUTS AT 104.5   10.61 AT 10611
106.11   9.03
104.6 2.01   5.02 7.08 4.02
106.4 (100)
9.8   5.02 7.08
9.1 6.0   94.92   3.91 LINE CUTS AT 94.79
RUINED D.S. WALL   7.7   2.2   80

7.7   2.2   80
(60)
5.0 24 0.4   58.2   RUINS OF D.S. WALL
4.3   23 0.3   54.0
ANGLE → 3.4 1.6   45.3
(40)
3.6   39.8
4.3   24.0   99,
4.4   20.0   4.1 NAT. SLOPE
17.93   A. AT TOP OF SCARP
3.0   A
MOD. WALL 0.8 W → L 5.35   11.51   A
9.22 → 20   8.07   A
D.A.   3.73   A

CB   O   Ⓒ
132.36   25

bearings along the main chain lines, or at very least along two of them. On the sketch S indicates a subsidiary station which will not be marked by a peg. The site is named, with grid reference and any other relevant details such as the name and address of the tenant; the date of the survey and the names (or initials) of L and F noted. After this, another page if necessary is used for a list of chain lines, with space for columns to record magnetic bearing, length and page reference at least; columns for slope and corrected length are also useful. You may consider this an unduly meticulous waste of time; but it does not in fact take very long, and I have found (all too often) that scamping these notes almost always adds a lot of unnecessary work later.

5.3 *Measuring and Booking, Preliminary Remarks.* Suppose that you decide to start at C and measure the line CB, in that direction. Since you cannot see B from C, you will need to line in a temporary pole, sighting from B towards C.

The chain book is held with the spine away from you and zero is at the foot of the page nearest to you, so that when you are facing in the direction of measurement the detail on the right-hand half of the page corresponds to that to the right of the chain line, and *vice versa*. In windy weather two rubber bands will help keep the pages under control, but in ordinary conditions they tend to be a nuisance, for they seem almost invariably to lie over the point one wishes to plot. In good conditions an HB pencil is best for booking (carry a spare, for they vanish without trace if dropped in long grass), but when the pages are wet a black ball-point pen is better; numbers and details should then be drawn extra large.

One point, though obvious from the field notes reproduced, nevertheless needs emphasis. The over-riding essential is legibility. The fieldbook is handheld, and notes are often taken in adverse conditions, so prize-winning calligraphy is not to be expected; the ideal is something which will still be clear even after the book has been dropped in a muddy puddle. A beginner will often make a careful and fairly accurate sketch for the whole length of a chain line, and then, using small neat numerals, will try to fit the records of measurement into that plan. This is an entirely mistaken approach. The sketch in the field notes is solely a convenient way of recording measurements; for example, a featureless straight wall 100 m long may require less space than a complicated feature only 10 m across. This will become obvious in the explanation which follows.

5.4 *Booking Detail* (Figures 5.2, 5.3). Suppose that you are
chaining line CB (Figure 5.2) including detail. Put the name of the
line, ringed, at the bottom of the page, with a space for the total
length when measured. Station C is at chainage 0; *chainage of*
stations on the measured line, and their names, are always ringed.
It is helpful to indicate the directions of adjacent lines (for
example, DA here), but this is often neglected. Some methods of
fixing important detail are illustrated between chainages 80 and 120
on line CB (Figure 5.2), and separately in Figure 5.4 (see Para. 5.6).

To start with, you are ascending a steep slope, so you will
measure in steps, measuring the horizontal distances with the tape
to the nearest centimetre. Do not try to get these to some pre-
selected length, but record the steps alongside the central pair of
lines and add them up to get the actual chainages. Thus the first
four horizontal distances between the points marked by arrows (A)
are 3·73, 4·34, 3·44, and 6·42 m, giving the corresponding chainages of 3·73, 8·07, 11·51, 17·93. Fortunately there is not much
detail to record. The third arrow (11·51) is put in to get an offset
(5·35) to the corner of the modern wall, but as it is difficult to
square off accurately on a slope, this is also fixed (after the 20 m
arrow has been put in) by a diagonal of 9·22 to 20. Because of the
awkwardness of working on a steep slope, the point where the top
of scarp cuts the wall is fixed by measurement from that corner.
The fourth arrow (17·93) has been put at the top of the natural
scarp. *Remember, when you are booking this, that the pair of red*
lines in the chain book corresponds to the single line of the chain on
the ground, so the line representing the top of scarp leaves the pair
of lines on the right exactly opposite where it enters on the left. (For
an example of what not to do, see Para. 7.4, Figure 7.3.)

You have now reached fairly level ground, so you can start
following the proper routine for chaining. If your arithmetic is
right, the 20 m mark should be 2·07 from your last arrow, so
measure this distance and put in a red arrow; return all the rest to
L. Record the 2·07 distance; it happens to be right, but it is surprisingly easy in the field to make a mistake such as 20·00 − 17·93 =
3·07. If the distance is booked, such a mistake can be put right
without returning to the site.

L now takes his end of the chain to the 40 m point, and having
been lined in by F marks it with a red arrow, as described earlier.
When released, the ends of the tightly-stretched chain will move a
few centimetres towards each other owing to the roughness of the

ground. The aim should be to allow the same movement at each end.

The chain is left lying on the ground, and forms in effect a ruled line from which measurements can be taken. It is heavy enough to be unaffected by wind (which is one reason why it is used rather than a tape), and is unlikely to be disturbed except by one of the surveying party tripping over it.

To measure offsets, F takes the zero end of the tape and goes to the point to be recorded, L stays at the chain. If F has a loop of string through the ring of the tape, he can keep it hooked round a finger, leaving his hands free. Depending on the nature of the site, it may be an advantage for L and for F to carry a pole for plumbing to the relevant points, but in general any extra burden is to be avoided.

F holds the end of the tape at the point with which he is concerned. L estimates the point at which the tape is perpendicular to the chain (see below), and reads off the offset and chainage, for example, '3·6 at 19·8' or 'at 19·8, 3·6'. F repeats this and records it, and L says 'Right' (if it is). F, however, is carrying one arrow, so he knows that he must add 20, which makes the chainage 39·8. It is very advisable not to rely entirely on this system, but to book every 20 m point, putting the figure in brackets if there is no offset at that chainage, as at 40, 60, and 100.

The offsets are always measured from the chain line (not built up in steps). Thus at '54' the readings might be 'at 14·0, 4·3', 'Same chainage, 2·3', 'Same chainage, 0·3', the face of the modern wall and the ancient wall being 4·3 and 2·3 m respectively *from the chain line*.

The first page of the booking continues to chainage 80. Plotting is simplified, and the risk of mistakes reduced, if the final measurements at the top of one page are repeated at the bottom of the next; but it is not essential to do this. The main feature which needs comment on this page (Figure 5.2) is the cottage. It is assumed here that only the outline is needed. Complicated buildings are discussed more fully in Para. 7.7.

Since it is a sharply defined structure, measurements can be made to a centimetre. All sides are measured, and a diagonal is taken across the re-entrant angle to determine whether it is a right angle. The points where the sides produced cut the chain line are noted, and where appropriate the distance of the corner to the chain ('9·21 to cut at 114·1'). The faces which cut at 94·79 and 104·50 are too nearly perpendicular to the chain line for it to be worth taking these distances as well as the offsets. Only three corners are accessible for offset measurements, and the most distant ('10·61 at 106·11') is annotated to avoid confusion. A diagonal (say '17·4 to 120') would have been quite useful as a check on this point.

Few other comments are needed on this chain line. The modern track has been booked by recording its centre line and its width, and the continuation of the modern wall by an offset, which is long and therefore also fixed by a diagonal; the resulting triangle is not very 'well-conditioned', but the feature itself is not important. Note that the name of the station and its chainage are ringed.

As soon as you have completed this line, 'index' it by noting at the beginning of the survey 'BC 132·36; p. 25. This only takes a moment, and will save a lot of bother when you start plotting.

There is no need to go through all the chain lines of this imaginary survey in such detail, but three of them, BA, EF, and F to subsidiary S3 will illustrate some points which deserve note.

Three occur on line BA (Figure 5.3). The distance measured 'backwards' from B to the shorter modern wall is booked as ' − 4·5'; it would be legitimate to take zero at the wall, when B would be booked at 4·50, E and A at 23·35 and 86·41, but if you use that method you will almost certainly some time find yourself trying to plot the network with BA = 86·41 m. The other points are: the width of the gateway (or any similar feature) is booked, not left to be inferred from the offsets; and the junction of the two walls (which cannot be fixed directly by an offset because the main wall is too high) is located by measurement along the wall face.

The line EF exemplifies three fairly important principles or techniques. The first is that a feature such as a hill-fort entrance should, so far as possible, be surveyed from a single line. The end of the inner rampart to the right of EF could theoretically be fixed by an offset from BA and the other side of the entrance by one from ED; but if these offsets are rotated only slightly in opposite directions, quite a large falsification of the plan will result.

Second, the use of a subsidiary station (S on plan) is to be noted. The rampart north of EF can be measured much more conveniently from a line 'Subsid. 5 at 21·82 on EF to A' than it could be from BEA, for the offsets are much shorter. A subsidiary is (normally) only marked temporarily, not pegged.

Finally, so far as EF is concerned, attention needs to be drawn to the method of booking. Standard practice is to take offsets on both

5.3 Field Notes, Chain Survey

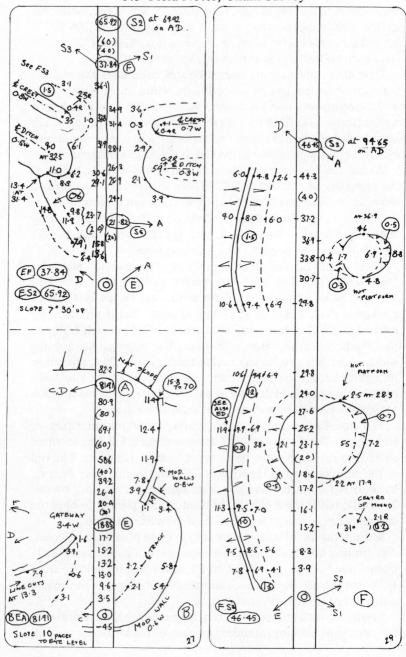

sides of the line as they are reached, and to record the corresponding chainages in order; line CB has been recorded in this way. In many archaeological surveys, though, it is a nuisance to have to keep on moving from one side of the chain line to the other and back again; it is much less trouble to finish off all the work on one side, and then to deal with the other. The chainages at which offsets are booked will not be the same for both sides. There are two ways of indicating this: either a mark can be made on the appropriate red line to show on which side the offset was taken (as for FS3), or the central column can be divided by a line along its middle, and the two sides booked quite independently (as for EF). The former arrangement is probably the more convenient when only a few chainages are involved, the latter if they are numerous.

The line FS3, from F to the subsidiary on AD, is for the most part self-explanatory if considered in conjunction with the conventions (Figure 4.2). Alternative methods for booking a hut-platform or similar feature are shown; but make sure it *is* nearly circular before you record it as such, for a square with rounded corners can be very deceptive.

A mark is supposed to be left at '11·9 at 25·2'. It is a good precaution to duplicate a few measurements off nearly parallel chain lines, either to the same feature such as a line of bank, or as implied here to some quite temporary mark such as a stick.

5.5 *Completing the Survey.* As noted earlier, a site of this size may well take more than one day. It will be instructive to go briefly through an imaginary account of two days' work, but without describing the measurement of each line in detail. To exemplify the extra work caused by a shortage of poles, it will be assumed that only six are available.

During the first day's work already discussed, the general shape of the network has been fixed, the stations A, B, C, D and E chosen and marked, and lines CB and BA measured. Returning on the second day, you will inevitably be unable to leave poles at all the stations, so you bring half a dozen or so 'wands' — fairly straight twigs preferably peeled to make them conspicuous — which will serve as expendable markers. You can *start* a line from a wand, but generally they are neither straight enough nor easily enough visible to run a line *towards* them.

Of the remaining stations, F, G and H, F might be worth a peg, if there is any prospect of further work on the site, but provided the work can be finished on the second day, G and H could merely be marked by poles.

Poles are needed at A, D, E and F. A sensible first step might be to chain ADC booking detail. In default of poles, wands must be left at the four subsidiary stations. In placing S_2, L would line his pole on EF produced, while the follower would keep him on the line AD. In this particular case the distance to F is less than 30 m and could be taped and booked, but in general a link of this kind would be chained as a continuation of EF. The other subsidiaries are chosen so that chain lines can be run close to the back and front of the defences. If this can be done conveniently, it gives a better result than trying to measure right across the bank and ditch.

H and G are then marked with poles, the pole from F is 'borrowed' temporarily for use in chaining (unless conditions permit the use of L's arrow for lining in) and HS_4, GS_3, S_1G and HD, all booked, with detail. Wands are left at G and H; there are now enough poles available to mark out all the remaining stations including S_5, so the order in which the remaining lines are measured does not make much difference. A convenient run would be DE, EFS_2, FS_3, and AS_5, perhaps with GS_2 as an afterthought, which requires no detail but is a useful extra check.

Ideally, if you have not already done so, you should now check the measurements of all chain lines, though without detail. What you would do in fact would depend on many circumstances, such as the time of day, the weather, and how quick you are at chaining. Obviously it would not, in general, be sensible to come back the next day merely to do this checking, since the object of the check is to make sure that you do not need to come back another day. Probably the next best compromise is for L to mark with pegs as many stations as possible, including subsidiaries, and for F to take the magnetic bearings of all lines measured. This at least permits the identification, with fair certainty, of any line which contains a mistake.

5.6 *Supplementary Notes on Accuracy, Booking, and Squaring Off.* Most earthworks or ruined dry-stone structures cannot be measured more accurately than to the nearest 0·1 m at best, and it is simplest to book measurements to that accuracy rather than to worry about whether such a length can be represented on the final plan. Buildings can be measured much more accurately, but if say the final plan is to be at a scale of 1/2,500 it may seem rather absurd to record lengths to 0·01 m. Nevertheless, it is usually more sensible to do this than to spend time deciding what is the nearest 0·1 m.

As noted earlier, it is tempting to sketch the whole plan in advance, and then to add the measurements as they are taken; but it is a mistake. If you do this, you will almost certainly find in places that you have not enough room for the entries. In practice, the sketch-plan should only be drawn a little way ahead of the measurement.

Although the offsets are defined as perpendicular to the chain line, nothing has been said so far as to how this is ensured. The method depends on circumstances. Usually, quite an accurate right angle can be estimated by looking down at the tape, and judging whether the two angles it makes with the chain are equal. Moreover, provided that the feature being recorded is linear, and at an acute angle to the chain line, quite a large departure from perpendicularity has little effect (Figure 5.4). The method of fixing an important point by a diagonal has already been noted (Para. 5.4). If, though, the position of the truly perpendicular offset is needed very accurately, it can be fixed by swinging the tape in an arc, and noting the points at which a radius rather greater than the offset cuts the line. The average gives the correct chainage (Figure 5.4). It is advisable to record all the measurements, rather than to rely on the average chainage being worked out correctly.

5.4 Offsets to Chain Line

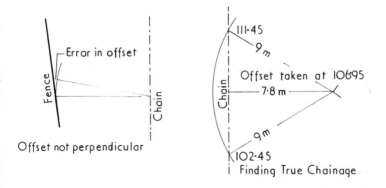

Error in offset

Fence

Chain

Offset not perpendicular

111·45

9 m

Offset taken at 10695

7·8 m

Chain

9 m

102·45

Finding True Chainage

This discussion of an imaginary chain survey has implied the assumption that no serious problems have arisen. What may happen in practice, and the necessary precautions which result, are discussed in Chapter 7, but first an explanation will be given of the work needed to arrive at the finished plan.

6 Plotting and Finishing the Plan

6.1 *General Remarks.* Preparation from the field notes of a finished
plan for publication falls into two parts: a pencil draft is plotted;
and this is traced in ink for reproduction. It is convenient to
consider these two procedures separately.

6.2 *Equipment for Plotting.* The following items are either essential
or desirable.

Accurate scales, 30 cm (or more) long, one graduated in millimetres (that is, a metric 1/1,000 scale); and preferably a metric
1/2,500 scale. Similar scales graduated in 1/500 and 1/1,250 are
useful, and perhaps 1/2,000 also, but these are not essential for one
can easily divide or multiply by two mentally. The sort of ruler
available in stationery shops is not adequate; and note, incidentally,
that the edge of a scale should be treated carefully and can be
damaged by use as a ruler.

Corresponding to each of these scales an 'offset scale' is needed
(for its use see Para. 6.4). This is a short length of scale, usually 5
or 7·5 cm long, similar to the longer scale but cut off truly square at
each end. The graduations start from these cut ends.

It is *absolutely essential* that both main and offset scales are
trapezoidal (that is, flat-faced) in section. Scales of oval section are
no use for this type of work.

You will also need: a 60° and a 45° set square, of transparent
material. The size is not crucial, but 17 cm shortest side is
convenient. It is often useful, but not essential, to have a smaller
(10 cm shortest side) 60° set square.

A 15 cm diameter protractor (transparent). The full circle type is
marginally more useful than the half circle, but preferably get both.

A metre straight-edge (of rustless steel) is necessary unless all
your drawings are going to be very small. Graduation in centimetres is useful, but not essential. If you get a T-square (see below)
you can manage without a straight-edge.

A drawing-board is not essential, for any flat surface will serve as base, but it is very useful indeed. Size is a matter of choice, depending on the dimensions of the plans you are likely to make. Probably the most generally useful, without becoming excessively cumbrous, is the Imperial size (80 × 58 cm).

If you have a drawing-board, it is well worth while to get a corresponding T-square (which can serve in place of the metre straight-edge). You will not use the T-square much for plotting an ordinary chain survey, but it can be very useful when finishing the final tracing.

If you need to fix the paper in place, drafting tape is usually preferable to drawing pins; but if you prefer the latter those with very large heads are worth the slight extra cost. Pins should only be used near the edges of a drawing-board; the centre should be kept undamaged.

Finally you will require pencil and paper and an eraser. The pencils should be 'drawing' quality, and either H or HB. My own preference is for HB, but experts usually prefer H. For almost all purposes, good quality white cartridge paper is adequate for the pencil draft; thin card has a better drawing surface, but is more expensive, and cannot be used with a tracing table if you have that equipment. There is, though, one difficulty in using either of these materials. Paper, and to a lesser degree card, is not dimensionally stable. That does not usually matter for a small drawing, say up to 50 cm across, but for a larger one precautions have to be taken. If, as on the excavation of a site with complex stratification, you need to be able to superimpose successive plans of the same area, dimensionally stable transparent material is needed. If tracing plastic is used, a very hard pencil (4H, 5H) may be required.

6.3 *Plotting the Network*. The first step should always be to plot this on a small scale say 1/1,000 or 1/2,500 for the example given here; lengths need not be corrected for slope. This plot should be on tracing-paper, for a reason which will appear subsequently. Any gross mistake should be revealed by this plot, so it is a good idea to do it before you leave the area where you are working, if you are away from home. Sketch on this plot, very roughly, the outermost features which will appear on the plan; and mark the true north point. The margin of the relevant 1/50,000 map gives the magnetic variation (Para. 25.3).

Next, you need to decide on the size and scale of your plan. Two factors have to be taken into account. First assuming that you accept the desirability of keeping to a set of rational scales (Para. 6.8) what is the smallest of these which will allow you to represent clearly the significant features of the site? And second, what is the page size of the periodical in which you hope to publish? Most of the major publications include 'Notes to Contributors' which give details of this kind. 'Throwouts' (folding plans) are expensive and should be avoided if possible.

Consider Figure 5.1. Note incidentally that this represents not a finished plan but a stage in plotting the pencil draft; the hachures, for example, are merely sketched roughly as a guide to the eye when tracing. It is size and scale, though, which are being discussed here. As plotted, at 1/500, with title and scales as shown, it can be enclosed in a rectangle 34 × 21 cm with the longer sides north-south. On a page measuring 17·5 × 13·5 cm, which is fairly typical, it could comfortably be reproduced at 1/1,000 with the north point 'upright'. Some periodicals are smaller, perhaps 15 × 10 cm. In that case, by setting the north point at about 10° to the page edge, reproduction at 1/1,000 is still possible, though the title and scales would need to be rearranged and crowded together. In my view this is in every way preferable to using an odd scale such as 1/1,300 to keep the north point 'upright'; but this problem is discussed in more detail in Para. 6.8. The exact arrangement does not have to be decided until the plan is ready to be traced.

A linear reduction to one half the original size is probably the most favoured for block making; you can go as far as one quarter, but rather special care is then needed to make sure that thin lines do not vanish in reproduction. You will therefore need to plot at 1/500, so if you have not got a scale with that graduation use a 1/1,000 scale and mentally double all your measured distances.

First, work out the corrected lengths of all the chain lines. If you have indexed them in your chain book, as suggested earlier (Para. 5.2) you can write the corrected figures there. Three different methods are given in the specimen bookings. Reference should be made to the tables in Appendix IV.

For the line EFS_2 the slope was measured with a clinometer, and found to be 7° 30'. Each 20 m step, therefore, is 20 − 0·17 m or 19·83 m. The deductions for 37·84 and 65·82 will be 0·33 and 0·57 respectively, making the corrected lengths 37·51 and 65·25.

Line FS_3 had its correction found by levelling. The difference in level between the two ends was 6·2 m and the measured length

46·45 m, corresponding to a fall of 2·66 m in each 20 m. The approximate correction for 20 m is therefore

$$\frac{(2·66)^2}{2 \times 20} = 0·18$$

or 0·41 in the whole length. The exact corrected length is

$$\sqrt{46·45^2 - 6·2^2} = \sqrt{2119·2} = 46·03$$

Finally, the correction for BEA was found using the rough 'by eye' method. The second table in Appendix IV gives a correction of 0·36 per 20 m for a slope of ten paces to eye level. Thus BE is 18·85 − 0·34 = 18·51, and BA = 81·91 − 1·47 = 80·44.

You can now start to draw the network, but if the plan is large and you are working on cartridge paper or other dimensionally unstable material you should either draw on the paper a scale rather longer than the longest chain line or better draw a faint grid, of sides of 20 cm or as convenient, covering the whole sheet (Para. 18.1). This will allow any dimensional change to be detected and allowed for in later drawing or in tracing. If the drawing of the network is not finished in a day, the plotted lengths of chain lines should be determined from this drawn scale, not from the boxwood scale. For small plans, up to about 30 or 40 cm square as drawn, these precautions will seldom be needed; but a background grid is always desirable if co-ordinates are being used for plotting.

Now mark the positions of B and C at the corrected distance apart; you then have to fix A, by measurements from these two points. AB = 80·67 m and AC = 154·82 m. If you have a beam compass you can strike these off directly, but it is just as easy to use the following method, which has the further advantages that you do not have to buy an otherwise unnecessary compass and you do not make holes in the paper at B and C.

By superimposing your small-scale tracing on the main plan with, say, C on both coincident, you can get a fairly accurate indication of the direction of CA (Figure 6.1). With the straight-edge draw three or four lines in about that direction and measure 154·82 m to scale along each; there is of course no limit to the distance. You then have three dots, indicating the arc of radius 154·82 m. Repeating this from B gives the position of A, though in this case, as BA is less than the length of your scale, you can measure direct.

Check all three lengths, and if they are correct stations A, B and

6.1   Plotting Intersection of Chain Lines

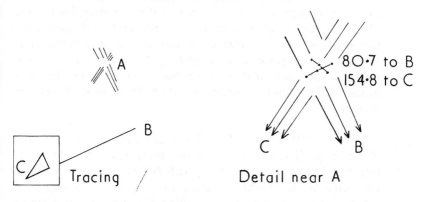

C are presumably fixed, but you have several other lines which should fit the network. Do not try to use too many of these at once, but choose those which seem likely to give the best check, perhaps DE and S_2E in this case. These lengths, as measured on the plan, ought of course to be exactly the same as on the ground, when corrected for slope; but in practice there may well be a *small* difference. (If the difference is large, something is wrong.) In chain surveys the errors are usually balanced out subjectively, though systematic methods can be used (Para. 17.9). In this example, it might be found that DE on plan was a little too short, while S_2E was exactly right; you could then assume that DE, only, needed adjustment. Alternatively, both DE and S_2E might be too long on the plan, in which case it would be more reasonable to move B as plotted a little towards C, so that the plan-lengths of DE and S_2E are still too long but not by so much, while BC is now a little too short. It is essential to realise that this sort of adjustment, which is of rather doubtful legitimacy anyway, must *only* be applied to 'errors'. If for example S_2E and DE both turned out to be about 8 m too long as plotted, you would not 'adjust' the line AB so that those two lines were 4·5 m too long and CB 4·5 m too short, but you would search for a 'mistake' either in measurement or in plotting.

Having fixed ABCDE and S_2 to your satisfaction, the rest of the network can be completed. Before plotting detail, choose a part of the paper well outside the plan and mark on it the north point.

If you are using a board with a T-square, then for each line for which you have a magnetic bearing measure the angle it makes with the T-square edge. You can then average the corresponding bearing of the T-square relative to magnetic north, and by deducting the magnetic variation the true north can be drawn. Alternatively, through a single point draw parallels to all the relevant lines, and measure from each of them to get the magnetic north. This will usually differ slightly according to which line is used, so take an average.

6.4 *Plotting Detail* (Figure 5.1). The 30 cm scale is placed along the plotted chain line, and the offset slid along it, the booked points being marked with a faint dot (Figure 6.2). The dots are then joined up to give the plan, using the same conventions as for booking, but drawing accurately instead of sketching. Explanatory notes can be added to help with the final tracing. It is easier to plot one side of the chain line at a time, and if you have several features running roughly parallel, as perhaps in a multiple-rampart system, you will often find it less confusing to dot out and complete two or three lines at a time, rather than to try to plot all at once. The modifications needed when you have to deal with a feature such as the building near BC are obvious.

If the line has required correction for slope, no attempt is made

6.2 Use of Offset Scale

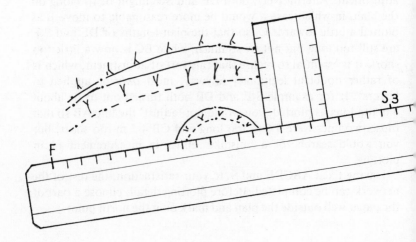

to work out the adjusted length for every chainage. Taking BA as an example, the corrected length was 1·24 m less than the measured length, but each 20 m section is only 0·3 m less. Marks are therefore put at points corresponding to 19·69, 39·38, 59·07, 78·76 m from B; detail from 30 to 50 m is plotted with the 40 m point on the scale against the 39·38 metre mark, and similarly for other sections of the survey. If greater accuracy is needed, the points corresponding to every 10 m can be marked.

6.5 *The Finished Drawing: The Materials.* This section requires some introductory comment. Everything described elsewhere in this book is within the competence of anyone who can measure a length and write down the result; but to produce a really attractive finished plan requires a natural gift which not everyone has been fortunate enough to receive. Nevertheless, even if you are (like me) thoroughly ham-handed, you may need or wish to finish your own plan rather than to rely on a draughtsman; this section is intended to help you to do so. The result will not be as decorative as you may hope, but should at least be workmanlike and inoffensive. If, on the other hand, your pen tends to obey your wishes, you will probably be able to reject much of what is said here; but do not skip it entirely, as it may contain some points worth your consideration.

Your choice of drawing equipment will depend on how often you are likely to need it, and perhaps also to some extent on whether you have to buy it yourself or can order it through the organisation which employs you. You will require a set of pens and either pen-stencils or adhesive sheets for lettering.

You will require a mapping pen, and a pen with a fine but soft nib, with some spare nibs for both of these. A ruling pen (resembling a pair of tweezers) is useful but not essential.

You will also need a range of stylo-type drawing pens of the type used with pen-stencils. This is where choice becomes difficult. There are several different brands, but essentially they fall into two types: an open or lightly covered reservoir, holding a small amount of ink, the writing point being a tube with an accessible sliding rod; and a more elaborate device resembling a fountain-pen, with a much larger reservoir, both it and the sliding rod being enclosed. The latter types are beautiful examples of precision engineering but have the disadvantage that they need to be treated as such. If allowed to clog, for example, they can be very difficult to clean; but a special stand is available to minimise this risk.

If you are going to do a lot of drawings, and if expense is unimportant, then a full range of the more elaborate pens, with the stand and other accessories, is certainly desirable; they give about ten line thicknesses. If on the other hand, you only produce half a dozen or so drawings a year, then three or four of the simpler type will be adequate.

Lettering, again, offers a choice. The first decision has to be whether to use pen-stencils or adhesive lettering. Most professional draughtsmen now prefer the latter, which offers a very wide range of letter forms and is easy to apply (it is important to remember that most types require a fixing spray, to prevent them from coming unstuck). Nevertheless, my own preference is for pen-stencils; they are more versatile, and there is no risk that just as you finish a drawing you find that you have run out of an essential letter. An adequate set, to start with, would be a range of four sizes, the largest with capitals about 10 mm high; in the smallest two, at least, you need numerals. The necessary pens will serve also for drawing.

There are now several different makes of stencil, and availability is as good a reason as any for choosing one rather than another; but keep in mind that when you choose your first half-dozen you are almost committed to go on using that make for ever, since the appropriate pens cannot be used with another make.

Finally, rather obviously, you will need ink and tracing material. The ink should be a really good quality black drawing ink; the small saving on a cheaper type is more than counterbalanced by its defects.

There is now an embarrassingly wide choice of tracing material. Tracing-paper is not durable enough for a final drawing. Tracing linen is now out of fashion, but has many good qualities. It is durable, erasures (by careful use of a razor-blade) are easy, and if creased it can be flattened with a domestic iron (also a hopelessly botched drawing, if washed and boiled, can be made into a very high quality handkerchief). Its chief defect is that it is dimensionally very unstable. Drawing is done on the matte side.

Synthetic tracing films are mostly dimensionally stable (a few which claim to be are not) but do not stand up to rough treatment as well as tracing linen, being more liable to tear or crack, and if creased they cannot easily be flattened. Erasure cannot be done with a razor-blade, but requires special erasing fluid. Some makes will give almost as clear a line with pencil as with ink; this property, combined with dimensional stability, makes them the obvious choice for use on an excavation where several successive strata have to be compared.

Alternatively, the finished drawing can be traced on to ordinary thin cartridge paper. Save for its lack of dimensional stability, this is in many ways the most convenient material to use; but it requires a tracing table. Essentially, this is merely a sheet of hard heat-proof translucent material supported over a light source. Commercially built tracing tables are (unduly?) expensive, and are unlikely to be available except in a fairly well equipped drawing office, but a perfectly adequate makeshift for small drawings can be constructed using a sheet of thick plastic from a derelict television set supported above a couple of electric lamps; household aluminium foil will serve as a reflector. Fluorescent tubes are to be preferred, as they give out less heat; if ordinary lightbulbs are used they should be of low wattage and only switched on when actually in use to avoid overheating the plastic sheet. The surface *below* the bulbs will also need protection from heat.

The question of dimensional stability has been rather over-emphasised above, because it is so often forgotten; but apart from the particular case of a multi-stratum excavation it does not cause much practical difficulty. The effect is negligible for a small plan, and even for a large plan it will usually be unimportant, *provided the scale is drawn at the same time as the basic network and is traced*, not redrawn on the tracing to the nominal scale. This will obviously correct automatically for most of the dimensional change, though not completely since the effect is not always exactly the same along and across the sheet. In any case, your attempt at scientific accuracy is quite likely to be frustrated by the block-maker. Some are careful to avoid any distortion, but surprisingly often, even in publications of a very high standard, what was presumably drawn as a rectangular frame turns out in reproduction to have opposite sides of slightly different lengths. This is perhaps one reason why frames are now unfashionable.

6.6 *The Finished Drawing: Tracing.* Continuing with the assumption that you are a complete novice, your first step must be to decide on a style. The best way of doing this is to look through several volumes of recent national periodicals, such as *Archaeological Journal, Antiquaries Journal, Britannia, Archaeologia,* and *Medieval Archaeology*, or perhaps better still the *recent* volumes of the three Royal Commissions on Ancient Monuments. Local periodicals may be useful, but are not of such high quality though some are very good indeed. Having picked out some examples which you think look pleasant and not too difficult, examine them carefully under a magnifying glass (for they will have been reduced at least to one-half for reproduction, possibly to one-third or one-quarter). Then when you have a fairly clear idea of the technique used, practice reproducing bits of the 'model' to their supposed original size, and invent some imaginary earthworks to draw.

Most earthwork plans depend almost entirely on the use of hachures, even on a closely contoured site. It is difficult to understand why this curious convention gives an immediate impression of banks and ditches, but no really satisfactory alternative has been devised so the labour it involves has to be tolerated.

The form most commonly used resembles an emaciated tadpole (Figure 6.3). This can, with practice, be drawn quite quickly using the fine but soft nib. If depressed heavily this gives a broad line (the head) and as the pressure is reduced the line thins out to form the tail. In this as in all hachuring, the thicker end represents the top of the slope. Slightly less common, and slower to draw, but rather easier to give a neat result without a lot of practice, is the thin wedge, with a flat or slightly concave top and slightly concave sides. Other types can be devised. These can be outlined with a mapping pen, and then blacked in. The thicker the heads of the hachures and the more closely set they are, the steeper and higher the scarp represented; but there is no standard formula relating the two. Some sort of consistency is desirable, and although you can get a fairly good result by relying on your subjective estimate of what is needed you may find it useful to draw out three or four imaginary scarps of different (but uniform) horizontal width in which the hachures steadily increase in intensity. You can then assign an arbitrary vertical height to correspond to each point on the 'scarp', which taken in conjunction with your field notes will serve as a rough guide to how heavy the hachures should be at various points on the plan. The variation of vertical height along the 'scarp' need not be linear but should follow a smooth curve, and need not be the same for all plans unless they form a set.

Next to hachuring, the most useful convention is stipple, used mainly to represent rubble. This can be bought in the same material as adhesive letters, and will give a much more uniform result, but that unfortunately can be a disadvantage, as the variation in the

6.3 Simple Conventions for Finished Plans

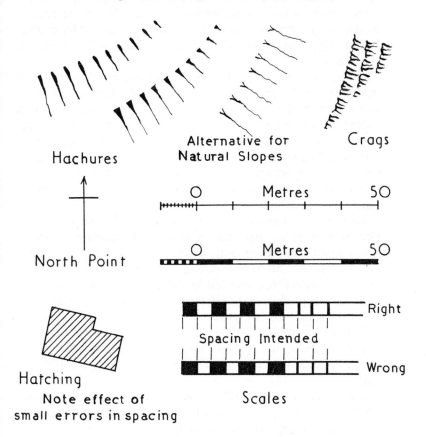

Hachures

Alternative for
Natural Slopes

Crags

North Point

O   Metres   5O

O   Metres   5O

Hatching
Note effect of
small errors in spacing

Right

Spacing Intended

Wrong

Scales

height of the surviving ruins of a wall, for example, cannot be represented, nor can the way in which the stones may fade out into the surrounding turf be shown. It is preferable therefore, though laborious, to do the stippling by hand.

Hatching is very difficult to do neatly, for a single mistake in spacing shows up glaringly. Cross-hatching is even worse. It is helpful to put up a sheet of squared graph paper under the tracing, and to use that to give uniform spacing to the lines.

Continuous or broken lines are conveniently drawn with one of the stencil pens, though a sharper and more uniform result can be got with the ruling pen. If you are ruling a line, the set square should be raised by resting it on a sheet of card or another set square so that the edge in use does not touch the paper. Otherwise there is always a risk that the ink will run under the set square, even though you may be using a pen designed to prevent that happening.

Lettering, scales and north point are best left until the plan itself is finished.

Before starting to trace, linen and some tracing films need to be dusted over with french chalk, to remove minute traces of grease which prevent the ink from adhering uniformly. The ink bottle should be stood on a tray where it cannot easily be knocked accidentally, and should *always* be kept corked except when actually filling your pen. Not only does it become clotted if much exposed to the air, but a bottle of drawing-ink displays to a very high degree the universal malevolence of inanimate objects, at any rate if being used by an amateur draughtsman.

Bear in mind constantly that the ink takes some time to dry, and plan your work so that there is no risk of smearing it. Several minutes wait is always necessary before you can work over a recently inked area, and even then it is very advisable carefully to blot the drawing although you may feel sure that it is completely dry, and although no professional draughtsman would sink to the use of blotting-paper.

It may be helpful to outline the scarps of banks and ditches *very* faintly in pencil, and to avoid irregularity in spacing faint pencil lines can be drawn indicating the position of every third or fifth hachure.

Having completed the plan, the direction of the north point should be traced lightly in pencil, and the original draft removed from beneath the tracing. The draft and tracing are then very carefully compared to make sure that nothing has been missed or incorrectly represented.

North point, scales and lettering should be kept as simple as possible (Figure 6.3). For the north point (which should of course show true north) a simple arrowed cross is perfectly adequate. The easiest scale to draw is the upper one, but the lower, with alternate black and white divisions, perhaps looks better. Note when drawing this that the lines dividing the sections before they are inked in must be completely within the black section, or the divisions will be of unequal length. It is customary to include one unit (say 10 m) of the main scale drawn to the left of zero and subdivided into smaller units (metres). This allows measurements to be made to one metre without the need to subdivide the main scale; but it is only needed if someone is likely to require these more accurate measurements, and it would obviously be out of place on a sketch-plan. Two scales should be given, one metric and the other in feet, to simplify comparison with plans published before metrication. It is now becoming fashionable to include a simple areal scale, a square equivalent to one acre or one hectare in area; my own view is that there is little or no advantage in this, for direct visual comparison of areas is difficult, and the linear scale gives all the information necessary. The area of an enclosure is better given in the descriptive text. Finally, so far as scales are concerned, always give a drawn scale; *never* rely on a simple statement such as 'Scale 1/250' or '1 cm to 5 m' for that will appear without alteration when the plan is reduced for publication.

If stencils are being used for lettering, all titles and other details should be first stencilled on a spare piece of paper, to the size chosen but without bothering too much about such matters as evenness of line. These can be inspected, and pencil notes made of desirable improvements such as changes in spacing. This draft can then be placed under the finished tracing, and moved until it seems to be in a satisfactory position; it can then be used as a guide to the finished lettering. Some editors prefer to put the actual name of the site in type, and it can then be omitted from the plan; but this is undesirable, for the drawing or the line-block has then nothing to identify it if it is needed for future use. In an organisation where several staff are engaged in similar work it is advisable to note, outside the area to be published, the division of responsibility, for example, S.AH 1973 Bk 5 D WG 10 vi 74 T DR 12 viii 74; S, D and T indicating Surveyed, Drawn, Traced, with initials of those responsible and dates of work.

The final tracing should always be carefully compared with the pencil draft, the scale should be checked by using it to measure some distance which is known from the *original record in the chain book* (to make sure there was no mistake in plotting), and the drawn metric and Imperial scales should be compared.

When lettering a drawing using a T-square as guide, keep in mind the probable orientation of the drawing as it will be published. Good quality drawing-boards have a hard edge along one of the shorter sides, and for geometrically accurate work the T-square should only be used with this; but for lettering the other edges can be used.

6.7 *Publication*. Usually, your plan will be intended for publication. If, as assumed above, you have prepared the drawing with regard to the page size of the periodical concerned and with the intention that it shall be reproduced at a rational scale (Para. 6.8) you will need to specify the reduction as appropriate, for example, 'Reduce to ½'; alternatively you can make two marks below the drawing at (say) 20 cm apart and mark on a line between them 'Reduce to 10 cm'. Editors and block-makers (provided they take any notice of your instructions) will tolerate reductions such as 1/2.5, ⅓ or ¼. They can be persuaded, reluctantly, to use others; for example, you might draw a plan at 50 ft to 1 inch (1/600) and wish it to be published at 1/1,000, so you place the marks 33.33 cm apart (= 200 m at 1/600) and state 'Reduce to 20 cm'. This will probably be done less accurately than for one of the integral reductions such as ½ or ¼.

Some editors, printers, and publishers interpret their functions rather too widely and may ignore instructions of this kind, believing that some different size of plan will look prettier on the page, and never mind whether the scale is rational. A few may even alter the drawing itself. If you feel strongly about these possibilities, you should put in the margin of each drawing, 'Do not depart from these instructions or alter this drawing in any way without the author's permission'. These dangers are not imaginary: in a recent excellent book the publishers decided, without consultation, to 'improve' the appearance of the drawn scales; their art department not only believed that a metre was exactly equivalent to a yard, but saw nothing surprising in a child burial where the skeleton measured 24 ft from head to toe. The discredit for this, of course, fell upon the innocent author.

Some editors prefer to have the whole plan redrawn. In that case, they will sometimes accept a pencil draft. Whatever arrangement is made, though, the final drawing will need to be checked very carefully against your original, by you.

6.8 *Rational Scales*. Archaeological opinion in Britain is moving slowly towards acceptance of the view that plans should be reproduced to a standard series of scales. Of the three Royal Commissions on Ancient and Historical Monuments, the English Commission now uses a scale of 1/5,000 for all hill-forts, the Scottish has for some time aimed at 1/1,000 for earthworks and 1/250 for houses, and the Welsh, which has a larger size range to cover, uses the largest appropriate scale from the sequence 1/10,000, 1/2,500, 1/1,000, and so on, with a preference for 1/2,500 for earthworks and 1/250 for most buildings. It is arguable that 1/2,000 and 1/200 should be included, but on the whole that seems unnecessary.

The advantages of this system seem obvious, especially in simplifying comparison of plans of similar structures. To those accustomed to such a rational scheme the appearance of a volume with a random selection of scales dictated merely by convenience or by misguided aestheticism is as offensive as the presence of misspellings and grammatical mistakes, and is much more of an impediment to the use of the work. Nevertheless, there are still many archaeologists who do not hold the views expressed here, and you will not be regarded as having committed a gross solecism if the scales of your plans as published are not rational. Indeed, there is a strong possibility that many people will not notice even if they are obviously wrong; the eight-metre child mentioned above escaped the attention of most reviewers.

7 Problems and Precautions

7.1 *Hazards*. The description of the imaginary survey in Chapter 5 assumed that nothing went wrong and no particular difficulties arose. For any site that takes more than one day to survey, you will be exceptionally fortunate if that is true. This chapter goes through the difficulties which are likely to be experienced in a real survey, and the ways of overcoming them. The special problems, of setting out a rectangle with a chain, and of surveying buildings, are also discussed. Until you have worked in the field, you will think some of the risks envisaged are so improbable that they can be ignored, but every recommendation made here is based on personal experience.

Apart from difficulties of terrain, the main hazards to surveying are children, other humans, and cattle. Children can hardly be blamed for finding that ranging-rods make admirable javelins, but after a day's work on even a lightly infested site you will feel that there was much to be said in King Herod's favour. Farmers and farm workers too may claim some justification, in that pegs can injure animals' feet and that as a matter of principle any apparently official activity ought to be frustrated; but it is hard to understand why, as happens quite often, an apparently sane adult should lift a pole, look at its point, and then replace it upright in the wrong position. Cattle merely knock poles down by rubbing.

So far as daily work is concerned, all that can be done is to try to keep all poles where they can be under constant observation, and preferably within shouting range. At stations, they can be supplemented by wands, which are less likely to attract attention and may remain even if the pole is shifted. It should be your invariable practice, at least if there is the slightest chance of disturbance but preferably always, to check that the pole to which you have chained is in fact at the station peg. If it is not, record the position of the station relative to the chain line (as Para. 7.3, Figure 7.6d) and correct when plotting.

Poles and arrows which are not in use should *always* be stuck *sloping* into the ground. It is annoying, when working towards a station, to be faced with a choice of three or four upright poles, any of which may be the one required.

As routine, always note what equipment you have taken on to a site and make sure that you collect it when you leave. A fallen pole can easily be forgotten. Similarly, when moving from one chain line to the next, always check that you have the full set of arrows.

7.2 *Locating Stations.* As noted, pegs are very liable to be removed, and the loss of a station before a survey is finished can be a major disaster, possibly making several days' work valueless. All pegs used to mark stations should therefore be driven down slightly below ground level and their tops smeared with dirt. The pegs can usually be made on site (Para. 3.2).

On most sites this precaution is absolutely essential; but having made the peg almost invisible you have to provide for its redis-covery, either by yourself *or by someone who takes over the work from you.* A wand may with luck remain in place for a few days, and this can sometimes be supplemented with a small heap of stones, but these latter should not be used where there is any risk of damage to farm machinery. These temporary marks, though, cannot be relied upon, and some more permanent method of recovery is needed.

The simplest solution is to drive the peg at some recognisable corner of a conspicuous boulder, or some other obvious and immovable feature. Incidentally, do not use an anthill, however easily recognisable; after a week or so the peg will be buried some centimetres deep, and the inhabitants resent disturbance.

More commonly, the peg will be within 20 m or so of two (or better three) landmarks. Examples of the sort of sketches recording such locations are given in Figure 7.1. Every station ought to be recorded in this way. In stony country, a thick red or yellow wax crayon can be used to make long-lasting marks. This will help to save time in identification, but should not be relied on exclusively. Measurement should be made along the ground, to the nearest centimetre.

To recover a station, as for example station M in Figure 7.1, two or three arrows are put in at 1·84 m from the corner of one gatepost

7.1   Field Notes to Locate Stations

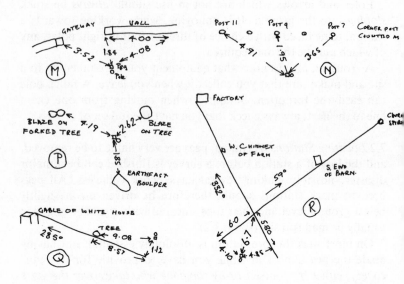

to indicate the line of an arc passing over the peg. Then 3·52 m from the other gatepost should give the exact position of the peg; the third measurement is a safeguard against mistakes, and will probably not be needed. In practice, the peg will usually be a few centimetres away, but can be discovered by slicing the turf with a blade held nearly horizontal.

Sometimes quite elaborate constructions may be needed to locate the peg (Figure 7.1, Q and R). These will not usually fix it as accurately as direct measurements from adjacent points, and a bigger area will need to be searched to recover the peg. At such stations, it is helpful to use a peg of large diameter.

Occasionally, no amount of ingenuity will guarantee the peg's recovery. In that case, every effort should be made to record *all* chain lines which involve that station on the first day, even if this requires a departure from the simplest programme of work.

It is useful, whenever possible, to run chain lines towards some conspicuous landmark well away from the site, such as a church spire, a factory chimney, the gable of some building, or even the junction of hedges or a line of roadway. Provided one peg on that line survives, the whole can be recovered. This is particularly useful on a 'salvage' site, where a sudden change in programme of earth-moving may destroy pegs without warning.

7.3 *Difficulties in Chaining.* The most usual obstruction in chain survey is a wall or hedge which does not prevent sighting but stops the chain from lying flat. This is easily dealt with, in a way essentially the same as chaining up a steep slope 'by steps'. Two poles are set up on the chain line, one on each side of the obstacle (Figure 7.2a). The first is chained in and booked. The horizontal distance from the first to the second is measured, with a tape or if more convenient with a pole, *and booked*, so that it is on record in case of an arithmetical mistake caused by working in the field. The chainage of the second pole is found by addition and the chaining is then continued, starting with the appropriate point on the chain at the second pole. This simplifies plotting, as the chainage runs on without interruption.

This type of obstruction is simple, and the way to deal with it is obvious, but some of the problems which arise are more difficult to solve. Standard works on chain surveying give various ingenious constructions for carrying a line past or across obstacles without breaking the continuity of measurement. This latter requirement does not apply to the type of work considered here, and almost all the difficulties these constructions are intended to overcome can be evaded by a suitable arrangement of the network. For example, Figure 7.2b shows how a survey could be linked up across a wide river. The broken lines, supposed to be too long to measure, enable a new starting-point to be fixed by lining in across the water.

Nevertheless, there is one method which is often useful. It provides a way of 'lining in' between two poles which are not intervisible.

The procedure is illustrated in Figure 7.2c. Stations A and B are not intervisible. The leader L, say, takes a pole to point 1a, from which B is visible, and F takes one to 2a from which A is visible; 1a and 2a should be as far apart as possible. L then lines F in towards B, so that 1a, 2b and B are in line. F then lines L in to A, so that 2b, 1b, A are in line. The procedure is repeated, L and F lining each other in with the appropriate station alternately. Poles 1 and 2 rapidly arrive at the line AB. You will find it worth while to carry out this procedure once on fairly level ground where A and B *are* intervisible; you will then accept that it really works.

The same procedure is possible with any even number of

7.2 Difficulties in Chain Survey

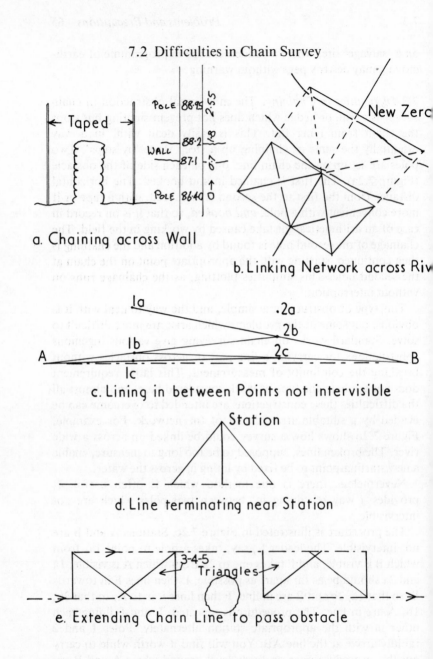

a. Chaining across Wall

Taped

POLE 88.95
2.55

88.2
.8

WALL
87.1
1.1

POLE 86.40
0

b. Linking Network across River

New Zero

la   .2a
                    2b
    lb   2c
A _____ B
    lc

c. Lining in between Points not intervisible

Station

d. Line terminating near Station

3-4-5
Triangles

e. Extending Chain Line to pass obstacle

intermediate poles; odd poles line in even, then even line in odd. In practice though, this is very seldom necessary, and as there is a possibility of a small divergence at every pole the line may not be quite straight.

Occasionally, you may know the general direction of a station but the pole has been displaced. Preferably of course it should be re-erected, but this is not essential. Run the chain line towards some obvious feature which is in about the right direction, and fix the station relative to this chain line by an offset and two equal diagonals of rather more than one-and-a-half times the offset in length (Figure 7.2d). The true distance station to station can easily be worked out, so that the network can be plotted; and the actual chain line used can be drawn in without difficulty to provide the detail.

Sometimes part of the site may be obstructed by a thicket. You can often run a straight line into and through this by sighting back on the way you have come step by step without knowing where you are going to emerge. For preference of course, the end of the line which you finally reach should be made a station, but if that is not convenient it can be marked, and surveyed in relation to the rest of the framework. This way of working is often convenient to use in conjunction with a closed traverse enclosing a wooded site.

The catch with this sort of randomly-oriented straight line is that after penetrating some way into the thicket it runs up against a tree. This can be got round by setting out a subsidiary line, or preferably two, parallel to the main line and a short distance from it. After passing the obstruction, the main line can be recovered (Figure 7.2e).

Another possibility is that woodland is penetrated by a path which is almost straight but does not provide a line of sight. A prismatic compass traverse (as Para. 25.7, but with the distances chained) will give the *distance* between points at each end quite accurately, so a line of that kind can be used to connect two stations and thus to fix a network, provided no detail is needed.

Sometimes it may be necessary to anchor the end of a chain or tape. The marker arrow should *never* be used as such an anchorage, for if it is displaced the measurements along the chain line up to that point have to be repeated. A satisfactory anchorage can generally be obtained by a spare arrow passing through the loop at the end of the chain and with its head inclined away from the direction of pull and a second arrow stuck vertically through the loop of the first.

Both should be pushed as far into the ground as possible. If available, a heavy rock resting on the chain and against the anchorage may be helpful.

A final problem which sometimes arises during a chain survey is breakage of the chain. This is a nuisance, but not disastrous. Join the broken ends firmly with several turns of string or wire (most field boundaries contain loose strands, if nothing better is available), and remeasure one line (without detail) to determine the new length. Note this, and note on every page of the remainder of the survey 'broken chain'. If the break is small, involving the loss of one or two of the small intermediate links, nothing else is needed. If several of the main 0·2 m links are lost, as may result from damage by farm machinery, the position of the loss should be indicated on each 20 m length of booking; there can be no certainty that it is always on the same side of the 10 m point.

7.4 *Booking.* Two types of difficulty may arise in booking. The first, by far the more common, is the result of carelessness; the second is caused by the need to record exceptionally complex detail.

If conditions are good, a single minor mistake can be rubbed out; but often the paper will be damp or dirty and any attempt at erasure will produce a smear surrounding a hole. Normally therefore, it may be better to cross out the mistake. A very common example, particularly among beginners, is to draw a line which crosses the chain line obliquely as in Figure 7.3 chainage 10·45. If you have done this, you should devise some way to indicate that the lines are really the same, either by arrows or by writing the chainage obliquely. Note that any such method is 'wrong' and would lose marks in an examination but it will serve to ensure that the detail is plotted correctly despite the mistake in booking.

This mistake is not very harmful in practice, and will not be repeated after a little experience. A much more usual difficulty is to discover that you have made a sketch of the detail to be recorded and when you come to book the necessary measurements there is no room to put them in. Examination of line EF (Figure 5.3) will show how easily that could happen. When it does, do not try to fit the information in by using very small figures, and do not rub out your sketch and redraw it. Merely draw bold lines across the page at each end of the botched section and start afresh with a new and larger sketch. If there is room for this on the same page no other information is needed, but sometimes you may need to write over

7.3 Dealing with Botched Entries in Chain Book

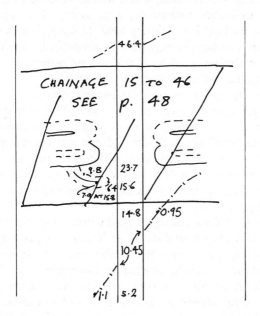

the abandoned section between the two cross-lines something such as 'Chainage 15 to 40 see p. 48' (as Figure 7.3). The separated section could refer only to one side of the chain line, or to a particular feature such as the building near line CB if that had been more complicated. There will be no difficulty in devising expedients of this kind once you have fully understood that the function of a chain book is solely to give an unambiguous record of measurements and other data from which the plan can be drawn. It is *not* a sketch roughly to scale to which dimensions have been added.

Sometimes there is so much detail to record that with no amount of care or skill can it be booked legibly using conventional methods. When there are merely a lot of linear features running roughly parallel to the chain line, the offset measurements can be kept to an adequate size by using two lines, indicating by a bracket that they refer to a single chainage (Figure 5.3, at 23·7 on ES_2). It is always better to do this than to use very small figures.

When the detail is really complicated, as for example with a group of numerous contiguous irregular stone-built huts, recording can be done more conveniently by plotting direct on to squared paper. A4 size is convenient, and a similar sized backing board of plywood, preferably waterproof, is necessary. The paper is best attached to the board by drafting-tape. Bulldog clips can be used, but in windy weather you may need an almost unbroken run round the whole perimeter. If there is risk of rain a flap of transparent plastic may be useful protection. Alternatively, if only a few sections of the survey are complex enough to require this method of booking, the drawing can be made on a sheet of tracing plastic sealed over a background of squared paper. This makes the whole arrangement practically weatherproof, but whether the appreciable extra work involved is worth while will depend on what conditions are to be expected, as well as on the number of sheets needed. If you use this method, be sure to mark on the plastic the details noted in the next paragraph.

A line is ruled along one of the graduations of the squared paper, not necessarily central, and the 10 or 20 m chainages marked, also the stations where necessary. Records are made of the 'name' of the line, and of the total chainage when measurement is completed; this is not left to be inferred from the drawing. Details are then measured in by offsets in the usual way, but instead of being recorded as numbers in the chain book they are plotted direct. There is of course no need to do the whole of a chain line by this method. It would be quite possible to book most of 'line xx' in the ordinary way, with a note in the relevant place such as '40-80, see squared paper sheet 3'.

No attempt need be made to cover the whole of the complicated area from a single chain line, but where the parts covered from adjacent lines overlap it is useful to record a few points from both. Where possible, as for example on stone-built huts, these points can be marked and numbered in crayon on the actual remains.

The scale to be used for the squared-paper plot needs to be considered. Ideally, it should be larger than that of the final pencil draft, and should be replotted in the office to the required scale. This is almost unavoidable if the pencil draft is to be to a scale of 1/250, for example, for paper with 4 mm squares ($=$ 1 m) is difficult to obtain, if indeed it exists. For scales such as 1/100, 1/500, or 1/1,000 circumstances may sometimes justify yielding to the temptation to make the field plot the same scale as the pencil draft, so that it can be traced directly; but it is important to remember that drawing in the field is never likely to be as accurate as it can be in the office.

For most work, paper with only centimetre divisions permits accurate enough plotting, and it is easier to use than that showing millimetres. The fine graduations tend to be confusing. If you intend to replot you can of course use squares of any size.

7.5 *Setting out a Rectangle with a Chain* (Figure 7.4). It is very much easier to make an accurate plan of existing points than to set out points in specified positions. Nevertheless, it is sometimes necessary to set out a true rectangle, as for example in preparation for an excavation. A theodolite should be used if at all possible, but if one is not available the job can be done with a chain. A prismatic compass is far too inaccurate for the work, but if the site is not too large and the ground is fairly level the little horizontal circle fitted to some levels may be adequate; accuracy to at least 5 minutes is needed, which corresponds to a possible error of about 1 m in 700.

Whatever method is used to set out the right angle, the accuracy of the result cannot be better than the accuracy of the linear measurements. So the first essential is that the chain used must be correct; if available, a steel band may be better. Further, the ground must be free of irregularities, and every chain length should be corrected for slope. Finally, all lines should be measured at least three times and averaged. These preconditions are assumed in what follows; they can of course be relaxed if the resulting inaccuracy is acceptable.

To avoid algebraic symbols, assume that you wish to set out a rectangle of 200 by 100 m. The same principles apply to any size and shape, save that a long narrow rectangle will involve 'ill-conditioned' triangles with the resulting risk of error. It should therefore be dealt with as two shorter rectangles.

The line AB, 200 m long, is supposed to have been chosen as base and established.

The next step is to set out *approximate* right angles at A and B. Anchor the end of the tape at A, and measure 12 m along the line AB. One surveyor then holds 24 m on the tape at that 12 m mark, and the other puts a pole at 9 m from A. Since 9.12.15 is a 3-4-5 triangle (Para. 16.5), the angle at A is a right angle and the pole is on the line AD. So at least it ought to be, but in practice the inevitable presence of errors means that it is not, exactly. Nevertheless, as a first approximation to the required point, measure 100 m in that direction, and put in a mark at D_1.

Repeat the process for B to fix C_1. Now measure AC_1, C_1D_1, and D_1B.

AD$_1$ and BC$_1$ are very nearly perpendicular to AB, so C$_1$D$_1$ is almost exactly parallel to and at the correct distance from AB; but the true positions of C and D are not yet known. If the rectangle were 'true', then AC and BD would each measure $\sqrt{100^2 + 200^2} = \sqrt{50000} = 223\cdot61$ m (or using excessive accuracy 223·607). Suppose in fact AC proves to be 223·32, that is 0·29 m too short.

Put in a mark at C$_2$ on the line AC$_1$ and 0·29 m from C$_1$, that is at the correct distance from A, and set out a perpendicular to AC$_1$C$_2$ to cut C$_1$D$_1$ at C$_3$. This is equivalent to drawing an arc of radius AC$_2$, centre A; the angle involved is so small that the straight tangent C$_2$C$_3$ is practically indistinguishable from the curve. C$_3$ should therefore coincide with C as required.

As a check, or as an alternative way of fixing C$_3$, similar triangles show that C$_1$C$_3$/C$_1$C$_2$ = AC/AB. In this case, C$_1$C$_3$ = 0·29 × 223·61 ÷ 200 = 0·32 m. If you are making the corrections by calculation alone, careful regard must be paid to sign. If the diagonal as measured is too short, as in this case, the corrected point is outside the first approximation; and conversely.

Having fixed C$_3$, and D$_3$ similarly, all measurements are made again. If any appreciable error should remain (which is unlikely) the whole procedure is repeated, taking C$_3$ and D$_3$ as the second approximation to C and D.

7.4 Setting Out Rectangle with Chain

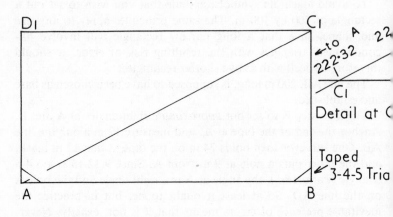

D₁

C₁

←to A   22

222·32

C₁

Detail at C

Taped
← 3-4-5 Tria

A   B

As a check, C_1C_3 plus D_1D_3 should, when allowance is made for sign, equal the 'error' in C_1D_1.

7.6 *Buildings*. For a surveyor with a professional conscience, standing buildings offer a particularly difficult problem. It is hardly ever possible to follow the fundamental principle of breaking down a large rigid network into smaller elements. Fortunately most houses are basically rectangular with walls of uniform thickness, and the plans of these can be worked out without much disquiet as to the validity of the result. For mansions and castles of irregular plan and incorporating alterations which may have taken place piecemeal over five centuries or more, a really accurate plan may be impossible without the use of a theodolite, to run traverses through the winding corridors with single lines of sight penetrating otherwise inaccessible rooms; and it is in this type of structure that accurate knowledge of details such as wall thicknesses may be crucial to a proper interpretation of its history. When, as often, the necessary equipment is lacking or circumstances prevent its use, one can only stifle one's conscience and fit the available incomplete jigsaw together as well as possible, partly comforted by the high probability that one's professional sins will never be discovered.

For an extensive establishment, such as a castle or abbey, the main outline should be surveyed as for an earthwork, but with all measurements taken to a centimetre; a theodolite is always a great advantage in this type of work, and is often essential, but sometimes, perhaps thanks to a single convenient putlog-hole, a satisfactory network for a chain survey can be laid out. In addition to fixing all corners and other exterior features with particular care it is often useful or even necessary to run lines of sight into rooms, linking them to the chained framework by a taped quadrilateral. The individual buildings, surveyed separately, will be fitted to this framework.

Since the plan of a building is usually built up from measurements of the individual compartments, these have to be recorded with particular care, and in this case, in contrast to the records of a chain survey, the sketch-plans should aim at being a reasonably correct representation of the structure, so far as that can be done before measurement.

7.7 *A Building Survey* (Figures 7.5 – 7.8). A fairly typical building survey follows, which exemplifies the general approach. Since most of the measurements are noted directly on to sketch-plans, a field book rather larger than a chain book and containing blank paper is to be preferred; double lines can be ruled as required for the few chain lines needed (Figure 7.6). In a building, a firm support is often available, so the outlines of many of the sketches can be ruled, but they are still to be regarded as diagrams to which dimensions are added, not as anything approaching accurate plans. Most of the detail and measurements, though, will have to be recorded in a hand-held book, and legibility rather than neatness remains the primary aim.

The first step, before starting any measurements, must be to make a complete sketch-plan of the whole building (Figure 7.5), showing all obvious features such as doors (D) and windows (W), but merely as square-sided openings, with no attempt to indicate shape. All rooms or other compartments are outlined, and identified by numbers, letters, or names; but fine details, such as fireplaces or recesses, are omitted. It is customary to draw house-plans with the main entrance towards the bottom of the page, but the approximate direction of north should be shown.

Next, when possible, a controlling framework should be established. In this example two lines, EG and JG, can be laid out touching projecting corners of the building, and E and J can be lined in along the east gable-end of the main block. Although direct measurement there is impossible, the external length of the gable-end can be estimated fairly accurately from internal measurements, so the triangle EGJ is quite reliable. The line CD gives an additional check.

In less favourable cases a theodolite traverse such as EFHJ might be used, either closed by measurement through room 3 or even left open, relying on the accuracy of the angular measurements. A theodolite can also be used to fix the position of otherwise inaccessible points, by triangulation. The magnetic bearings merely give the direction of north; they are not reliable enough to establish the outline.

A framework of this kind, if accepted as reliable, is taken as fixed, and subsequent measurements are adjusted 'by eye' to fit into it.

In addition to the external frame, some long internal lines are desirable. In an occupied building permanent marks can seldom be made, and the lines are linked to each other by recording shared features. Thus AB is connected to the running measurements on the

7.5 Field Notes, Survey of Building: Sketch Plan

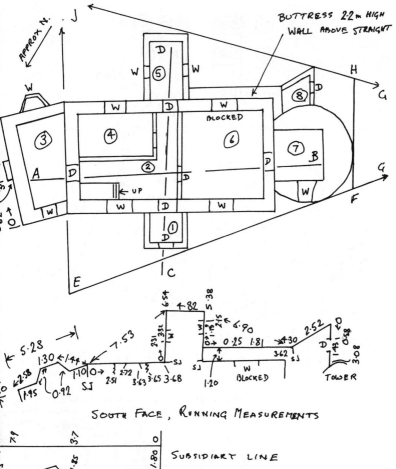

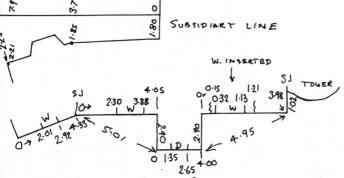

SOUTH FACE, RUNNING MEASUREMENTS

SUBSIDIARY LINE

W. INSERTED

NORTH FACE, RUNNING MEASUREMENTS

TOWER HOUSE   OWNER-OCCUPIER   J. JONES

AH; J.S 10.VI.79

7.6 Field Notes, Survey of Building: Chained Control

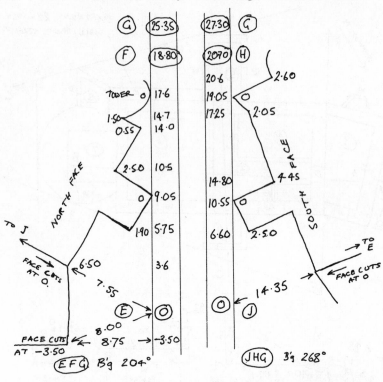

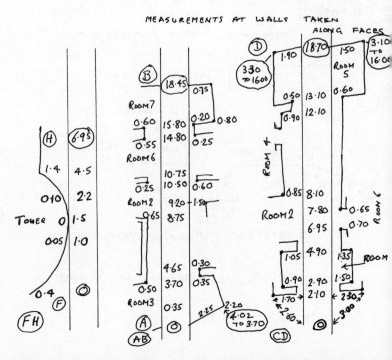

north face and hence to EFG by measuring the positions of windows and wall thicknesses; CD is linked to EFG by the external angles of the porch (room 1), to AD by detail of room 2, and to GHJ by the wall thicknesses, positions of windows, and external running measurements of room 5. Subject to the external frame, these internal lines form overriding controls to which the remaining detail must be fitted.

Note that along these controlling chain lines only the main features of the building are booked (Figure 7.6). External detail, which would be plotted next, is recorded by measurements noted against sketches of the relevant walls. These can either refer to single facets, as on the south side of room 3, or they can be running measurements. The latter are indicated by a small arrow beside the zero, showing the direction in which they have been taken. Subsidiary lines can be used if they are likely to be helpful, such as that which gives the direction of the south wall of room 3; this was not accessible from line GHJ. The tower would be recorded by a running measurement round its outer face (not reproduced), noting the points of contact with EF and FH which would have been marked with chalk or crayon.

Finally, the detail for each internal compartment is recorded as a separate sketch (as Figure 7.7). These should be drawn as large as conveniently possible, and all walls and diagonals recorded; a diagonal may sometimes have to be measured to a point near but not at an angle. Corners and other important points should be lettered (independently of the main control lines, otherwise the alphabet will prove too short), and measurements which have no associated detail can be listed. The letters can also be used to separate out information which would overcrowd the sketch-plan, as for DC in room 2. Important features can be recorded as separate dimensioned sketches, as for the window in room 2, or they can be described verbally, like the stair. Note that the sketch-plans of all compartments should be continued into the adjacent rooms, which should be numbered. The wall thicknesses must be recorded. As stated earlier, the inevitable small discrepancy which will be found in plotting should be distributed among the internal measurements; the shape established by the controlling chain lines should be kept fixed.

A complete 'snapshot' cover of the exterior of a building can be very useful both in interpreting it and in drawing the plan, and despite possible opposition from professional photographers can

7.7 Field Notes, Survey of Building: Internal Detail

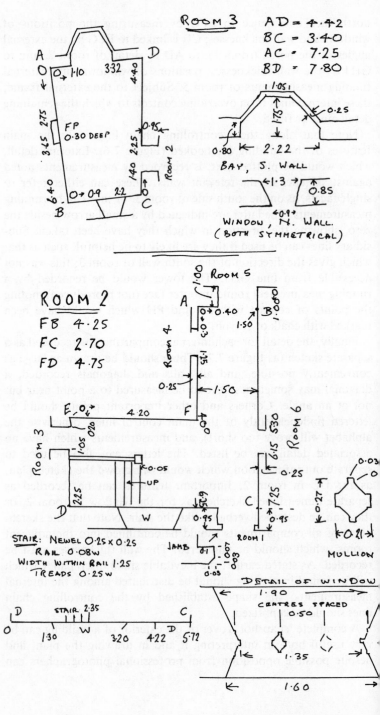

properly be regarded as an extension of the surveyor's note taking. As its purpose is to save time, a separate visit by specialists seems unjustified.

Upper floors are usually linked to the ground floor by assuming the walls to be vertical, unless there is good reason to suppose otherwise. On particularly difficult sites a theodolite may be needed.

Some types of building, notably churches, tend to be much longer than they are broad. In such a case, the interior should be subdivided into several shorter quadrilaterals (as Figure 7.8) to avoid the use of ill conditioned triangles.

7.8 Long Narrow Building: Network for Interior

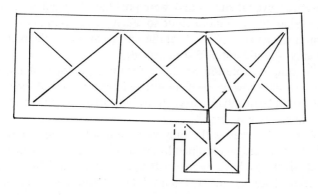

If the building is known to be rectangular, some time can be saved by omitting the diagonal measurements. For some purposes, such as recording vernacular house-plans, the builder may reasonably be supposed to have aimed at a rectangular plan even if he did not achieve it. The house can therefore be drawn as if it were rectangular, even where it may not be. If this is done, it should be stated in a note ('house treated as if rectangular', or 'angles assumed to be right angles'); for someone might wish to use your plan to examine one aspect of the competence of vernacular builders, and he could be misled.

7.8 *Sites on Chaotic Terrain.* Sometimes, perhaps on no more than a dozen sites in Britain, the terrain on which a structure has been built makes an objective survey almost impossible. Rough Tor, in Cornwall, is one such, and can be taken as typical. I am greatly indebted to Mrs Henrietta Miles for the following suggestions as to how a place of this kind might be treated.

The Tor may be visualised as a huge loose dump of granite boulders, ranging in size from a football to a small house; they tend to be slabs rather than spheroids. Round the top of this dump are lines of rough walling. Two are certain, but as both were formed by tilting slabs on end to form a double row of orthostats, many of which have now fallen, details of their exact lines and limits, and especially of the entrances through them, are doubtful. Archaeologists of equal competence disagree as to whether the third apparent rampart is artificial or natural.

On a site of this size it would in practice be impossible to survey every stone, or even to sketch them against a surveyed framework. Moreover, even if such a task were possible, the result would be of little value, for it would include so much 'background noise' — the natural scatter of rocks — that the 'information' — the plan of the remains — could not be distinguished.

The simplest solution would be for the surveyor to make a plan which would show his own subjective interpretation of the site; but that would be unsatisfactory, for as indicated very wide differences of opinion are possible.

If ground survey is the only method available, an approach to objectivity could be obtained by surveying every stone which seems at all likely to have been artificially placed, and indicating by different shading, ranging from solid black through heavy and light stipple to outline only, an estimate of the likelihood that they were so placed; the remaining purely natural rock scatter would be represented by some mechanical stipple or other appropriate pattern.

The best system would be to use a photogrammetric survey as base, to which the actual aerial photographs would be fitted as a mosaic. Stones likely to have been artificially placed would then be shown in heavy outline, with differential stippling as suggested above. The finished plan, reproduced as a half tone plate, would probably give as good a representation of the site as could be hoped for in practice; but it would be a laborious and expensive procedure, difficult to justify except for a structure of major importance.

8   Single-handed Chain Surveying

8.1 General; 8.2 Chaining; 8.3 Lining in; 8.4 Measuring Detail;
8.5 Arrangement of the Network.

8.1 *General.* Sometimes you may need to make a survey single-handed. This is quite easy, especially for a small site, and is not as laborious as might be feared. Using the tricks described here, the time required is only likely to be increased by a quarter to a half.

8.2 *Chaining.* The main source of delay is in chaining. The procedure is as follows: assume that you have put in a marker-arrow and wish to move the chain on for the next 20 m. Take the leading end of the chain and pull it on for rather *more* than that distance (say 25 paces). The method of keeping in line is described below.

   Return to the following end, and pull it back to the marker-arrow. Anchor it there, firmly, but *do not* use the marker as part of the anchorage; if that is displaced, the disaster is considerably greater than for normal chaining, with an assistant, for to re-establish the point takes much longer single-handed. Do not remove the marker.

   Then return to the leading end, pull the chain tight and straight, and put in the marker-arrow on line.

8.3 *Lining in* (Figure 8.1). The other main modification is to place an intermediate pole about mid way on each chain line (if longer than one chain length). Suppose that you are chaining from A to B, I being the intermediate pole. If you are between A and I, you line yourself in by sighting forwards along the line IB, if past I by sighting back along IA. The ways in which the necessary intermediate poles can be fixed are explained in Para. 8.5.

8.4 *Measuring Detail.* Detail is booked in the ordinary way. Short offsets, up to perhaps 6 m depending on the feature being recorded, can be measured step by step with a 2 m pole, preferably one with 0·2 m divisions. Larger offsets, and diagonals, must be taped, the end of the tape being anchored *at the feature*, not at the chain.

The other modification of normal practice required when working single-handed is merely that, to save time, detail on one side of the chain is booked working backwards from the leading end. On reaching the following end the position of the chain relative to that marker-arrow is checked. If, as sometimes happens, it has moved, the distance is recorded in the chain book. The record of this should be made conspicuous, for example, by enclosing the figure in a square 'box'. There is then no need to remeasure the line; those corrections can be inserted when plotting.

The end of the chain is then freed, the marker-arrow lifted, and the remaining detail booked. The process is then repeated for the next chain length.

8.5 *Arrangement of the Network* (Figure 8.1).

For a simple and small enclosure, especially one without much internal detail, a polygon is the obvious choice. A description of marking out such a network for a single-handed survey will make the basic principles clear.

Choose a roughly central station O, and another A on or just outside the enclosing bank. Put Intermediate I_1, to give a convenient direction for your chain line AB, and then choose

8.1 Networks for Single-handed Chain Surveys

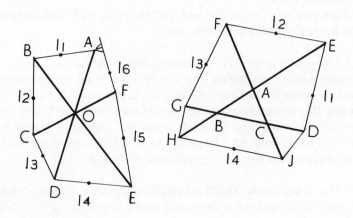

station B, lining in on AI$_1$ produced. Proceed similarly with I$_2$ and C, and I$_3$ and D, but for D, if you are working with a hexagonal grid, you have to line in with OA as well as I$_3$C. E and F are fixed similarly, and you will have a network in which you can line yourself in along any line except FA.

If FA is short, the necessary intermediate can be located by putting up two poles roughly on line near the mid point, going to A (say), sighting towards F and estimating relative to them where the intermediate should be. A pole is then put up in the estimated position, and checked from A, repeating the procedure if necessary. If a recumbent pole near the mid point is not hidden by grass the correct position can be read off against its graduations.

Alternatively, the first 20 m length could be run from F in roughly the right direction, a pole put up at its end, and the line continued by sighting back. Station A is then fixed by an offset with diagonals as in Para. 7.3.

For a larger site, the central point can be replaced by a triangle (Figure 8.1). A side of less than 60 m can often be measured with the tape anchored near the mid point, provided no detail is needed; this is quicker than chaining from one angle to the other. It is very important, if this construction is used, to make sure that the radial lines are collinear with the sides of the triangle (cf Figure 4.1, j - m).

Part III
THE LEVEL

9 The Level: General Description

9.1 Essential Features; 9.2 Choice of Instrument; 9.3 The Staff;
9.4 Setting Up; 9.5 Checking the Level; 9.6 Adjustments;
9.7 Precautions.

9.1 *Essential Features.* Telescopic levels are widely used, especially on excavations. All have the same primary function, to provide a horizontal line of sight (also termed line of collimation). The intersections of this line with a levelling staff held vertically allow the relative heights of different points to be determined.

Much ingenuity has been employed in constructing devices for this purpose. A useful account has been published by M. A. R. Cooper (*Modern Theodolites and Levels*, Crosby Lockwood and Son, 1971); it is perhaps a little too technical for the archaeologist who merely wishes to use the instrument.

There are many variants, but levels fall into three main types. The simplest is illustrated diagrammatically in Figure 9.1; it comprises:

(a) The telescope (see also Para. 9.4). This is fixed through semipermanent adjusting screws (S) to

(b) A sensitive spirit-level and

(c) The stage, which is integral with the spindle (Sp); this rotates in a bearing in the upper parallel plate (u.p.p.) or tribrach, which is connected by the levelling screws (l.s.) to the lower parallel plate (l.p.p.) which screws onto the tripod head (g).

The levelling screws now almost always number three, but old instruments may have four.

In the telescope, the line of sight is indicated by cross-hairs (now almost always engraved on glass) just inside the eyepiece end. The eyepiece can be moved to focus on the cross-hairs, either on a screw thread or in older instruments by sliding (see Para. 9.4). The spirit-level is parallel to the line of sight, and both are perpendicular to the spindle and its bearing. These last can be set vertical by the levelling screws; the detailed technique is described in Para. 9.4. It is assumed here that the instrument is in adjustment; checking and correction are described in Para. 9.5.

9.1 The Level: Diagram of Essential Features

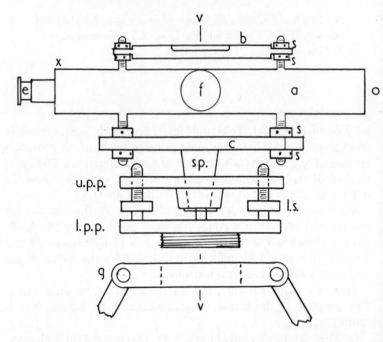

In many dumpy levels the lower semi-permanent adjusting screws are eliminated, and the telescope is fixed rigidly to the spindle.

The tilting level is essentially the same in principle, but the lower semi-permanent adjusting screws are replaced by a pivot and screw with which the telescope is levelled for each reading.

The automatic level works on a radically different system. It contains a freely-pivoted mirror, prism or lens (the compensator), which is acted upon by gravity so that the line of sight is always horizontal. Tilting and automatic levels both have to be levelled roughly before use; this is done either by three levelling screws or by a ball-and-socket tripod head.

In modern levels the essential features are often concealed by a casing, and prisms or mirrors are used to simplify reading the spirit-levels.

9.2 *Choice of Instrument.* You will probably have to take what you can get, but if you have any choice the following notes may be of use.

My own choice is a standard dumpy level. I am no doubt biased through having learnt surveying fifty years ago, but this type has the advantages that you can see whether it is working properly, adjustment is easy, and provided that the lenses, cross-hairs, and spirit-level are intact it can always be used, even if it has suffered other damage.

The automatic level is slightly easier to use, but much more expensive, and if anything does go wrong (admittedly unlikely) a professional overhaul is unavoidable.

The tilting level suffers from the great disadvantage that the telescope has to be relevelled before every reading (see below). If you cannot avoid using one, then provided it has three levelling screws the best thing to do is to fix the tilting screw with a piece of adhesive tape so that it cannot be moved accidentally, and then to use the instrument as if it were a dumpy. Before fixing the screw it must be used as if it were a semi-permanent adjustment to make the telescope perpendicular to the spindle (see Para. 9.5).

Cooper (*Modern Theodolites*, p. 81) cites rates of progress for running a line of levels, comparing an automatic with a tilting level. Allowing a walking speed of 5 km/hr, the figures show that to set up and take two readings consistently takes two minutes longer using the tilting level; for sights up to 60 m in length, the automatic required one-and-a-half minutes. Unfortunately the time taken in setting up, as distinct from taking readings, is not given, but a quarter of a minute would seem reasonable, as against the half-minute needed to set up a dumpy.

In archaeological work, to take twenty or more readings from a single setting-up is much more usual than to run a long line of change points. Using the above figures, to set up and take twenty readings should require twelve and three-quarter minutes with an automatic level, thirteen with a dumpy, and thirty-two and three-quarters with a tilting level; obviously the quarter-minute precision is absurd, but these figures show very clearly the great delay caused in this type of work by the need to relevel for each sight.

To sum up, the automatic level is preferable, provided someone else is paying for it; but it costs roughly twice as much as a dumpy, and the advantage is very small. Further, since the dumpy is now regarded as obsolescent (Cooper, *Modern Theodolites*) recon- ditioned instruments tend to be rather cheaper than other types.

Of the various optional extras, the only one which shows any real advantage is a tripod with telescopic legs. This is helpful when setting up on rough ground, but that is less important with a level than with a theodolite. The main advantage is that transport is much easier.

There are other extras which at best offer no benefits to the user.

(a) A graduated horizontal circle permits measurement of the angles between sights, but for the type of work envisaged here the lack of movement in a vertical plane makes this almost useless; if you need these angles, you need a theodolite.

(b) Tacheometric cross-hairs (Para. 14.2). These are occasionally useful, but generally if you need distances it is quicker and more accurate to measure them with a tape or chain. Moreover, if conditions are bad you may read against the wrong line. Unless the alternatives are easily available, though, it is not worth a fuss to alter whatever is fitted as standard.

(c) A ball-and-socket tripod head. The supposed advantage of this is that you do not have to bother about getting the tripod head even roughly horizontal. In practice it tends either to work loose during use or to jam immovably, whichever is likely to cause the greater inconvenience.

(d) An erect image. Most levels, and nearly all theodolites, show an inverted image. Very little practice is needed to get used to reading this, so the supposed advantage of an erect image is imaginary. Moreover, there is the considerable disadvantage that if you have to use the more usual type, or if someone accustomed to that has to use your level, work will be slowed down and the risk of mistaken readings greatly increased. The same objection applies to levelling staffs numbered upside-down.

A new instrument, or a reconditioned one bought from a reputable firm, should be in correct adjustment when bought. Casual purchase is a gamble, though for a level the risk is less than for a theodolite. Apart from obvious defects such as broken lenses, cross-hairs, or spirit-levels, the most likely faults are worn spindles or levelling screws. If the instrument can be set up properly, the focusing screw works smoothly, the spindle does not stick and there is no relative rotation between the upper and lower parallel plates, it is probably capable of giving adequate results. If there are small defects, the level will only be worth consideration if you can repair them yourself, for the cost of a professional overhaul is now very high indeed. Spare spirit-level tubes can be bought, but are not always easy to fit.

9.3 *The Staff.* Besides the level itself, a levelling staff is essential. These are now graduated (Figure 9.2) in metres, decimetres and centimetres (but see Appendix I). The telescope inverts the image, but you will get used to this after a few readings. *Do not* get a staff which is graduated upside-down (they are obtainable) for if you learn on one of that kind you will make numerous mistakes when you use the normal type; and the apparent advantage is illusory.

The choice of staff is unavoidably a compromise. It has to be transported to the site, and carried about when there, which makes

9.2 Graduation of Levelling Staff

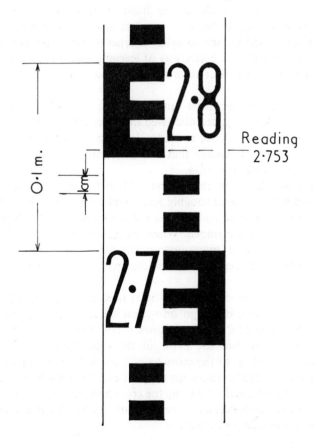

a light, short staff desirable; but the longer it is the less often will your line of sight run a few centimetres above its end. Four metres is about the shortest acceptable. The most convenient type now is probably that made in detachable sections of light metal alloy; these are not affected by damp or corrosion, but care must be taken to make sure they do not get bent. A small attached spirit-level is useful for tacheometric work, but is not needed for levelling. Handles are quite unnecessary. In general, the choice of a staff is very much a matter of personal preference.

Before you do any actual levelling, you should familiarise yourself with the graduation and numbering of the staff, always looking at it upside-down. Note that some numbers are in Roman figures to reduce the risk of confusion, and that some small numerals indicate the metre with which you are dealing. It will be useful, also, to get a colleague to indicate points on the staff (preferably with most of the face concealed), which you will read and then verify with a tape to discover whether you have got the reading correct. This is a better way of learning than by starting at once with the level, for your accuracy can be checked.

9.4 *Setting up.* Observation and booking, and the various applications of levelling, are discussed in succeeding chapters, but the first step must always be to set the level up ready for use. The following description assumes that you are starting the day's work, by setting up at the first station.

Set the tripod firmly on the ground, with its feet pressed into the surface and with the head roughly level. Make sure that the fixing screws between the head and legs are not slack and that the sliding legs (if any) are firmly clamped. When taking the level from its box note how it is arranged; many instruments have only one position in which they can be replaced. Screw the level firmly to the tripod head.

Before using the level, the cross-hairs need to be brought into focus. There is no need to go into great detail as to the optics involved, but in brief the main focusing screw is used to bring the image of the staff into the plane of the cross-hairs; so if the eyepiece is focused on to the cross-hairs there will be no apparent relative motion (parallax) between the staff and the cross-hairs even if the eye is moved a little. To bring the cross-hairs into focus, point the telescope towards the sky or some featureless blank surface and move the eyepiece gently in and out.

This setting is specific to one observer, but two different persons often have eyes sufficiently alike for one to be able to check the other's readings without refocusing. In theory, the setting of the eyepiece will remain right indefinitely, but in practice the characteristics of one's eye change during a day's observation, so occasional refocusing may be needed, preferably when the level is moved to a new position.

The instrument is then levelled.

The telescope, with its attached spirit-level, is placed parallel to a pair of levelling screws, and these are turned in opposite directions until the bubble is central. The rule as to which way to turn the screws is 'the bubble follows the left thumb', which may seem obscure in print but which will reveal its meaning unequivocally the first time you try to set up a level. The telescope is then turned through a right angle and levelling repeated, using *only* the third, previously untouched, levelling screw. (With four screws, opposite pairs are used together, and must be kept just tight.) The telescope is then turned back to its first position and relevelled if necessary, and the process is repeated until the bubble remains central. Provided the instrument is in adjustment, the axis of the spindle is now truly vertical, and the line of sight of the telescope, which is parallel to the spirit-level, will be horizontal in whatever direction it is pointed.

This reads as a slow and laborious procedure, but in fact it takes far less time to do it that to read about it. After a day's practice, or less, the average time for setting up a level on reasonably good ground will be about half a minute; so there is no reason to worry about the need to move the instrument during a series of readings (Chapter 10).

9.5 *Checking the Level.* There is no obvious reason why levels should ever go out of adjustment, unless brutally ill-treated; but they do. The most usual indication is that the instrument cannot be levelled so that the bubble of the spirit level remains central; but apparently inexplicable mistakes in reduced levels may also suggest faulty adjustment.

To check the accuracy is simple. Two firmly driven pegs or other suitably immovable stations are established, on fairly level ground, as far apart as conveniently possible up to 100 m or so. The level is then set up as accurately as its condition permits *exactly* midway between the two pegs; two of the levelling screws should be on that line. Sight on the staff on one peg (A, say), and using those two screws turned in opposite directions (and thus not altering the height of instrument) bring the bubble to the centre of its run and read the staff. Sight towards the other peg B, and repeat, having centred the bubble again. The difference between these readings gives the true difference in level between A and B, even if the instrument is not in adjustment (see Figure 9.3); so if A is taken as at 100·000, B's level can be worked out.

9.3 Checking Level

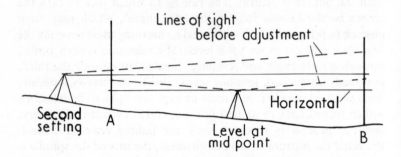

The level is then set up on BA produced, as near to A as possible consistent with clear focusing. The bubble is centred as before, and the staff reading taken for A. Provided, as almost always happens, the inaccuracy of adjustment is small, this will give the height of instrument above A, so the correct reading at B is easily worked out. The staff is held at B, and using the levelling screws but paying no attention to the spirit-level, the cross-hairs are brought to that reading. The reading for A is checked, and if it has altered from its first value the procedure will have to be repeated. When finally the readings at A and B give the correct difference, the line of sight is horizontal.

If the level is out of adjustment, the bubble will no longer be central, but this does not mean that further work must be abandoned until time has been found to make the adjustment needed. If for example the bubble is displaced from the centre towards the eyepiece by 5 mm, then so long as it is in that position the line of sight will be horizontal. If the bubble-tube is graduated, the readings of the ends of the bubble can be noted; alternatively, pieces of adhesive tape can be fixed to the sides of the tube, and the ends of the bubble marked on them.

The second check is whether the axis of the spindle is perpendicular to the line of sight. This is tested by setting up in the ordinary way (Para. 9.4 above). Make sure the bubble is central or that it is between the appropriate marks as explained in the last paragraph; that is that the line of sight is horizontal. Then turn the telescope through 180° about its vertical axis. If it is in adjustment, the line of sight will remain horizontal.

If this adjustment is wrong, again the level can still be used, but will have to be relevelled with a levelling screw for each sight, which is a nuisance. This would not be legitimate in really accurate work, for moving one levelling screw changes the height of instrument a little, but the effect is very small and can be neglected for the type of surveying considered here.

9.6 *Adjustments.* Before attempting any adjustment make sure that you understand exactly what needs to be done, and work through the whole procedure in imagination before you touch any of the adjusting nuts. If you have the slightest doubt about your ability to do the work, do not attempt it; as explained above the level can be used without being exactly adjusted. Nevertheless, the method is simple.

The first step is to set the telescope truly horizontal, as described above. The spirit-level can then be moved by means of the adjusting screws between it and the telescope. These screws are usually capstan-type nuts, turned with a small tommy-bar. They should be moved smoothly and if possible gently; only a small movement will be needed. It is important that these nuts are left tight when the adjustment is finished, but avoid excessive force.

To adjust so that the line of sight (and thus, now, the spirit-level) is perpendicular to the spindle, the instrument is set up as well as possible and the bubble centred. The telescope is then rotated through 180°. Any displacement of the bubble which results is *half* got rid of by the levelling screws, and the adjusting screws between the stage and the telescope are used to make the bubble central again.

After adjustments, the level should again be checked, as before.

In some levels, the spirit-level is attached to the stage instead of directly to the telescope. In that case, adjustment is in the reverse order: the spirit-level is first brought perpendicular to the axis of the spindle, and afterwards the level is adjusted relative to the stage so that when the line of sight is horizontal so is the spirit-level.

Occasionally, though very seldom, the spirit-level has no adjustment relative to the telescope. In that case the line of sight is brought parallel to the spirit-level by adjusting screws which move the diaphragm carrying the cross-hairs; but in general these screws should be left alone.

9.7 *Precautions.* In principle, when the level is screwed to its tripod it should be carried upright, so that the spindle is roughly vertical; this avoids strain on the levelling screws. In practice, levels suitable for the sort of work envisaged here are robust enough to stand being carried over one's shoulder. If you are passing through openings, have the instrument in front of you, and if you are working amongst traffic always carry it upright, for if it is over your shoulder there is an even chance that impact with a moving vehicle will break your neck as well as the level.

When the level is in use, you should try to avoid any contact with it at all when you are taking a reading. Never try to steady it (or yourself) by holding the tripod.

In some conditions, typically a sunny day with a cold wind, you will find that the level drifts slowly out of adjustment, owing to differential expansion of the levelling screws and tripod legs. This effect can be reduced by always setting up with the same leg towards the sun. The movement of the bubble will be small, and for the type of work envisaged here it is legitimate to correct it by means of the levelling screws. A large movement is an almost certain indication that the level has been knocked out of position, and it should be relevelled and a check taken back to the last change point (Para. 10.1).

10 The Level: Observation and Booking

10.1 Booking; 10.2 Reducing Levels; 10.3 Adjustment of Errors.

10.1 *Booking.* There are several purposes for which levelling may be used, and these are discussed in the next chapter; but the methods of observation and booking are always the same. To fix our ideas, assume that we are starting from a 'bench mark' having a known level, and determining a run of levels at points 1 to 8 (Figure 10.1). The bench mark (BM) may either be related to ordnance datum (OD) or may be given some arbitrary value relative to site datum (SD) as for an excavation; abbreviations for these are OBM or SBM.

Observations are recorded in a level book, preferably purpose-made though you can laboriously rule your own. This is similar in

10.1 Run of Levels

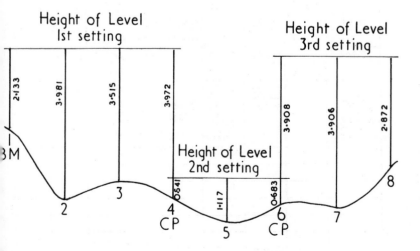

10.2 Booking and Reducing Levels
(a) Height of Instrument Method   (b) Rise and Fall Method

B.S.	I.S.	F.S.	H.O.I.	R.L.	Point	Remarks.
2·133			125·393	123·260	1.	SITE B.M.
	3·981			121·412	2	
	3·515			121·878	3	
0·541		3·972	121·962	121·421	4	C P
	1·117			120·745	5	
3·908		0·683	125·187	121·279	6	C P
	3·906			121·281	7	
		2·872		122·315	8	
6·582		7·527		− 123·260		
−7·527				0·945 ✓		
− 0·945 ✓						

(a)

SPINE

B.S.	I.S.	F.S.	Rise	Fall	R.L.	Point	Remarks
2·133					123·260	1	SITE B.M.
	3·981			1·848	121·412	2	
	3·515		0·466		121·878	3	
0·541		3·972		0457	121·421	4	C P
	1·117			0·676	120·845	5	
3·908		0·683	0·434	0·676	121·279	6	C P
	3·906		0·002		121·281	7	
		2·872	1·034		122·325·315	8	
6·582		7·527	1·936	2·981	−123·260		
−7·527			−2·981	2·881	−0·955 ×		
−0·945			−1·045 ×		−0·945 ✓		
			−0·945 ✓				

(b)

size to a chain survey book but bound along the longer edge. The pages, ruled horizontally, are also divided into columns, usually by red lines. The abbreviations in Figure 10.2a stand for backsight, intermediate sight, foresight, height of instrument, reduced level. These occur on the left page; the right-hand page, only partly indicated in the figure, may carry additional columns but these are not necessary. In some books two columns, headed Rise and Fall, may replace the HOI column (see Figure 10.2b and Para. 10.2).

The observations are imagined to start from a firmly driven peg which forms the site bench mark, 123·26 m above site datum. You set up (Para. 9.4) at any convenient point and look *back* to the staff held on this, so this is a 'backsight'; the reading is 2·133. In fact, you could seldom be sure of the last figure, but it is much less bother and rather more accurate to make a rough estimate of the third decimal place than it would be to try to make up your mind as to whether it is really nearer 2·14 or 2·13. The reduced level of site BM is therefore recorded as 123·260, although the third decimal place is in fact unknown. The line of sight (or line of collimation) cuts the staff at 2·133 m above the BM. Similarly, points 2 and 3 are 3·981 m and 3·515 m below the line of sight. These can be observed without moving the instrument, and are booked as intermediate sights.

It is important that the staff should be vertical when read. Even when a spirit-level is fitted, there will almost always be slight movement, so a much better way of achieving this is to sway the staff slowly backwards and forwards well past the vertical; the *lowest* reading is then booked. This method cannot be used, though, if the readings for three (tacheometric) cross-hairs are needed.

There is no automatic check to detect mistakes; it is easy at the end of a day's work to misread a metre, or even, surprisingly, having *read* a number such as 3·081 correctly to *book* it as 3·801. As a precaution, having read the staff *and booked the reading*, you should always verify it by a second look. If you have a helper to do the booking, he should read the number back to you after he has booked it, for checking. Even when you are alone, you may find it helps to say the figures to yourself out loud.

Point 4 is the last visible from the instrument as now set up, so it will be used as a change point (CP). A 'foresight' is taken to it (3·972, say) preparatory to moving the instrument *forward*. The level is then set up again, a backsight taken back to point 4, and levelling continued. Note that each line in the level book corresponds to a single point (*not* to a single *observation*), so both backsight and foresight to point 4 are entered on the same line.

A CP need not be part of the run of levels which is being surveyed. In choosing a CP, it is important that it should be firm and well-defined, for if the staff is not resting at exactly the same level for both backsight and foresight a mistake is introduced which is carried forward throughout the rest of the run. In really bad ground it may be worth while to carry a metal plate, preferably with a knob on top and with spikes which can be forced into the earth.

For a reason explained later, the last reading in a run is recorded as a foresight (also, you should record the last reading on a page as a foresight and repeat it as a backsight at the beginning of the next page). The booking and reduced levels might then appear as in Figure 10.2.

10.2   *Reducing Levels.* Having taken the necessary readings the 'reduced' levels have to be worked out. There are two methods. Of these, the 'height of instrument' method is more easily understood and is quicker to use than the theoretically preferable 'rise and fall' method.

Referring to Figure 10.2, the level as first set up is 2·133 m above the BM, which is itself 123·260 m above site datum (SD); so the line of sight ('height of instrument') is 125·393 m above SD. Point 2 is 3·981 m below the instrument, so it is at 125·393 − 3·981 = 121·412 m above SD, and similarly for the remaining points. Point 4, used as a change point, is at 121·421, and for its second setting up the level is 0·541 above this. 'HOI' is thus 121·962; and so on.

With the rise and fall method, the difference between each successive staff reading is worked out, and the levels found from those differences. Thus the staff reading on the site BM is 2·133, on point 2 3·981. So point 2 is lower than the BM (a fall) of 3·981 − 2·133 = 1·848. The BM is at 123·260, so (2) is at 121·412. At (3), the staff reads 3·575, so the rise from (2) to (3) is 0·466 and (3) is at 121·878.

The advantage of the rise and fall method is that it provides a check on the arithmetical accuracy of every level calculated:

(sum of backsights − sum of foresights)

= (sum of rises − sum of falls)

= (last reduced level − first reduced level); it is to permit these checks that the last reading on a page is entered as a 'foresight'. With the height of instrument method only the levels of the change points can be checked in this way. This advantage though, is counterbalanced by the disadvantage that 'rise and fall' requires twice as much arithmetic as 'height of instrument'. Much will depend on how quickly you can do arithmetic, but my own preference is for the theoretically inferior method; I find that I am almost always able to work out the reduced level while the staff is being moved from one point to the next, so that the levels are all worked out as soon as the fieldwork is finished. The arithmetic can be made almost as reliable as in 'rise and fall' by a second check in which each reduced level is added to the relevant reading, to make sure that the total gives the height of instrument; this is better than repeating the original subtraction, for if any calculation is repeated exactly, the risk of repeating a mistake is increased.

It is very important to realise that 'rise and fall' does not and cannot detect a misreading, only a mistake in arithmetic.

Examples of the two modes of booking are given in Figure 10.2. Arithmetical mistakes have been included in each.

Note that with 'height of instrument' the mistake at point 5 goes undetected. The two mistakes in the rise and fall example are more likely to be made, but all are identified. Some time is saved if the rise and fall columns are worked out and checked before the reduced levels are filled in.

10.3 *Adjustment of Errors.* For accurate work, any run of levels should start *and finish* on a known level, but even when no mistakes have been made there will almost always be a small error to distribute. In the last example, suppose that point 8 is known to be at 122·30 m above OD; the closing error is therefore 0·015 m. This is built up from errors in the backsights and foresights; the intermediate sights make no contribution. There are six backsights and foresights and each is equally likely to be wrong, so the adjustment to each should be 0·0025 m, but since half a millimetre is insignificant 0·002 and 0·003 are used alternately. The backsights need to be decreased, to 2·131, 0·538, and 3·906, and the foresights increased, to 3·975, 0·685, and 2·875. The corresponding HOI values are 125·391, 121·954, and 125·175. The adjusted intermediate levels are worked out from these without altering the intermediate sights.

11 The Level: Applications

11.1 *Establishing a Site Bench Mark*. The main applications of a level in archaeological fieldwork are for drawing profiles and sections and for contouring, but as a preliminary it is often necessary to establish a site bench mark.

The accuracy with which that needs to be tied in to ordnance datum depends on the circumstances. To do this is always an advantage, but is sometimes not worth the work involved, as, for example, when a site is to be completely destroyed. Otherwise, in order to ensure that present and possible future work can be related accurately, site levels should either be based on ordnance datum or on a *permanent* site datum. If the SD is really permanent, a rough link with OD may be acceptable, such as the intersection of a contour with a road, but the value assigned to the SD and the way in which it has been fixed should always be recorded. The merit of OD is that it is an accepted standard, though even when that is used the basis should be defined (see Para. 27.5).

The nearest OBM is often quite a long way from the site, and special care is needed to establish the site BM. The main precaution is rather obvious: the line of levels is run from the OBM to site BM *and back again*. If done correctly, the closing error will obviously be small. In order to locate mistakes, the change points used should be the same (so far as possible) for both outward and return runs; to work out the reduced levels as you go may save time. Two other points are perhaps less obvious. An OBM is normally the crossbar of a broad arrow cut on a vertical surface. The staff cannot easily be supported at the right level, so rest it on the ground and take the reading against the crossbar (0·224 say). Then the first entry is made as 0·000 backsight against the OBM and the second as 0·244 foresight against 'CP1. Ground below OBM'. The second point to remember is that after reading the staff held on the SBM *the level should be lifted, moved a little way, and reset.* If you do not do this, and you have made a mistake in reading the staff held on the SBM, you are likely to repeat the mistake, so despite the long run of levels you have no real check on your accuracy. An example of a short run of this kind is given in Figure 11.1; the rise and fall method is slightly preferable for this sort of work.

This exemplifies a general rule, that any run of levels should start *and finish* on a point for which the height above datum is known. Thus if you were taking levels at stations A to F in a polygon, starting at A, you would not stop at F but would continue back to A, to make fairly sure that you had made no mistakes. You can only hope that you have not made two which cancel out. Note that these precautions only check the CPs, not the intermediate points.

11.1 Establishing Site Bench Mark

B.S.	I.S.	F.S.	Rise	Fall	R.L.	Remarks.
0·000					201·450	◯ BM
3·821		0·224		0·224	201·226	CP1 Ground below BM
3·903		0·107	3·714		204·940	CP2
3·622		0·081	3·822		208·762	CP3
0·048		0·147	3·475		212·237	Site BM
0·066		3·517		3·469	208·768	CP3
0·124		3·889		3·823	204·945	CP2
0·225		3·832		3·708	201·237	CP1 below OBM
		0·000	0·225		201·462	◯ BM
11·809		11·797	11·236	11·224	− 201·450	
−11·797			−11·224		0·012	
0·012 ✓			0·012 ✓		Rise OBM to SBM	10·787, 10·775
					Average 10·781	
					Accept S BM as	212·23

11.2 *Profiles.* A profile (to be distinguished from a section) is the trace of the intersection of the ground surface with a vertical plane. A line is chosen, and a zero point on it fixed; spot levels are then taken at measured distances from zero along the line. The points, on a scale drawing, are joined up usually with a smooth curve.

Linear measurements for preference should be horizontal, but they can be taken along the ground and either measured thus in plotting or corrected for slope. If all levels can be taken from one setting of the instrument, there is often no need to reduce them; they can be plotted as measurements down from the line of sight (see also Paras. 13.4 and 27.6).

11.3 *Sections.* The strata exposed in the side of an excavation will normally be plotted in the field, the vertical measurements being taken from a horizontal string at some defined level. This application is described in more detail in Para. 27.6.

11.4 *Direct Contouring.* The easiest method is to mark out the contours directly on the ground, using 'wands'; these are then recorded by chain surveying. Two or three contours can be run at a time. Different types of wand (for example, peeled, unpeeled, and with a tuft of leaves) can be used to distinguish the contours, but these are usually widely enough spaced not to get confused. Contours should be booked separately from other detail. The wands are put in by the staff man, who is directed 'up' or 'down' by the man at the level. Thus, with HOI = 125·393, points on the 125 m contour would be found by moving the staff to obtain a reading of 0·39. Time is saved if a broad rubber band is put round the appropriate reading. When you have finished chaining a run, the last wand in each contour line should be left in place, and checked when marking out the next stretch. This method is appropriate when the slope of the ground is fairly gentle.

11.5 *Contouring with Profiles.* This method is useful for fairly small features of marked relief, such as hill-fort entrances or burial-mounds. Lines for profiles are chosen, running mostly at right angles to the contours. These are surveyed, care being taken to record the positions of the 'zeros'. The diagram (Figure 11.2) shows the sort of arrangement which might be used, but in practice about three times as many profiles would be taken, and to measure in the tops and toes of scarps is often useful.

The profiles are drawn on a separate sheet of squared paper, using the same horizontal scale as the plan, but an exaggerated vertical scale; paper can be saved by overlapping the profiles, taking a different zero datum for each, as in the diagram. The points at which the contours cut each profile can then be marked,

11.2 Contouring with Profiles

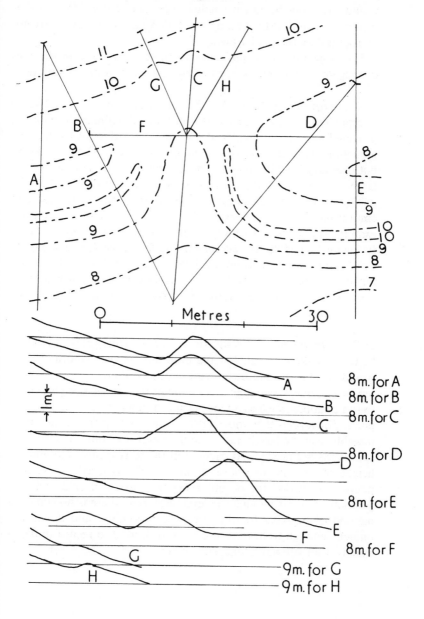

and joined up to give the plan; in a real case, the vertical interval would probably be much smaller than one metre. The profiles themselves, and the lines along which they have been taken, are not reproduced on the final drawing.

The same method is applicable when the profiles follow the lines of a regular grid which has been set out as a preliminary to excavation.

11.6 *Contouring with Random Spot Levels.* Contours can also be interpolated among a scatter of spot levels distributed irregularly, provided they have been placed with some regard to the form of the ground. Usually, the levels are fixed by tacheometry (Paras. 14.3 – 6), but ordinary levelling may be more convenient if, as in a town, a large-scale plan is available with plentiful detail, so that the positions of the spots can easily be fixed. Incidentally, the value of contouring in a town survey is often not realised; compare for example the plans of Conway in the *History of the King's Works* (I, Figure 35) and in the *Caernarvonshire Inventory* (I, Figure 58). As a piece of draughtsmanship, the latter is the less elegant of the two; but it is of far greater value, as it carries contours, which show clearly how the defences were arranged to take advantage of the form of the ground.

11.7 *Single-handed Levelling.* In an extreme emergency, levels can be taken single-handed; but the procedure is very laborious, and would be quite unsuitable for a lot of observations.

Since no one is available to hold the staff, it is tied upright, either to some support such as a fence post or using a makeshift tripod of poles. The *level* is then moved around, and set up first as nearly as possible over the bench mark and then over the points at which the spot levels are needed. At each point the staff is observed and the height of instrument above ground level measured. A 'change point' is provided for by observing the staff in its old and new positions without moving the level. Naturally there is no standard method of booking for this eccentric procedure, and if you are unlucky enough to have to use it you will need to record in detail exactly what you have done, step by step.

Part IV
THE THEODOLITE OR TACHEOMETER

12 The Theodolite: Essential Details

12.1 *Description* (Figure 12.1). The Theodolite, though a very versatile instrument, is essentially simple. A telescope (or in the most elementary forms a sighting tube) is attached to a graduated circle and supported so that it can rotate about a horizontal axis, thus permitting measurement of vertical angles. The supports of the telescope stand on a plate which can rotate about a vertical axis, so horizontal angles can be measured on another graduated circle. By providing three cross-hairs at the eyepiece end, distances can be measured directly by readings on a levelling staff, and the instrument becomes a tacheometer or tachymeter. Since almost all theodolites now have tacheometric cross-hairs the terms are effectively interchangeable.

From this simple basic idea, instruments of great accuracy and of corresponding complexity have evolved. Some can be read to one-fifth of a second of arc, roughly one centimetre at 10 km distance. For our purpose, one minute of arc is quite accurate enough. This gives an accuracy of about three parts in ten thousand, without any difficulty; to obtain half that precision in linear measurements quite laborious precautions are needed. Astro-archaeology is the only research handicapped by this limitation. For all other archaeological work instruments of greater precision can be a positive disadvantage, for the measurements take much longer.

There are many different makes and types of theodolite, and some recent modifications are very useful, but the nature of all such instruments is essentially the same, and can best be understood by describing a simple type (Figure 12.1). Some features are the same as for a level, and to avoid repetition reference back should be made to these.

The telescope (a) is essentially the same as for a level (Para. 9.1) but should, for choice, have three cross-hairs, converting the instrument into a tacheometer (Chapter 14).

12.1 The Theodolite: Diagram of Essential Features

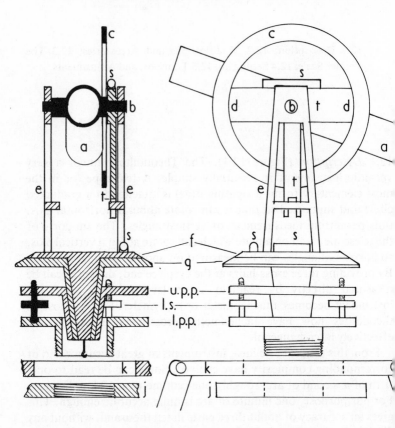

Fixed to the telescope, and rotating with it about the horizontal (or trunnion) axis (b) is the graduated vertical circle (c). Sometimes, but very rarely in modern instruments, the telescope has an attached spirit-level, which simplifies the use of the instrument as a level.

The horizontal axis passes through a T-piece (t) with an attached spirit-level (s). The arms of the T carry vernier scales (d) (Para. 12.3 below) which read against the vertical circle. When the instrument is properly set up and the line of sight is horizontal the vernier may read 90° and 270° (by far the best), 0° and 180°, or 0° and 0° (worst). Make sure what system is used on your instrument.

The T can be clamped to the vertical circle, and there will be a fine adjustment of some kind (usually a tangent screw) which allows fine controlled movements. There are several alternative arrangements, and for simplicity they are omitted in Figure 12.1.

The ends of the horizontal axis rest in bearings in the A-frames or standards (e). The upright of the T is slotted, and fits over a projection on one A-frame. The slot is clamped to this projection, either by capstan screw or by a tangent screw, so that relative adjustment is possible.

The A-frames are rigidly fixed to the vernier plate (f), also known as the upper limb or upper plate. This plate carries a spirit-level (S) with axis parallel to the horizontal axis, and sometimes a second spirit-level at right angles to it. The plate is fixed to a slightly tapered spindle, the inner axis, corresponding to the vertical axis of the instrument.

The vernier plate rests on the lower plate (or limb), (g) which has a graduated circle round its circumference, and is attached to a hollow spindle, the outer axis, within which the inner axis can rotate.

The outer axis rotates in a bearing in the upper parallel plate (u.p.p.) The upper and lower plates can be clamped together, and the lower plate can be clasped to the upper parallel plate; both clamps have tangent screws for fine adjustment.

The lower parallel plate (l.p.p.) is not screwed direct to the tripod head (k) but to a sliding plate (j) which can move relative to the tripod head and can be clamped to it.

The tripod head and the sliding plate are pierced so that a plumb-bob can be suspended from the lower end of the inner axis.

The vernier scales are provided with small magnifiers to assist reading them, not shown in Figure 12.1.

12.2 *Modifications and Accessories*. All theodolites incorporate the features described above, but in most modern instruments they are more or less masked by a protective casing. In general, for the type of work envisaged here, complications should be avoided, but there are some modifications or accessories which, at least in some circumstances, are really useful.

The most valuable of all, which should be obtained if at all possible, is the modification which replaces the vernier scales. The graduated scales are engraved on glass and totally enclosed, and a system of prisms brings their images to one or two eyepieces, where they can be read through small magnifiers which are focused in the same way as the telescope eyepiece. This device cuts down the time needed to read angles to about a quarter of that taken when working with verniers.

Theodolites can also be obtained with automatic levelling devices connected to the vertical circle. These save some time and improve accuracy in tacheometric work, but for the sort of surveying envisaged here the gain is not very great, and the considerable extra cost would be hard to justify.

For most field surveying, the limited vertical range of an ordinary theodolite (some 30° or 40° above or below horizontal) is no disadvantage. If, though, you are working inside a tall building, such as a ruined castle keep, a prismatic eyepiece is almost essential. With it, observations can be made to elevations up to about 80°.

If you are working a lot in very bad light, as for example underground, a properly made device to illuminate the cross-hairs will be useful; but this is not essential if the need only arises occasionally (Para. 24.4).

If you need magnetic bearings more accurately than can be read on a prismatic compass, you can get a compass to attach to the theodolite; this will usually allow readings to about 15 minutes or better. Again, the need for this is only likely to arise in underground work, where you need all the checks you can get.

The optical plummet, which replaces the plumb-bob and string, is seldom available except for instruments which would be excessively accurate for the type of work envisaged here.

As noted earlier (Para. 9.2) the purchase of a second-hand theodolite, except from a reputable dealer, is a gamble. In addition to the checks described there you can see whether the tangent screws work smoothly, and measure the horizontal angle between two well-defined marks using different parts of the horizontal circle; but a much used instrument can often conceal faults which could only be detected by an expert instrument technician.

12.3 *The Vernier Scale.* Most readers will be familiar with this, but it is described here for reference. In the diagram (Figure 12.2) the main scale is divided into half degrees. The vernier scale has 30 divisions, corresponding in total length to 29 of the main divisions, so when the 17th vernier graduation, say, coincides exactly with a division of the main scale, zero on the vernier scale has moved $^{17}/_{30}$ ths of half a degree, that is, 17 minutes, from the adjacent

12.2 Vernier Scale

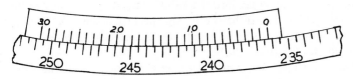

preceding graduation on the main scale. The same principle applies to any system of subdivision; those most commonly found are 1', 30'' or 20''.

12.4 *Setting Up.* A theodolite takes rather longer to set up than does a level, for it has to be set vertically over the station. In reasonably good conditions, after a little practice, setting up should take about one-and-a-half minutes.

Remember that the stations are at the poles, not at the pegs; so a pole must always be replaced in the same position relative to the corresponding peg, and in setting up you plumb down to the hole in which the pole stood. Where grass or vegetation is long, a short length of rod to make a temporary mark is useful. The distinction between peg and pole will make no measurable difference on the finished plan, but can introduce inconveniently large closing errors when the angles are checked.

To set up, the plumb-bob is brought as nearly as possible into the right position by moving the tripod legs, at the same time trying to keep the tripod head roughly level. Using the sliding plate, the plumb-bob is then centred exactly over the required point, and the sliding plate is clamped. The instrument is then levelled, as for the level (Para. 9.4).

You will sometimes find that the tripod head is so far off level that there is not enough travel available in the levelling screws. The slope of the tripod head can be altered *without much movement of the plumb-bob* by moving the end of the appropriate leg *along the circumference* of the circle passing through the three tripod feet; *not* radially to that circle.

12.5 *Transport and Adjustments.* The extra weight of a theodolite puts more strain on its attachment to the tripod than occurs with a level, but most instruments are fairly robust. Nevertheless, there is an additional risk, in that in some types fixings such as the clamp of the sliding plate or the upper bearings of the horizontal axis may come unscrewed; so get into the habit of making sure, as routine, that everything is safe before lifting the instrument. Also, make sure when putting it into its case that it is correctly arranged; never exert any force to close the lid.

The adjustment most often needed is to ensure that the spirit-level on the vernier plate is perpendicular to the vertical axis. This is done in the same way as the second adjustment of the level (Para. 9.6). The same warnings apply.

The accuracy of the vertical readings can be checked as for the first adjustment of the level (Para. 9.6), the vernier being set at zero. In the older type, the spirit-level on the T-piece can be adjusted, but in modern instruments all that can usually be done is to note the zero-error; they are, however, very unlikely indeed to go wrong.

Apart from these simple adjustments, it is almost always unwise to attempt to rectify faults in a theodolite, especially in a modern one.

13 The Theodolite: Observation and Booking

13.1 General Remarks; 13.2 Horizontal Angles; 13.3 Vertical Angles; 13.4 Profiles with a Theodolite.

13.1 *General Remarks.* The primary function of a theodolite is to measure angles, both horizontal and vertical. These measurements are much more accurate than most others in the type of survey considered here, and usually, though not always, form the basis for a numerical calculation; the various types of these are discussed in the next Part (V).

There are several different rulings for angle books, but probably the most common is that shown in Figures 13.1 and 14.2. Although this is designed for tacheometry, it can be used equally well for any angular measurements; as will be obvious from the examples, you are not obliged to keep rigidly to the headings as given. Except in one case, I have assumed throughout that the instrument reads to minutes, and that an estimate has been made of tenths. When booking minutes or seconds note that a single figure must *always* be preceded by zero, and where appropriate the zero after the decimal point must also be given. Thus 4 minutes exactly should be booked as 04·0, not as 4 or 4·0; if blurred by rain these could be misread. The same convention for degrees (for example, 082° rather than 82°) is good practice, but not essential.

A modern theodolite which has been well looked after will probably be in adjustment, so the procedure described later, designed to detect 'mistakes', is a sufficient precaution. If you suspect that the instrument is not in adjustment, errors can be eliminated by taking readings according to the following programme: 'right face' (rf) means that the vertical circle is on the right of the telescope, 'right twist' (rt), or alternatively 'swing right' means that the instrument is rotated clockwise as viewed from above, while lf and lt have corresponding 'left' meanings. Thus left face left twist (lflt) means that the vertical circle is on the left of the telescope and the instrument is rotated anticlockwise;

when the telescope is turned about its horizontal axis so that the vertical circle moves from one side to the other, the instrument is said to have 'changed face'. If four sets of readings are taken (rfrt, rflt, lfrt, and lflt), averaging the resulting angles will eliminate errors caused by slight maladjustment of the spirit levels and slight slackness of the supports. Even if you feel confident that the instrument is in adjustment you should do a full run of this kind occasionally as a check, and see whether there is any appreciable difference in the resulting angles. It is particularly desirable to 'change face' when you are taking vertical angles, for those depend on the vernier arm or its equivalent being truly horizontal. The change in 'twist' is usually less important.

13.2 *Horizontal Angles.* Many applications of the theodolite require horizontal angles only. The station at which the instrument is set up must obviously be noted, and it is sometimes useful to record bad weather conditions, as a guide to the reliability of the readings.

Three precautions should be invariable:

(a) A run of readings should *always* start and finish on the same point, for it is very easy indeed to move the wrong tangent screw. If the final reading does not check to sufficient accuracy (say less than 01 minute), the whole run should be disregarded and repeated.

(b) The run should start at some random reading; for if the first figure is near a simple value such as 0° or 90°, there is a tendency to book it at exactly that. Moreover, such a figure is easy to remember, so if a mistake has been made it is likely to be repeated at the end of the run.

(c) All runs should be taken at least twice, starting with different random angles.

Figure 13.1 exemplifies a round of bookings, and shows how a standard tacheometry angle book can be adapted when only angular measurements are needed; almost always, to keep one book for all theodolite and tacheometer observations is preferable to using separate books, even though many of the column headings will often be found to be irrelevant.

If only horizontal angles are being observed (Figure 13.1, top) everything except 'Angles; horiz.' can be crossed out in the first four column headings, giving ample room to book two runs of readings. The first run starts with the reading 319° 07·0' to the spire, and is taken clockwise (right twist), as indicated by the

13.1 Booking Angles

Station ___B___

Height of Instrument _____

No. of Point.	Angles		Reading of Wires	Reading of Axial	Rise	Fall	Reduced Level	Dist.	Horiz. Dist.	Remarks
	Horiz.	Vert.								
319°	070'	74°	30.3' ✓							SPIRE
105°	24.5'	220°	47.7'	↑						A
135°	258°85'ER	250°	49.0 ER			3m pole ① Top 1m Down 135°27.6' 270° ②	250°	51.1' 50.4'		E
230°	10.6'	345°	33.8'							F
319°	06.4'	74°	30.1'							SPIRE

Station ___B___

Height of Instrument ___1.33___

Unless noted, all poles 2m., with 0.1m in ground. All sights to top of pole

No. of Point.	Angles		Reading of Wires	Reading of Axial	Rise	Fall	Reduced Level	Dist.	Horiz. Dist.	Remarks
Vernier A	B	A	B							
319°01'00"	01'00"	—	—							SPIRE
105°24'00"	24'30"	86°3d00	30'00"							A
135°26'00"	26'30"	94°05'30	05'00"							E(3m.)
230°10'30"	11'00"	100°30'30"	30'30"							F
319°06'30"	06'00"	✓								SPIRE

arrow, closing with 319° 06·4' to the spire again. The second run can be booked in the remaining two columns, and is taken left twist, so the entries start at the bottom.

If horizontal and vertical angles are being taken, 'Angles horiz. and vert.' are kept as headings, and the readings are allowed to overflow into adjacent columns. There is no possibility of confusion. With a vernier theodolite, one vernier is booked in full, giving degrees, minutes, and seconds; only minutes and seconds are booked for the other.

If someone else is booking, he should compare the readings on the second run with those on the first before the observer sights another point. Thus in Figure 13.1 top, suppose that the second reading for A were given as 220° 37·7', then deducting from the reading to E, 250° 49·0' would make the angle ABE 30° 11·3', instead of 01·3' as previously. The booker would then say 'Check'. He would not say what he thought the reading ought to be, for that might cause the observer to repeat the mistake.

It is sometimes useful to take the first reading not to a station but to some permanent landmark, such as a church spire or the gable end of a distinctive building. This is advisable if your station poles are liable to displacement by humans, cattle, or wind. It is also useful if you are going to return for tacheometry, for you can then simply set up at each station in turn without the need to put up poles at the others.

You will often find that the pole on to which you are sighting is not vertical, and that the bottom is invisible. There is no need to go to the pole and reset it plumb. Observe the horizontal reading for the top and (say) halfway down; clearly the corrected reading at the bottom can easily be deduced. Both actual readings should be booked, so that the estimated correction can be checked in the office. An example is given in Figure 13.1, assuming a 3 m pole.

13.3 *Vertical Angles* (Figure 13.1 bottom). These are usually taken either to allow the chain measurements to be corrected for slope or to establish the levels of the stations; tacheometry is discussed below (Chapter 14). They can also be used to find the heights of inaccessible features in buildings.

The method of booking is similar to that for horizontal angles. The measurement involves the assumption that when the reading is 90° (or sometimes 0°) the telescope is horizontal, but quite a small maladjustment can have a considerable effect on the result; so if the levels to be determined are important, the readings should be taken right face and left face.

If all that is required is a correction for slope, measure the height of the horizontal axis above ground level (with the pole which marked the station) and then sight on the same height above ground on the pole at the station being observed. Since you will be making a corresponding observation from that station the final average will be accurate enough for the required purpose.

If more precise values are needed for the levels of the stations, two methods are available. Neither is quite as reliable as normal levelling, and indeed if the time spent in calculations in the office is taken into account theodolite observations show little advantage; but they save time in the field.

The simpler of the two methods is to observe the tops (or a known subdivision) of the poles marking the stations. A record must be made of the total height of each pole and of the length inserted in the ground. Since the distances between stations are known the differences in level can easily be calculated. The average difference found by observations taken in both directions will be accurate enough for subsequent contouring, but is not really precise. The method has the advantage that only one (of the assumed party of two) is needed; the second can be engaged in other work, assuming that the stations are already marked with poles.

Levels of greater precision, good enough for most purposes, can be obtained by sighting on the levelling staff, and recording also the vertical angle. If the height of instrument is also measured carefully observations may be made from every alternate station; but this is not good practice as the risk of an undetected mistake is increased.

The example given in Figure 13.1 bottom assumes the use of an instrument with vernier scales, nominally reading to 30 seconds. Once again, it is convenient to disregard most of the column headings.

13.4 *Profiles with a Theodolite.* Unless special care is taken, levels calculated by measuring vertical angles will be less accurate than those found by levelling; nevertheless they are adequate for most profiles (cf. Paras. 11.2, 26.9).

The theodolite is set up at 'zero' on the line of the profile, usually on the main rampart; its height above ground level is noted. The telescope is set to some convenient vertical angle, which is booked. If aimed at the ground just beyond the far end of the profile, all the necessary readings can often be taken with one setting, but the angle can be changed if desirable. The staff is then held up at suitable points and readings taken. Distances can be measured horizontally, using a tape anchored at zero, or they can be taken from the telescope to the relevant staff reading. An alternative, which makes measurement easier but needs some mental arithmetic, is to take the distance from ground level at zero to a point on the staff corresponding to 'staff reading minus height of instrument'.

The readings can be plotted as measurements down from the line of sight, and the distances can also be marked off directly, either horizontally or along the line of sight; no calculation is needed.

For most defensive earthworks a single setting-up as above is enough; but if the ditches are very deep points can be established on intermediate ramparts and parts of the profile observed from them.

14 Tacheometry

14.1 *The Instrument.* As usually available, a tacheometer (or tachymeter) is simply a theodolite with 'tacheometric' cross-hairs (Figure 14.1), which can therefore be used in conjunction with an ordinary levelling staff to measure distances. Almost all theodolites now have such cross-hairs, so in colloquial use the terms theodolite and tacheometer are practically interchangeable. The existence of variant types needs to be noted, but they are seldom encountered in archaeological work, so will not be described in detail here. If one should become available, the accompanying instructions must be studied. I have no personal experience of these instruments, apart from a very brief examination of the second type.

In the simplest variant, sighting is to a horizontal staff, instead of to a vertical one. The cost is similar to that for ordinary tacheometric equipment. The advantage is that swaying in the staff has relatively little effect on the readings; the disadvantage is that the ordinary levelling staff cannot be used.

Recently, a very ingenious (and correspondingly expensive) 'self-reducing' theodolite has been devised, in which the cross-hairs move to compensate automatically for the change in vertical angle. The distance is invariably 100 times the intercept between two cross-hairs and the 'rise' or 'fall' is a simple factor such as two or five times another intercept. Work in the field is about twice as fast as with an ordinary tacheometer, and work in the office is greatly reduced.

Finally, although it is not really the same type of instrument, mention must be made of electronic distance measurement. In very oversimplified terms, this can be regarded as a theodolite which measures distances directly, and with great accuracy, either by a form of radar or by interferometry. Such instruments are very expensive indeed, and require some experience in use. They would be of value in establishing a large network, but details would have to be filled in by other methods.

14.2 *Basic Principles* (Figure 14.1). For the ordinary tacheometer, the only one which will be discussed in detail here, the principle is simple. The lines of sight through the upper and lower cross-hairs diverge at one hundredth of a radian, so if the telescope is horizontal the distance from the telescope to the staff is 100 times the intercept on the staff. This is a slight oversimplification, for in some older instruments an additive constant is needed, and very rarely indeed the multiplier is not 100. These quantities can be checked by a few horizontal sights to the staff held at measured distances. The explanation which follows can easily be modified if necessary, but in practice, for this type of work, any additive constant is likely to

14.1 Tacheometry

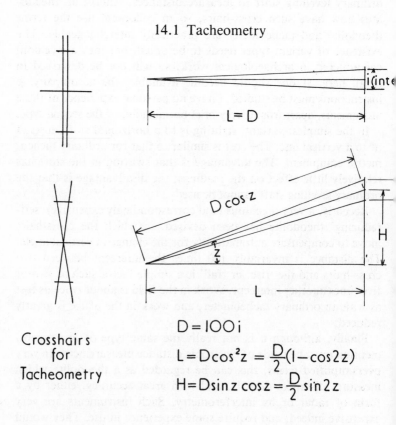

Crosshairs
for
Tacheometry

$$D = 100\,i$$
$$L = D\cos^2 z = \frac{D}{2}(1 - \cos 2z)$$
$$H = D\sin z\cos z = \frac{D}{2}\sin 2z$$

be negligible having regard to the inevitable inaccuracy of the measurements.

The relevant formulae are set out in Figure 14.1. Fortunately, tacheometric slide-rules and tables are available to simplify the calculations. Alternatively, they can be done very quickly with an electronic calculator; a programme is given in Para. 17.2, table 17.1.

For measurement, an ordinary levelling staff is used, but it must be held vertically and should therefore be fitted with a spirit-level. Unfortunately, in practice the staff-man is only able to hold the staff really steady under absolutely ideal conditions; this fact is the major source of inaccuracy in tacheometry, for as will be obvious everything depends on the precision with which the intercept between the upper and lower cross-hairs is known; any movement of the staff between taking those two readings will cause a disproportionate error in the final result. Even under ideal conditions, the distance measurement will usually be rather rough, for one can seldom read the staff to an accuracy of better than about 2 mm. Since there will be that sort of uncertainty in the readings for both upper and lower cross-hairs, the calculated distance may be nearly half a metre wrong.

The most useful application of tacheometry, therefore, is to fix spot levels for contouring. For accessible detail, the method is not only much less accurate than chain surveying but is also much slower. Nevertheless it can be of value in fixing isolated features around the perimeter of a survey, particularly, for example, as when a scatter of isolated huts spreads down a craggy hillside. Preferably in such a case two or more points should be taken on the feature to be recorded, and their distance apart noted by the staff-man. Otherwise, the precautions to be observed are the same as for spot levels.

14.3 *Contouring.* A possible method of contouring with a tacheometer is to keep the telescope horizontal and use it as a level; the distance and direction are fixed tacheometrically. This is considerably slower and less accurate than the alternative method, of marking out the contour with wands which are then located by chain surveying (Para. 11.4).

The real value of a tacheometer appears in dealing with a site, such as a hill-fort, where the variation in level may be considerable. The instrument is used to fix spot levels, and the contours are drawn by interpolation between these. Several hundred spot levels may be needed on a large site.

A survey of this kind will often be based on a trigonometrical network, and the observations will take more than one day. In that case, it will almost always be preferable to complete measurement of the angles for the network first, and to establish the levels of the stations, either by levelling or by measurement of vertical angles. The tacheometric survey of the spot levels is then treated as a separate operation. In what follows it is assumed that this programme is being followed, and that a 'landmark' (which may be another station) has been included among the angular observations. Alternative methods of booking are explained in Para. 14.4.

The instrument is set up over a station, and its height above that level is recorded, as well as the 'name' of the station (Figure 14.2).

The lower plate of the tacheometer is kept locked throughout the work.

A reading is taken to the 'landmark' or to a known and fairly distant station. This, which should be a random angle, is booked. Observations are then taken to the staff (desirable precautions are noted below). The reading to the 'landmark' should invariably be checked before leaving the station, and preferably at intervals during the round of levels. If it has altered appreciably, any observations since the last check will have to be scrapped and repeated.

Each position of the staff is given a number in the angle book. The staff-man also carries a note book, in which he records each number, together with any relevant notes, such as '20 top of scarp', 21E end of line of crags', '22 centre of doorway 1 m wide, of round hut, inner face, wall 0·9 m thick', '23 hut, inner face opposite doorway, 6·3 m to 22', and so on. The observer and staff-man can very easily get out of step, so at least at every tenth spot (for example, 90 in Figure 14.2) the staff-man should shout the number and the observer should confirm that he agrees. If he does not, observations on previous spots must be repeated until the mistake is found and eliminated. This regular check is essential.

Apart from keeping this record, the staff-man has only two responsibilities: to choose the spots so that interpolation will be easy and accurate; and to hold the staff vertical and stationary. This last is very difficult indeed, especially in any sort of wind.

The observer has to record the horizontal and vertical angles and the readings of the three cross-hairs. The angles present no problems, save that it is obviously important that the instrument should be level; otherwise an error is introduced into the vertical angle. In the type of work considered here, an occasional *small* adjustment by the levelling screws is permissible.

The main difficulty arises in reading the cross-hairs, for in practice the staff is almost always in movement, so that you need to observe two four-figure readings simultaneously. I have found the following approach fairly satisfactory, but I do not claim it as ideal. Much depends on how quickly you can read the staff and how many figures you can carry in your head long enough to record them accurately.

Having sighted on the staff, and clamped both the horizontal and the vertical scales, I try to read the *decimal* parts against the upper and lower cross-hairs to three decimal places, neglecting the whole metres. When I am satisfied that I have, in effect, got both readings simultaneously, I book them. Then I book the whole-metre readings for all three cross-hairs. I look again and verify whether the *intercept* between the upper and lower readings agrees with what I have recorded (the actual readings will almost certainly have altered). If that is correct, I read the decimals for the upper and *middle* cross-hairs; if the upper reading has increased by (say) 0·013 m I reduce the middle reading by that amount, and book it. If it is a particularly important point I may make a further check, by reading again the last two decimal places for all three cross-hairs, to make sure that the new readings all differ from those booked by the same amount; but usually I am content with the final, *essential*, check that the average of the two outer readings equals the reading against the central cross-hairs. Provided this check is satisfactory, I then signal to the staff-man to move to the next spot. While he is doing so, I read and book the horizontal and vertical angles, being particularly careful not to move the telescope before doing this. All this is not, in fact, anything like as laborious as it sounds.

14.4 *Booking and Precautions*. The columns in most angle books provide for recording as in Figure 14.2 top. I prefer to allow more space by putting the number of point in the 'remarks' column and using the 'rise' column to book one of the outer cross-hairs readings (Figure 14.2 bottom). No risk of confusion is caused.

As noted above, sights should be made occasionally to the starting station or landmark, as time permits, and this reading must

14.2 Booking for Tacheometry

Station ___B___   Level 292·63 OD
Height of Instrument ___1·28(GL)___ = 293·91 OD

No. of Point.	Angles Horiz.	Vert.	Reading of Wires	Reading of Axial	Rise	Fall	Reduced Level	Dist.	Horiz. Dist.	Remark
SPIRE	319°07'	—	—							
88	197°16'	74°30'	3·352 / 1·274	2·314	5351	—	345·11	207·8	192·86	
89	148°13'	110°40'	3·160 / 2·119	2·638	—	3438	256·90	104·1	91·13	
90✓	135°25'	98°35'	1·935 / 0·240	1·087	—	2501	267·81	169·5	165·72	
91	113°28'	88°45'	1·881 / 0·105	0·994	19·22	—	312·14	177·6	178·50	
92	111°35'	90°00'	2·702 / 1·465	2·083	0	0	291·83	123·7	123·70	
SPIRE	319°06'✓	—	—							

Station ___B___   Level 292·63 OD
Height of Instrument ___1·28(GL)___ = 293·91 OD

No. of Point.	Angles Horiz.	Vert.	Reading of Wires	Reading of Axial	Rise	Rise Fall	Reduced Level	Dist.	Horiz. Dist.	Remark Point
	319° 07'	—	—							SPIRE
	197° 16'	74°30'	3·352	2·314	1·274	R 53·51	345·11	267·8	192·96	88
	148° 13'	110°40'	3·160	2·638	2·119	F 34·38	256·90	104·1	91·13	89
	135° 25'	98°35'	1·935	1·087	0·240	F 25·01	267·81	169·5	165·72	90✓
	113° 28'	83°45'	1·881	0·994	0·105	R 19·22	312·14	177·6	175·50	91
	111° 35'	90°00'	2·762	2·083	1·465	L	291·83	123·7	123·70	92
	319° 06'✓									SPIRE

always be checked at the end of a round of observations. The spirit-levels should also be checked fairly frequently.

When taking spot levels, to diminish the large errors arising from the uncertainty of distance measurements, you should try to get the line of sight roughly parallel to the ground surface. Also, keep in mind that the effect of sway in the staff is less when the readings are low, and that it is easier for the staff-man to hold the staff steady if he is only using two sections instead of three. If readings near the top of the staff cannot be avoided, a useful check is to take two (or better three) sets of readings, with different vertical angles. As a special case, if the staff is not too far away, it is almost always worth while to have the telescope horizontal if possible, for it greatly decreases the subsequent work of reducing the observations.

On the outskirts of the survey, especially if these include a steep hillside, contouring can often be extended accurately enough if the staff-man measures the slope with a fairly accurate clinometer, and records it against the relevant point number in his notes.

14.5 *Reducing Readings.* Unless a suitable electronic calculator is available, the first step in reducing the readings is to fill in the 'Distance' column. This is simply 100 times the difference in readings between the outer cross-hairs. Then, if you have used up the Rise column for one of the readings, write R or F as appropriate down the edge of the Fall column. If, for example, 90° on the vertical circle is 'horizontal', angles less than 90° correspond to 'R', and similarly those over 90° to 'F'. This is the rise or fall relative to the telescope, not as in levelling relative to the previous point.

Calculation of the horizontal distance and of the rise or fall is facilitated by using either 'tacheometric tables', or a tacheometric slide-rule, which may either be the normal ruler type or circular. The slide-rules are almost always accurate enough, and are much quicker to use than the tables. Tables and slide-rules are always accompanied by instructions, so there is no need to describe them here.

Rarely, usually if the vertical angle is approaching 40° or more, the formula has to be used. The necessary calculations are described in Para. 17.2.

Having filled in the rise or fall, the reduced level is given by height of instrument above datum minus the axial reading plus rise (or minus fall).

If an electronic calculator is available all the calculations can be done as quickly as with a slide-rule, and more accurately (Para. 17.2).

14.6 *Plotting.* This can almost always be done using a 25 or 30 cm diameter circular protractor, and a scale. The protractor is placed so that the appropriate reading lies on the line joining the station to the 'landmark' or starter station, and the angles corresponding to the points are marked and numbered. The positions of the various spot levels can then be scaled off. The corresponding level should be marked against each spot.

Contours are filled in by interpolation, either by eye (if no great

14.3 Contouring with Spot Levels

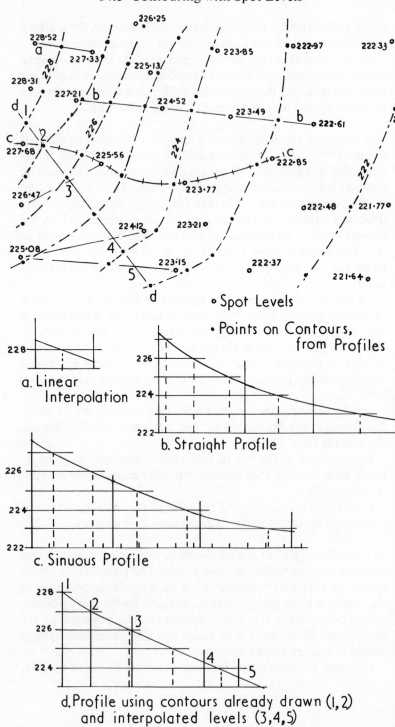

- Spot Levels
- Points on Contours, from Profiles

a. Linear Interpolation

b. Straight Profile

c. Sinuous Profile

d. Profile using contours already drawn (1, 2) and interpolated levels (3, 4, 5)

accuracy is needed), by slide-rule, or by sketching profiles on squared paper. The last is probably the simplest method; note that a contour which has already been drawn can be used in sketching the profile, also that a profile can be drawn following a gently sinuous line in plan; in this last case, measurements must be taken step by step along the curve. Examples are given in Figure 14.3.

Although rather more work is involved, you will probably find it best to complete one contour at a time. This avoids the risk of straying on to the wrong line of dots. Also, if there is much detail on the main plan, confusion can be avoided by plotting the spot levels and resulting contours on a separate sheet, the two plans being combined in the final tracing.

Except on very large-scale plans, as for example of a burial-mound, it is probably better to reserve contours to represent the form of the natural ground surface, using a convention such as hachuring or stippling to indicate artificial structures; but there is no general rule about this.

15 Setting Out a Rectangle

15.1 General Remarks; 15.2 Equipment and Materials;
15.3 Corrections; 15.4 Setting out; 15.5 Examples of Measurement;
15.6 Detached Base Lines: 15.7 Transfer Pegs.

15.1 *General Remarks*. Many excavators now use a rectangular co-ordinate system as a basis for their records. Although a theodolite is not absolutely essential (see Para. 7.5), it greatly simplifies setting out the necessary frame. One minute of arc corresponds to 3 parts in 10,000, and if used with care a theodolite, reading direct to one minute, can give an accuracy of 1 in 10,000 without much trouble. To get the same accuracy in linear measurement is laborious, so the first thing to decide is what sort of precision you need. Working over smooth ground cleared of irregularities, taking levels at every change of slope, and averaging at least two measurements, the accuracy of ordinary chaining can be raised to about 1 in 1,000, assuming of course that the chain itself is accurate. With a steel tape under similar conditions, and using pegs as described below but driven flush with the ground, this can be improved to about 1 in 5,000. If that is not good enough, the measurements must be made 'in catenary', that is with the tape raised free of ground and its irregularities.

This method is described in detail below. It is not quite as laborious as it sounds, but is obviously to be avoided if lesser accuracy is acceptable. If measurement in catenary is replaced by measurement along the ground the necessary modifications are obvious. For really precise work corrections would also be needed to allow for comparison with a standard tape, height above sea level, the stretch of the tape under tension, and its temperature; but the corrections for sag and slope are adequate to give 1 in 10,000 accuracy.

15.2 *Equipment and Materials*. For measurement of angles and slopes, the theodolite and the levelling staff are necessary. The level is useful, but not essential.

For linear measurement, a *50 m steel band*, graduated throughout in millimetres, is to be preferred (not a studded band chain, which is not closely graduated). One of 100 m is rather inconveniently long, but a 30 m steel tape can be used. This band should be reserved exclusively for accurate work. To accompany this, you will need a *tension handle* reading to 10 kg, and a *roller grip* which allows a handle to be attached at any point on the band.

If not measuring in catenary the tension handle and the roller grip are not necessary, but the band should be of heavier section.

Other equipment required is a heavy hammer to drive pegs, and a light claw-hammer to drive and extract nails. A pair of pliers is also useful.

Another very useful accessory is a builder's level, sometimes called a bricklayer's level or simply a long spirit-level. This is essentially a solidly made straight-edge about a metre long, fitted with spirit-levels so that it can be held either horizontal or vertical. It should be painted along *one angle only* with alternate red (or black) and white strips on the broad face and contrasting strips on the adjacent narrow face; this is far easier than a plumb-line to sight on and to manipulate. It is not mentioned specifically in what follows, but should be used for any distant sight and wherever a measurement needs to be plumbed upwards or downwards.

Finally, an ample supply is needed of properly made pegs of about 5 cm square and 40 cm long, also some 3 or 4 cm (1½ inch) nails.

If not working in catenary, the pegs should be shorter, so that they can be driven flush with the ground surface.

Most of the necessary corrections can be worked out longhand, but time will be saved if a table of logarithms or (preferably) an electronic calculator is available on site.

15.3 *Corrections.* The expressions for these are given in Appendix IV. Assuming that a high degree of accuracy is desired, exact or closely approximate formulae should be used. The correction for slope needs no further discussion. That for sag is probably best determined in the field, though it can be worked out provided the weight of the band per metre is known, as well as the applied tension. Once found it does not alter, provided the tension is kept the same.

As part of your preparation for measurement you have pegs nos. 2, 3, and 4, say, equally spaced at 24·9 m (see Para. 15.4); the level of the top of peg 3 is the mean of those for pegs 2 and 4. Preferably

they should all be at the same level, but this is not essential.
Temporary pegs are driven nearly to ground level midway between
2 and 3, and between 3 and 4, and levels taken on them.

One end of the steel band is anchored on the nail on peg 2 (do not
use peg 0); the other end passes over the top of peg 4, and the
middle over peg 3. The same tension is applied as will be used when
measuring the line (probably 5 or 10 kg), and the sags are found by
measuring up from the intermediate temporary pegs. Then the
correction in each half length is $\frac{8}{3} \times (\text{Sag})^2 \div$ length; for a numerical example see Para. 15.5. Note that if the tension or length is
altered, the correction will vary inversely as the tension, or directly
as the cube of the length.

In this work the nails on the pegs should not normally be used as
anchorages, for the pull may displace the pegs. The sag correction
should therefore be determined before the main measurement is
started. It is for this reason, also, that peg 0 is not used in
determining this correction.

15.4 *Setting out.* Whether or not you are aiming at a high degree of
precision, the corner points should be established first, the
intermediate pegs being put in later.

To fix our ideas, suppose that a rectangle ABCD 300 × 200 m is
to be marked out, using a graduated 50 m steel band; in practice the
area is usually likely to be much less, but the principles remain the
same. Initially, you have one corner (A) fixed, and the direction of one
side AB; the corner A is marked by a nail driven into the top of a peg.

Having set up the theodolite over A and sighted along AB with
the horizontal angle reading zero, pegs must be driven at intervals
of about 24·95 m along this line; the *exact* distances are not at this
stage crucial, but they should be kept nearly equal. For convenience
call these pegs 1, 2, etc, the corner A being at peg 0 and peg 12
being about a metre short of the required position of B.

The even numbered pegs are lined in and then driven firmly into
the ground leaving 20 or 30 cm standing above the surface. Note
that, because the image in the telescope is inverted, if you want the
image of the peg to move to the right you must signal for the peg to
be moved to the left. Note also that if the peg starts to lean
sideways while being driven it must be corrected by *hitting the earth
close to the base of the peg* (perhaps with a stone rammed in to give
extra effect). The peg itself should never be knocked sideways, as

this loosens it. Having got a peg in line, a nail is lined in and driven into the top, thus marking the alignment; enough should be left projecting to allow it to be withdrawn, for these pegs can be reused. The odd numbered pegs are lined in, but are only driven in lightly at this stage; their function, as will be seen, is merely to reduce the correction for sag. In windy weather, additional pegs may be useful to help keep the tape on line, but such conditions should be avoided if possible.

Levels are taken on the even numbered pegs, and the odd numbered pegs are driven down so that when the staff is held on (say) peg 3 the reading is the average of that for pegs 2 and 4. The theodolite can be used for this, and may if convenient be set to some definite vertical angle.

Measurements are made between the nails on the even pegs, with the steel tape under some definite tension (say 5 kg) and passing over the top of the intermediate odd peg (two nails in its top may serve as a guide). *No attempt is made to get either end of the tape to read zero against the nail*, but readings on the tape are taken simultaneously at each end, and recorded. Three sets of such readings should be taken, or more if these do not all agree.

If measurement is being made along the ground, only the even numbered pegs are used, and they are driven flush with the ground. There is of course no correction for sag.

The distance from A (peg 0) to peg 12 must now be worked out (see Para. 15.5); the difference between this and the total distance (300 m) gives the remaining length to the corner peg B. That peg is carefully lined in with the theodolite, and driven at the appropriate measurement from peg 12. Mark three points in line on the top, and then mark three others at the right distance from peg 12. A nail is driven where these two lines cross. This method is easier than trying to measure and line in at the same time, and is rather more accurate. If peg 12 has been driven flush, but the station peg is to project above ground level, the builder's level may be used for plumbing.

To fix AD, the horizontal angle is set at zero (with the theodolite still at A), and using the lower plate adjustment the telescope is sighted on B. Keeping the lower plate clamped, the angle is turned to 90° (or 270°) and a peg driven on that line a little beyond the intended position of D. The top is then marked. The telescope is transited (turned through about 180° vertical angle) so as to 'change face', and the procedure is repeated. Provided the two marked lines on the peg are almost coincident, their average is accepted as giving the required line for AD, which can then be marked out and measured.

The theodolite is then moved to B, and BC is set out; and finally, with the instrument at C or D, line CD is marked out.

Assuming the distance CD proves correct, the accuracy of the setting out can be fairly safely accepted. Nevertheless, if any doubt is felt, all angles can be remeasured and the whole rectangle worked out as a quadrilateral (Para. 20.2). If this shows that the corner pegs are not quite correctly placed, the procedure for moving them (described in Para. 15.7) should be followed.

15.5 *Examples of Measurement.* To illustrate the procedure, a numerical example for measuring a 200 m line is given:

Line AD. Required length 200 m.

Tape 50 m steel band.

Pegs at average spacing of 24·95 m.

Sag under 5 kg, with 24·95 m span,
$$\text{found to be } 0\cdot11 \text{ m whence}$$

$$\text{Sag correction (per 24·95 m)} = 8 \times (0\cdot11)^2 \div (3 \times 24\cdot95)$$
$$= 0\cdot0013 \text{ m}$$
$$\text{or for 50 m tape} = 0\cdot0026 \text{ m}$$

Theodolite set at 88° vertical angle (2° elevation) giving a rise of $49\cdot9 \times \sin 2° = 1\cdot742$ m in each 49·9 m length.

The correction is then worked out as below. Since the differences in level are relatively small, the formula $h^2/2L$ gives results which are never more than a tenth of a millimetre wrong.

Peg	Staff Reading	Rise or Fall relative to Line of Sight	Rise of Line of Sight	Total Rise	Correction for 49·9 m.
0	1·321				
		0·018 R	1·742	1·760	0·031
2	1·303				
		0·243 R	1·742	1·985	0·039
4	1·060				
		0·076 R	1·742	1·818	0·033
6	0·984				
		0·772 R	1·742	2·514	0·063
8	0·212				

For each 50 m span three pairs of measurements (in mm) are taken from the ends of the band; in span 2 to 4 one pair was found to be apparently inconsistent with the other two, so a fourth pair was measured, and the doubtful pair (marked XX) rejected.

Peg 0	62	48	45		
Peg 2	34	45	51		
Total	96	93	96		Average: 95
Peg 2	52	61	51	50	
Peg 4	51	49	50	52	
Total	103	X110X	101	102	Average: 102
Peg 4	43	40	43		
Peg 6	41	42	43		
Total	84	82	86		Average: 84
Peg 6	77	29	53		
Peg 8	74	121	96		
Total	151	150	149		Average: 150

All corrections are then deducted from 50 metres.

Peg	End readings	Sag	Slope	Corrected Span	Cumulative Distance
0					0
	0·095	0·003	0·031	49·871	
2					49·871
	0·102	0·003	0·039	49·856	
4					99·727
	0·084	0·003	0·033	49·880	
6					149·607
	0·150	0·003	0·063	49·784	
8					119·391

Peg D, therefore, should be 0·609 m from peg 8.

The nails on the intermediate pegs 2, 4, and 6 are at 49·871, 99·727, and 149·607 m from A, so the intermediate 10 m pegs can be set out by measurement from them, using the theodolite for alignment. Finally, all the odd and even pegs are removed to avoid confusion.

15.6 *Detached Base Lines.* Suppose that the corner A of a rectangle has been fixed, and the directions of the sides AB, AD, but that the ground is too irregular for accurate linear measurement; points b and d, however, can be set out on those lines and close to the required points. It is often possible to set out a base XY near by on ground which does allow measurement to be made precisely. The points A, b, and d can then be connected to this base by a careful theodolite triangulation from which the lengths Ab, Ad can be worked out. B and D can then be fixed by short measurements, as in the last section. A pair of transfer pegs (Para. 15.7) can be driven on the line BC, using the theodolite set up at B to establish the direction; and a pair can be set out similarly on the line DC. The intersection of the two lines gives the point C.

Two possible arrangements out of many are indicated in Figure 15.1. In one, the network can be solved as a polygon centred on A (Para. 20.2); the directions Xb and Yd would be observed but would not be utilised in the calculations, though they might serve later as checks. Alternatively this network could be solved as two quadrilaterals XYbA, AYbD (Para. 20.6). Similarly, the other example can be treated as two quadrilaterals AXYd, AXbY; provided the angular measurements were made carefully, there should be no appreciable difference between the two calculated lengths found for AY.

15.1 Detached Base Lines

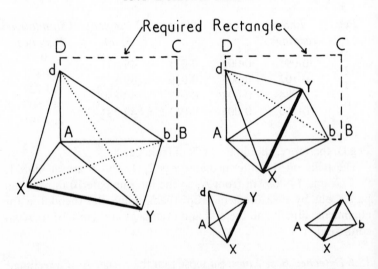

There are a great many other possible arrangements of this kind, and there is no need to list them all. For example, a single side AB could be the measured base.

A detached base line for measurement may be useful even where maximum precision is not needed, and indeed on very rough ground where measurement is difficult an ordinary chain-and-theodolite survey may be made more accurate by deducing all main measurements from a single carefully chained base.

15.7 *Transfer Pegs*. The correct and approximate positions for a station may be so near each other that the new peg cannot be driven without disturbing the old; or you may wish to dig round a correctly placed peg so as to embed it in concrete. Transfer pegs are used in those circumstances. These are merely four pegs preferably in a cruciform arrangement, driven at a safe distance from the peg to be disturbed; and marked with nails, so that string lines joining opposite pairs of nails cross at the mark which has to be displaced. The exact position can thus easily be recovered after disturbance.

Alternatively, two pegs on opposite sides of the mark can be used, their distances to the mark being recorded.

After use the transfer pegs are removed, to avoid confusion.

Part V
NUMERICAL AND
SEMI-GRAPHICAL METHODS

16 Introduction and Basic Formulae

16.1 *Introduction.* Few printed pages are drearier than those which
set out long numerical calculations, and since at least nine sites out
of ten can be easily and accurately surveyed using only the very
simplest geometry you may, with luck, never need to refer to this
Part at all. Nevertheless, provided that you do not allow them to
frighten you, numerical methods can often save time and labour,
and there are a few structures which would be very laborious to
survey without using them.

I have therefore given an example of every problem which is
likely to arise in practice; where two or more methods are available,
that which seems simplest has been chosen. I suggest that you
should skim through this section, so that you are aware of its
contents; but do not try to struggle through the numerical work.
If you are faced with a particular problem, first work through the
relevant example so that you understand what you are doing, and
then apply exactly the same procedure to your own data. Do not
allow the appearance of these calculations to discourage you; taken
step by step you will find that they are quite simple.

16.2 *Arrangement.* Survey calculations are based on a very few
trigonometrical formulae. These, accompanied by numerical
examples, are set out in this chapter, after the introductory
material. The next gives a miscellaneous collection of methods
which are sometimes useful. Chapter 18 deals with problems which
can arise when plotting the results, or subsequently. Finally,
because of their importance, the solutions of traverses and of
triangulated networks are treated separately in Chapters 19 and 20.

Six-figure logarithms are used, with positive characteristics; that is, 10 is added to log sin, log cos, etc, so that for example 9 appears before the decimal point instead of $\overline{1}$. No confusion can arise. For small sites five figures may be just adequate, but four-figure tables are not.

Save for a few obvious exceptions, all calculations are based on the network described in Appendix III. This will help in understanding how 'errors' and methods of 'balancing' affect the final results.

16.3 *Electronic Calculators.* For brevity, these are often called 'hand calculators'. The invention of these semi-magical devices has enormously simplified all types of surveying calculations. New and more versatile types are constantly being developed, so only general advice can be given here. The following facilities are desirable:

Seven- or eight-figure display.

Normal notation, with Scientific Notation available if needed; for example 131·22 and 0·0043 are 'Normal', 1·3122 + 02 and 4·3 − 03 are in 'Scientific Notation'.

Trigonometrical and Inverse Trigonometric functions.

Two memories at least. Four would sometimes be useful, but if you have too many you may forget what is stored in them.

Polar conversions are not essential, but are very well worth having, and can save a lot of time in some calculations. Several examples of their application are therefore given.

Finally, you will almost certainly find a calculator using algebraic notation preferable; it is indicated by the presence of an = key, and entries are mostly made as you would write them. The alternative, Reversed Polish notation (with a key marked ENT) is likely to be confusing unless you have been educated in its use.

Unfortunately, calculators have not yet evolved a standard key pattern, and their great variety and rapid development make it impossible to give programmes for all types. I have therefore not attempted to generalise the notation, but have kept to that of one calculator. The explanations which follow should enable you to translate the programmes to suit another calculator, if studied in conjunction with its instruction manual.

In the calculator used here, most of the keys will perform two alternative operations, one of which is given directly and the other by first pressing the F. key. For example, one key is marked x^2 in black, and has above it (in green) the symbol $\sqrt{x}$. Suppose we are operating on the number 16; then if the programme reads Figures x^2. the result will be 256, whereas if it reads Figures F.$\sqrt{x}$. the result will be 4.

The F. key is used here to obtain inverse trigonometrical functions; thus entering 0·5 followed by F. $\sin^{-1}$. will give 30 (degrees). Some calculators would use an Inv. key followed by the sin. key; others have a separate key for arc.sin.

There are also several different ways of referring to Memories. That used here has STO1 and RCL1, implying STOre in memory 1 and ReCalL from memory 1. Once understood, this is easily interpreted into another notation.

Finally, an explanation of Polar Co-ordinates may be useful to those not familiar with them. In these, the position of a point is defined by a radial distance measured from the origin at a stated angle to the x-axis. Thus the co-ordinates $\sqrt{3}$, 1 can also be written as 2, 30°. Using the programmes given, the P. key converts x, y co-ordinates to polars, the R. key Reduces polars to x and y. The potential advantages in survey calculations are obvious, but at least in the calculator used here the (. key must be pressed before any further work is done; otherwise nonsense figures are produced.

For programmes which are in frequent use, the ingenious arrangement devised by A. L. Allan may be useful (Program Cards for the Small Hand Calculator, *Survey Review* XXIV (1978) p. 233). The programme is written out step by step on a circular disc, which is rotated behind a cover with a single 'window' through which each step is seen in turn.

Two warnings must be given. In working through a long programme, the wrong key can very easily be pressed. This is by far the most usual cause of a mistake, but very occasionally (and very disconcertingly) the hypothetical little green men who operate within the device may go mad and start producing nonsense results. The course of a calculation, therefore, must be kept under review, with the possibility of a mistake in mind. A useful precaution is to copy down some crucial figures which appear during the course of calculation, even though they are not needed in the final result; this will save you from having to return to the beginning after a mistake.

Two programmes (Paras. 16.8 and 18.4) are explained verbally step by step. These will enable the others to be followed.

Addendum. During the preparation of this book, electronic calculators have fallen considerably in price, and many new models have been developed. In particular, programmable calculators have become relatively inexpensive; but to make really full use of these requires rather higher numerical ability than merely to tap out a programme step by step. Moreover, although in some types the programme can be preserved on a detachable card and is thus always available when needed, in most of the cheaper models it is lost when the calculator is switched off. In the sort of work envisaged here, therefore, the programming facility would probably not be used very often.

16.4 *Definitions.* Calculations are almost always used to find the co-ordinates of stations, which are normally measured East and North relative to some defined axes. For brevity, the co-ordinates of station P can be written E(P), N(P). If the axes chosen are not truly oriented, but are taken relative to 'site north', the risk of confusion is reduced if lower case letters are used, as e(p), n(p) or x(p), y(p).

A line, PQ say, has length and direction. The length can be written as PQ or as L (PQ). The Bearing, Bg (PQ), is measured clockwise from the meridian. It can also be expressed as the Reduced Bearing (RB or RBg), measured the nearest way from the meridian. Thus the bearings 32°, 117°, 206°, and 293° can also be written as N32°E, S63°E, S26°W, and N67°W. Note that the order in which P and Q are written is important. If Bg (PQ) is 109°, or S71°E, Bg (QP), is 289°, or N71°W.

A line can also be specified in terms of the difference between the co-ordinates of its ends. If P is at 120E, 275N, and Q at 360E, 350N, then the 'Easting' of PQ, (EPQ), is 240 and the 'Northing', N(PQ) is 75. Again, the order is important; E(QP) = −240, N(QP) = −75. To avoid negative signs these are usually called Westings and Southings, for example, W(PQ) = 240. Eastings and Westings are also termed 'Departures', Northings and Southings 'latitudes'.

16.5 *Trigonometrical Functions.* Most readers will be insulted by the suggestion that they do not know what follows; but a few may have forgotten these expressions, so they are given here. All refer to a triangle with sides a, b, and c, and the opposite angles A, B, and C; C is a right angle (Figure 16.1).

16.1 Notation of Triangles and Signs of Trigonometric Functions

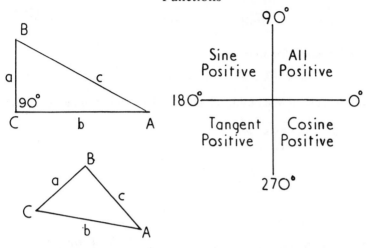

The Theorem of Pythagoras states that:
$$a^2 + b^2 = c^2$$
If a, b, and c are whole numbers, the triangle is called a 'Pythagorean Triangle'. Of these, the '3–4–5' triangle is the simplest, and is of considerable use in surveying.

The trigonometrical functions are:

sine A = a/c; cosine A = b/c; and tangent A = a/b.

These are abbreviated to sin A, cos A, and tan A; their reciprocals (cosecant, secant, and cotangent) will not be used.

The inverse functions can be written either as $\sin^{-1}$, $\cos^{-1}$, $\tan^{-1}$, as inv sin, or as arc sin, etc.

$$\text{inv sin } (a/c) \text{ or } \sin^{-1} (a/c) = A$$
$$\cos^{-1} (b/c) = A$$
$$\text{and } \tan^{-1} (a/b) = A.$$

The signs of the functions are important. In the first quadrant, with A between 0° and 90°, all are positive. Between 90° and 180° only the sine is positive, 180° to 270° only the tangent, and 270° to 360° only the cosine. A useful nonsense–mnemonic which I learnt at school is '*s*ome *t*all *c*aterpillars'.

16.6 *Trigonometrical Formulae.* The following are sufficient to solve all surveying problems. The notation is the same as above, but C is not necessarily 90° (Figure 16.1).

The most useful is the sine formula

$$\frac{a}{\sin A} = \frac{b}{\sin B} = \frac{c}{\sin C} \tag{16.6.1}$$

Angles can be found from

$$a^2 = b^2 + c^2 - 2bc \cos A \tag{16.6.2}$$

which is useful when using a hand calculator; but if using logarithms,

$$\tan \frac{A}{2} = \sqrt{\frac{(s-b)(s-c)}{s(s-a)}} = \frac{r}{s-a} \tag{16.6.3}$$

where $r = \sqrt{\dfrac{(s-a)(s-b)(s-c)}{s}}$

and $s = (a + b + c) \div 2$

This is preferable to the alternatives $\sin \dfrac{A}{2} = \sqrt{\dfrac{(s-b)(s-c)}{bc}}$
and $\cos \dfrac{A}{2} = \sqrt{\dfrac{s(s-a)}{bc}}$

for all three angles can be found using the same four logarithms.

Calculations using these formulae are the elements which are combined to give the solutions of surveying problems. Examples follow.

16.7 *Conversion of Minutes and Seconds to Decimals of a Degree.*
Most hand calculators require angles to be entered in degrees and decimals. Usually, to convert all the angles as a single operation is quicker than doing each as required. The programme is simple. Enter 60 and transfer it to STO 1. Enter seconds, and press keys ÷, RCL 1, +. Then enter minutes and press ÷, RCL 1, =. The result gives the minutes and seconds in decimals of a degree. The 60 is retained in STO 1 until all the angles have been converted.

The calculator gives results to eight figures, but unless you are working to exceptional accuracy there is no need to go beyond the fourth decimal place, for $0.0001°$ corresponds to 03.6 seconds, less than 00.1 minutes. Similarly, in linear quantities, the third decimal place, corresponding to 1 mm, is accurate enough. In long calculations, where errors may build up, another decimal place may sometimes be worth while, for there is then no need to worry about discrepancies in the last figure. Sometimes, if one number in a sequence of calculations is small, it should not be abbreviated, for the *proportional* effect of cutting off the last few decimal places may be unacceptably large; but this difficulty ought not to arise in a properly planned survey.

In all examples which follow, where the hand calculator is used, the angles are assumed to have been already converted to degrees and decimals of a degree.

16.8 *Co-ordinates, given Length and Bearing of a Line.* The formulae used are

E(AF) = AF sin Bg(AF)

N(AF) = AF cos Bg(AF)

The calculations are arranged as table 16.1, the necessary information being noted first, after which the logarithms are copied down, and the necessary arithmetic follows. The apparently unconventional arrangement saves writing down the log of the length twice, which is a worth-while saving if a lot of calculations have to be made.

With the calculator, the R key is used, which reduces polar co-ordinates to Cartesians. With polar co-ordinates, the angle is measured from the x-axis, and the R key gives x first, so we shall get the northing first. The procedure will be described in detail, since it illustrates clearly how the calculator is used; but the description takes much longer than the calculation.

As in any such calculation, the work can best be arranged in columns. That on the left sets out the programme, which is the same for any calculation of this kind. The others are specific to this particular problem, the second giving the data, the third the results, and the fourth the significance of the various quantities.

For any given problem the first and fourth columns are written out; the modification needed if one were dealing with a line PQ instead of AF is obvious. Then the data are entered, AF = 160·12 m, Bg (AF) = 150·6017°, and so on. Note that there is no need to work out the reduced bearing.

'Figs' in the Programme column indicates that the data are to be keyed in, 160·12 in this case. The F and x/y keys transfer this to the invisible y register. The bearing, 150·6017, is then keyed in.

Pressing the R key gives, directly, the x-co-ordinate of the Polars, which in this case is the Northing of AF, − 139·501; there is no need to record this, but it may be useful as a check.

Table 16.1 Co-ordinates Given Length and Bearing

```
Data: Length of AF  160·12 metres.
      Bearing  150° 36·1'  (150·6017°)
             = S 29° 23·9' E
      Coordinates of A: 169·10 E; 779·25 N.
Required: Coordinates of F.
```

(a) <u>Solution using logarithms.</u>

			E(A)	169·100
	1·895 420	whence	E(AF)	78·600
log sin 29° 23·9'	9·690 974		E(F)	247·700
log 160·12	2·204 446			
log cos 29° 23·9'	9·940 132		N(A)	779·250
	2·144 578	whence	N(AF)	-139·501
			N(F)	639·749

(b) <u>Solution using calculator.</u>

Programme	Data	Results	Notes
Figs.	160·12		AF
F. x/y.			
Figs.	150·6017		Bg.(AF)
R.		(-139·501)	N(AF)
(. +.			
Figs.	779·25		N(A)
).		639·749	N(F)
F. x/y		(78·599)	E(AF)
(. +.			
Figs.	169·1		E(A)
).		247·699	E(F)

Care is now necessary. If you try to add the north co-ordinate of A directly, you get a mysterious and meaningless number, so it is essential to use the (.key. Indeed, whenever you are doing any supplementary calculations on the results obtained with either the R or P key, the brackets should always be used. So the sequence is (, +, then key in the figures for N(A), and then). This gives the Northing for point F (which has nothing to do with the F key).

Pressing the F and x/y keys then extracts the y-co-ordinate, that is E (AF), from where it has been lurking in the y-register, and the same procedure as before gives E(F).

16.9 *Length and Bearing, Given Co-ordinates* (Table 16.2). This, the converse of the previous calculation, is used less often. The P

Table 16.2 Length and Bearing Given Co-ordinates

Data: Coordinates of A: 169·10 E, 779·25 N.
      Coordinates of F: 247·70 E, 639·75 N.
Required: Length and Bearing of AF.

(a) <u>Solution using logarithms.</u>
E(F)-E(A)= 78·60 E; log.= 1·895 423
N(F)-N(A)=139·50 S; log.= 2·144 574
  whence log tan (R.Bg) = 9·750 849

So Reduced Bearing of AF = S 29° 23·9′ E
   True Bearing   = 150° 36·1′

The Northing is larger than the Easting;
Log 139·50 = 2·144 574
- log cos R.Bg.9·940 132
So log AF   = 2·204 442   whence AF= 160·119

(b) <u>Solution using calculator.</u>

Programme	Data	Results	Notes
Figs.	639·75		N(F)
-.			
Figs.	779·25		N(A)
=. F. x/y.			
(.			
Figs.	247·7		E(F)
-.			
Figs.	169·1		E(A)
).			
P.		160·119	AF
F. x/y.		150·6013	Bg.(AF)

key on the calculator gives the result almost at once, but if logarithms are used the formulae are

$$\tan (\text{reduced bearing}) = \frac{\text{Easting or Westing}}{\text{Northing or Southing}}$$

and Length = either (Easting or Westing)
                          ÷ sin (RBg)
         or   (Northing or Southing)
                          ÷ cos (RBg)

Provided that the Easting and Northing are about the same it does not matter which is used, but if one is appreciably larger that should be taken as basis, for the *proportionate* error will be smaller. If only the length is needed, to add the squares and take the square root of the total (Pythagoras) is perhaps a little quicker, if the necessary tables are to hand.

With the calculator, the P key converts (x,y) co-ordinates to Polars. The only points to note are that the north co-ordinates must be dealt with first, and as previously a nonsense result is obtained unless the (. and). keys are used.

Table 16.3 Triangle with All Three Sides given

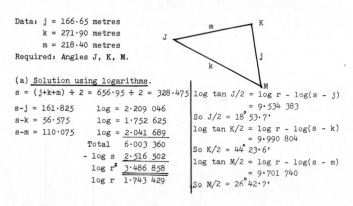

```
Data:  j = 166·65 metres
       k = 271·90 metres
       m = 218·40 metres
Required:  Angles J, K, M.
```

(a) <u>Solution using logarithms</u>.

s = (j+k+m) ÷ 2 = 656·95 ÷ 2 = 328·475

s-j = 161·825	log = 2·209 046	
s-k = 56·575	log = 1·752 625	
s-m = 110·075	log = 2·041 689	
	Total	6·003 360
	- log s	2·516 502
	log r^2	3·486 858
	log r	1·743 429

log tan J/2 = log r - log(s - j)
  = 9·534 383
So J/2 = 18° 53·7'

log tan K/2 = log r - log(s - k)
  = 9·990 804
So K/2 = 44° 23·6'

log tan M/2 = log r - log(s - m)
  = 9·701 740
So M/2 = 26° 42·7'

(b) <u>Solution using calculator</u>

Programme	Data	Results	Notes
Figs.	218·4		Side m
÷ . Figs. STO 1.	166·65		Side j
=. F. STO 2		(1·31053)	(m/j in Memory 2)
Figs.	271·9		Side k
÷.RCL 1.=.STO 1.		(1·63156)	(k/j in Memory 1)
x^2. +. F. RCL 2.			
x^2. -. 1.			$(k/j)^2 + (m/j)^2 - 1$
÷ . 2.÷ . RCL 1.			
÷ . F. RCL 2.			÷ 2 (k/j) (m/j)
=. F. $\cos^{-1}$.		37·7902	Angle J
RCL 1. x^2. +. 1.			
-. F. RCL 2. x^2.			$(k/j)^2 + 1 - (m/j)^2$
÷ . 2.÷. RCL 1.			÷ 2 (k/j)
=. F. $\cos^{-1}$.		53·4230	Angle M
F. RCL 2 . x^2. +.			
1. -. RCL 1. x^2.			$(m/j)^2 + 1 - (k/j)^2$
÷. 2 ÷ . F. RCL 2.			÷ 2 (m/j)
=. F. $\cos^{-1}$.		88·7868	Angle K

16.10 *Solution of Triangle, Three Sides Given* (table 16.3). This problem seldom arises, and is given primarily for completeness. Nevertheless, it can sometimes be used, with a hand calculator, as a quick check in the field, as for example on the central angles in a chained polygon, to see whether they total 360°; but it will not always locate small mistakes.

If logarithms are used, the most convenient formula is (16.6.3).

This is preferable to the sine or cosine formulae of the same type, as only four logarithms are needed to give all three angles.

This formula can also be used with a hand calculator, but unless four memories are available at least two of the quantities involved will have to be written down and re-entered as required; but as the whole calculation takes less than five minutes, this is counter-balanced by the advantage that there is no need to remember a special programme. The formula $\cos A = (b^2 + c^2 - a^2)/2bc$ is only slightly quicker, in that form.

The quickest method, for which a programme is given, is to use the same formula, but rearranged thus:

$$\cos A = \left(\frac{b}{a}\right)^2 + \left(\frac{c}{a}\right)^2 - 1 - 2\left(\frac{b}{a}\right)\left(\frac{c}{a}\right)$$

$$\cos B = \left(\frac{b}{a}\right)^2 + 1 - \left(\frac{c}{a}\right)^2 - 2 \cdot \frac{b}{a}$$

$$\cos C = \left(\frac{c}{a}\right)^2 + 1 - \left(\frac{b}{a}\right)^2 - 2 \cdot \frac{c}{a}$$

This takes about half as long to work out as the first method, so can be useful if the programme is to hand.

In any calculation of this kind, all three angles should be worked independently, and the total checked.

16.11 *Solution of Triangle, Two Sides and One Angle Given* (table 16.4). This problem may take two forms, which require different methods of solution. That considered in this section deals with an angle included between the two given sides. When the angle is not so included, the method is closely similar to that when one side and two angles are given (Para. 16.12) and indeed requires no separate explanation.

Table 16.4 Triangle with Two Sides and Included Angle Given, Using Calculator

```
Data: j=166·65 metres
      k=271·90 metres
      M= 53·423
Required: Side m.
```

(a) <u>Programme for Cosine formula.</u>

Programme	Data	Results	Notes
Figs. cos. x. 2. x. Figs. STO 1. x.	53·423 166·65		Angle M Side j
Figs. F. STO 2. +/-. +. RCL 1. x². +. F.	271·9		Side k
RCL 2. x². =. F. √x.		218·400	Side m

(b) <u>Programme using Polar keys.</u>

Programme	Data	Results	Notes
Figs. F. x/y. Figs. R. (. -.	166·65 53·423	 (99·307)	Side j Angle M (gives MX)
Figs.). F. x/y. P. F. x/y	271·9	(-172·593) 218·400 142·2098	Side k (gives JX) Side m External angle at J

With two sides and the included angle, the natural formula to use is (16.6.2)

$$a^2 = b^2 + c^2 - 2bc \cos A$$

The calculations, using logarithms and tables of squares, are obvious, and to set out an example seems unnecessary. Two programmes for a hand calculator are given. The first uses the above formula, altering the order of terms to reduce the number of entries. The second uses the Polar keys; it is slightly shorter, and gives the angles as well as the unknown side, but has the disadvantage that the programme must be at hand for reference.

16.12 *Solution of Triangle, One Side and All Angles Given* (table 16.5). Problems of this type arise very frequently (see for example, Chapter 20, on Polygonal Networks). The formula used is (16.6.1).

$$\frac{a}{\sin A} = \frac{b}{\sin B} = \frac{c}{\sin C}$$

Table 16.5 Triangle with One Side and All Angles Given

```
        Data: j = 166·65 metres.
              J = 37° 47·4′
                = 37·7900°
              K = 88° 47·2′
                = 88·7867°
              M = 53° 25·4′
                = 53·4233°
        Required: Sides k and m.
```

(a) Solution using logarithms.

```
                                    log k  2·434 411 whence k = 271·901
        log j      - log sin J│log sin K  9·999 903
        2·221 805 - 9·787 297 │    =       2·434 508
                               log sin M  9·904 748
                                    log m  2·339 256 whence m = 218·402
  Alternative arrangement:
                     log j 2·221 805
                 - log sin J 9·787 297
                             2·434 508
               + log sin K 9·999 903   + log sin M 9·904 748
                     log k  2·434 411        log m  2·339 256
                    whence k 271·901        whence m 218·402
```

(b) Solution using calculator.

Programme	Data	Results	Notes
Figs.	166·65		Side j
÷.			
Figs. sin.	37·79		Angle J
=. STO 1.			(j/sin J stored in memory)
x.			
Figs. sin.	88·7867		Angle K
=.		271·901	Side k
RCL 1. x.			
Figs. sin.	53·4233		Angle M
=.		21f·402	Side m

This is equally applicable to the case where two sides and an angle not included between them are given, as noted earlier; the necessary modifications are obvious.

In the table, two alternative arrangements are given for the calculation with logarithms. The arithmetic is the same in both. The second is slightly longer, but is perhaps easier to follow.

17 Applications, Including Semi-Graphical Methods

17.1 *Introduction*. Usually, ingenuity in surveying is misdirected; the more straightforward the observations and calculations, the better will be the results. Nevertheless, there are occasional exceptions to this rule; satellite stations (Para. 17.3) are an example. This chapter assembles a miscellaneous collection of methods which are sometimes valuable as stages in reducing the raw data to information which can be plotted. The semi-graphical approach (Paras. 7–10) is particularly useful.

17.2 *Tacheometry*. The tacheometer has been described in Chapter 14, and the formulae for height and distance were discussed in Para. 14.2, where reference was made to the availability of tacheometric tables and slide-rules. If a hand calculator is available, these can be dispensed with.

In the previous discussion, the vertical angle was measured from horizontal as zero, but most theodolites now measure from vertically upwards as zero, so that 'horizontal' corresponds to 90°. If so, the calculator gives the 'rise' or 'fall' automatically. The appropriate programme is given in table 17.1 (which also gives the full calculation using logarithms).

Necessary preliminaries are that the vertical angles have been expressed as degrees and decimals (as Para. 16.7), and the 'distances' (that is, 100 × the intercepts) have been worked out. At the same time, the middle reading should again be checked to see that it is in fact the average of the other two; if not, the sight should be rejected. The calculator could be used for these calculations, but normally they would be done mentally, for the risk of a mistake in such simple arithmetic is not much greater than that of keying the wrong number. Note that the height of instrument

Table 17.1 Reducing Tacheometric Observation

```
Data: (extract from fig. 32)    Height of Instrument: 293·91 OD.
```

Vert. Angle	Cross-hairs			Rise or Fall	R.L.	Dist.	Horiz. Dist.	Point No.
74°30'	3·352	2·314	1·274	R 53·51	345·11	207·8	192·96	88
110°40'	3·160	2·638	2·119	F 34·38	256·90	104·1	91·13	89

(a) <u>Full calculation using logarithms</u>.

```
Dist./2 = 103·9          log      2·016 616                    2·016 616
90° - 74°30' = 15°30' log sin 2z  9·711·839  log cos 2z        9·933 066
                                  ‾‾‾‾‾‾‾‾‾                    ‾‾‾‾‾‾‾‾‾
                                  1·728 455                    1·949·682
                         antilogs   53·51                        89·06
                                                          + 103·9 = 192·96

Dist./2 = 52·05          log      1·716 421                    1·716 421
110°40' - 90° = 20°40' log sin 2z 9·819 832  log cos 2z        9·875 571
                                  ‾‾‾‾‾‾‾‾‾                    ‾‾‾‾‾‾‾‾‾
                                  1·536 253                    1·591 992
                         antilogs   34·38                        39·08
                                                          + 52·05 = 91·13
```

```
In practice, a tacheometric slide-rule will almost always give
results of sufficient accuracy.
```

(b) <u>Using calculator</u>.

Programme	Data	Results	Notes
Figs. F. STO 2.	293·91		H. O. I.
Figs.	207·8		Dist. (Point 88)
x.			
Figs. STO 1.	74·5		Vert. Angle
sin. x². =.		192·96	Horiz. Dist.
÷. RCL 1. tan. -.			
Figs.	2·314		Axial Reading
+. F. RCL 2. =.		345·11	Reduced Level
(programme repeated)			
Figs.	104·1		Dist. (Point 89)
x.			
Figs. STO 1.	110·6667		Vert. Angle
sin. x². =.		91·13	Horiz. Dist.
÷. RCL 1. tan. -.			
Figs.	2·638		Axial Reading
+. F. RCL 2. =.		256·90	Reduced Level

above datum is retained in memory 2 for all calculations at a given station.

After the horizontal distance and level have been found for point 88, the programme is repeated for point 89, and so on as required. The repetitive part is indicated by broken lines. As will be realised, there is no need laboriously to write out the 'programme' and 'Notes' columns over and over again. They can be written on a mask with part cut out, and moved down the page; only the Data,

Results, and Point Number need to be filled in.

17.3 *Satellite Stations*. Sometimes a feature such as the angle of a building or a telegraph-pole may be located in a good position for a station. It has the great advantages of being vertical and permanent, but you cannot set up a theodolite over it. Nevertheless, at the expense of a little extra office calculation, it can be used.

The instrument is set up near the station, at a convenient point S 'the satellite station', and observations are taken in the usual way. The necessary adjustments to give the corresponding angles for measurements taken from the true stations can be worked out using the sine formula. The network can then be balanced, treating the adjusted angles as if they had been observed at the true station.

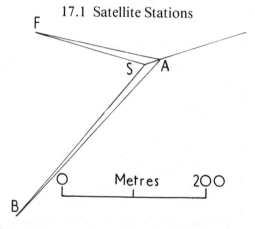

17.1 Satellite Stations

If A and S are the true and satellite stations (Figure 17.1), and sights are taken to B and F, then angles ABS (added) and AFS (deducted) are the adjustments needed to the observed readings. From the sine formula:

$$\sin ABS = AS \sin ASB / AB.$$

The percentage error in the adjustment is proportional to the percentage errors in AS and AB, so since the adjustment is normally small AB can usually be measured from a careful small-scale plot. AS, of course, must be measured accurately on the site. This can be done when the theodolite is set up; S need not be marked by a peg.

The calculations are so simple that there is no need to give a worked example, but the following numerical results will enable you to make sure that you understand the method: AS = 1·16 m, circuit of readings from station S:
B 220° 42'; F 286° 15'; A 72° 14'.
AB = 273 m; AF = 159 m (measured from draft plan).

By subtraction, the angle ASB = 148° 28', so by the sine formula angle ABS = 07·6'; and similarly the angle AFS = 14·0'. So if the readings had been taken from A they would have been:
to B, 220° 49·6'; to F, 286° 01·1'.

The most likely mistake is to add the correction when it should be subtracted, or conversely. The risk is less when a calculator is used, as it automatically gives the right sign, but nevertheless a diagram should always be drawn (as in Figure 17.1) with the length SA exaggerated. If working with logarithms the angles must be reduced to the appropriate values smaller than 90°, in this case 180° − 148° 28' for ASB and 214° 01' − 180° for ASF.

17.4 *Horizontal Angles with Sextant and Clinometer.* The sextant is so seldom used in ordinary surveying that a detailed description would be unjustified. Essentially, one object A is observed directly, the other B via its reflection in a mirror attached to an arm which moves against a graduated arc. When the image of B is brought into coincidence with A, the reading on the arc gives the angle between them. In the box sextant the mirrors are enclosed in a cylindrical box, in the naval sextant (which is capable of greater accuracy) the whole construction is visible.

For surveying, the instrument has two disadvantages. One, minor, is that the angle measured cannot exceed 120° so a complete circuit has to be measured in steps, with intermediate marks. More seriously, the angle measured is the true angle; to obtain the horizontal angle, this must be corrected using observations made with a clinometer.

Nevertheless, even the box sextant can give results to within 05', roughly 1 part in 700, so it is much more accurate than the prismatic compass; and since a sextant is sometimes available when a theodolite is not, the necessary formula for correction is given here (but without a worked example and without detailed explanation).

The standard formula is
$$\cos H = (\cos M - \sin a \sin b)/\cos a \cos b$$

where M is the measured angle, a and b the elevations of the two points observed, and H the required horizontal angle.

For a useful range of moderate altitudes, an alignment chart (Figure 17.2) can be used. I have described its construction in *Civil Engineering*, xxxvi no. 420, (June) 1941 pp. 484–90.

To use it, a transparent straight-edge is set to pass through the measured angle and the intersection of the curves corresponding to the elevations or depressions of the two points observed. The straight edge is then tangential to the curve giving the appropriate correction, the point of contact being shown by the radial guidelines. Two examples which will make the use of the diagram clear are indicated by fine lines.

With a measured angle of 56°, and altitudes of the same sign and both equal to 9°, the chart shows the correction as 48' to be added, and the same correction is indicated for altitudes of 15° and 8°, or of 20° and 8·5°; the calculated values, to the nearest minute, are 46', 50', and 49'.

With a measured angle of 70°, and both altitudes 8° but of opposite sign, the correction is found to be 1° 35' to be deducted, which should also apply for 17° and −2°; the calculated value for both is 1° 38'.

It will be evident that determination of horizontal angles with a sextant is laborious, and should be regarded as an emergency procedure, only applicable when not many angles are needed.

17.5 *Intersections: Plotting Angles.* A simple survey involving angular measurements can often be plotted directly without loss of accuracy. Consider as illustration triangle ABF (Figure 17.3) to be drawn to a scale of 1/500. The side AB is given as 273·00 m, and the angles A and B as 55° 11', 35° 14' respectively. A small-scale plot will show that AF and BF are roughly 160 and 220 m. An ordinary protractor, of say 10 cm radius, will not be adequate; for BF (to 1/500) will measure about 44 cm, so that any error is multiplied four times or more.

The method adopted, therefore, is to measure some length BP along BA, set up a perpendicular at P and mark off PQ = BP × tan B. Then QBA is the required angle. In this case a convenient length for BP would be 50 cm, and PQ would then be 50 × tan 35° 14' = 35·31 cm. The length BP is chosen to give a simple multiplier. Clearly any desired degree of accuracy can be attained, at least in principle.

If the angle to be drawn much exceeds 45°, the perpendicular

17.2 Alignment Chart for use with Sextant and Clinometer

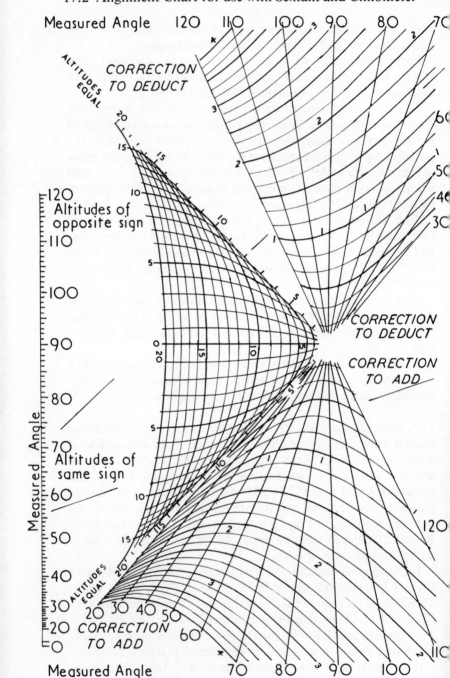

Measured Angle   120   110   100   3   90   80   70

ALTITUDES EQUAL

CORRECTION TO DEDUCT

Altitudes of opposite sign

CORRECTION TO DEDUCT

CORRECTION TO ADD

Altitudes of same sign

ALTITUDES EQUAL

CORRECTION TO ADD

Measured Angle

Measured Angle   70   80   3   90   100

17.3 Plotting Intersection

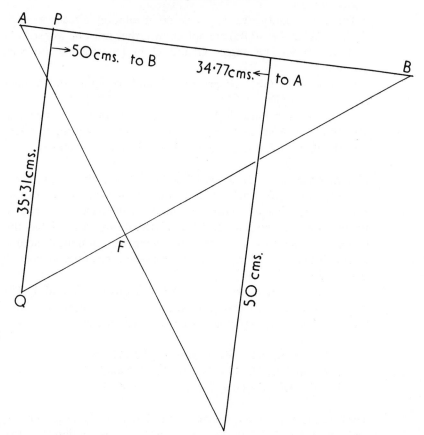

becomes unduly long; for 55° 11' it would be 71·90 cm at 50 cm from A. In such a case, therefore, the length of the perpendicular is chosen, and is divided by the tangent of the angle to find where it should be drawn. In the example, 50 cm divided by tan 55° 11' = 34·77 cm so a 50 cm perpendicular set up at 34·77 cm from A will give the required angle.

Angles drawn in this way should always be checked with a protractor, to detect possible mistakes. The same method is applicable when bearings are given.

17.6 *Intersection of Two Rays: Numerical Solution.* Two rays, which intersect at F, are observed from G and H, and have known bearings. The co-ordinates of F are to be found (see Figure 17.4, neglecting JF).

This is a straightforward application of solutions already given.

(a) If GH and Bg (GH) are not known, they must be worked out as Para. 16.9. The angles G and H in the triangle are then determined.

(b) The sides GF, HF are then found as Para. 16.12; their bearings are known.

(c) Then, as in Para. 16.8, the co-ordinates of C are calculated using line GF. Also, as a check, they are calculated using line HF. This should be invariable practice; a mistake is easy to make.

17.7 *Intersection of Three or More Rays.* Since errors are always present, three rays which should intersect at a point will in fact form a small triangle, so three calculations will need to be made if the previous method is used. If four observations are available, this number will increase to six. The following semi-graphical method offers an easier solution, and as will be seen it has other incidental advantages.

F is to be located using observations from G, H, and J. The 'true' co-ordinates are taken, but the bearings are worked out from the 'measured' angles (Appendix III) so the data are:

G at 114·75E, 622·75N, Bearing GF 82° 42·8'
H at 136·75E, 332·35N, Bearing HF 19° 49·5'
J at 470·00E, 455·00N, Bearing JF 309° 44·3'

These lines are plotted at a small scale (Figure 17.4); as drawn, the scale used was 1/2,500. To save space in reproduction, the two diagrams have been overlapped, so the point H appears close to the larger-scale plot; there would be no need for this economy in practice. This plot shows that F is near 250E, 642N; so a square enclosing that point is examined on a larger scale. The limits 245 to 255E, 635 to 645N seem suitable.

The distance from G to 245E is 130·75 m, and GF has a bearing 82° 42·8'. So the line GF cuts 245E at 130·75 ÷ tan 82° 42·8' + 622·75 (the N coordinate of G). This gives 16·719 + 622·75 = 639·47 m N. Similarly, it cuts 255E at 140·75 ÷ tan 82° 42·8' + 622·75 = 640·75N.

For HF, the line runs nearer N–S than E–W, so the intersections with 635 and 645N are used, giving 302·65 tan 19° 49·5' + 136·75

17.4 Intersection of Three Rays

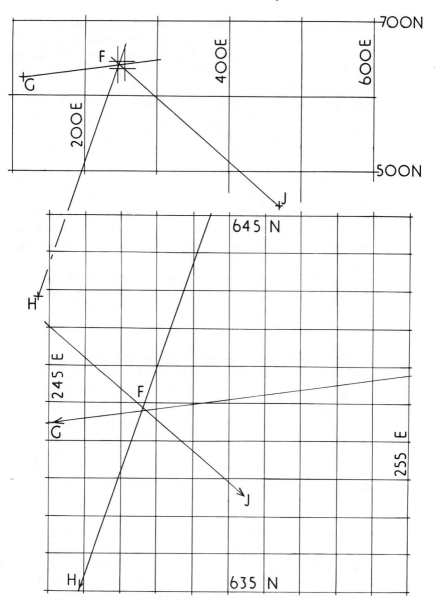

and 312·65 tan 19° 49·5' + 136·75, or 245·86 and 249·47 E.

For JF, the intersections with 245 and 255E are again calculated, bearing in mind that F is west of J. The results are therefore 225·00 tan 39° 44·3' + 455·00, 215·00 tan 39° 44·3' + 455·00, giving 642·05 and 633·74N.

Plotting these three lines, to an original scale of 1/50, gives a triangle of error with sides of less than 0·2 m, and by inspection the co-ordinates of F are about 247·6E, 639·8N; these seem unlikely to be much more than 0·1 m in error. In fact, the 'true' co-ordinates of F are 247·70E, 639·75N.

If greater accuracy were considered desirable, there would be no difficulty in applying the same method to examine the square 247–8E, 639–640N, which could be plotted to 1/10th. Logically, the point chosen should be placed so that its distances from the rays through G, H, and J are proportional to GF, HF, and JF, thus giving the same angular error for each.

Apart from its simplicity, and the ease with which it can be adapted to any number of rays, the great merit of this method is that it can display, to any scale desired, the actual magnitude of the uncertainty caused by the errors involved.

17.8 *Intersection of Chained Rays.* A straightforward chain survey is almost always plotted by direct measurement. Occasionally, though, to determine co-ordinates for the stations may be useful, as for example when the scale used is so large that the work extends to more than one sheet. This also is most simply done by a semi-graphical method similar to the last. The stations used in this example are the same, but the 'measured' distances are given instead of the bearings. GF = 134·05 m; HF = 327·15 m; JF = 288·75 m. As before, a small scale plot (not shown) indicates that F lies within the square 245–255E, 635–645N, so this is examined in detail (Figure 17.5).

The line 635N is 12·25N of G, so an arc of 134·05 m radius, centre G, will cut that line at $\sqrt{(134·05)^2 - (12·25)^2} = 133·49$ m E of G, that is, at 133·49 + 114·75 = 248·24. Similarly, the arc will cut 645N at $\sqrt{(134·05)^2 - (22·25)^2}$E of G, at 246·94. The short length of arc joining these two points is very nearly a straight line, and can be treated as such to a first approximation. For this centre only, a short length of the true arc is shown in the diagram. It cuts 640N at 247·69E, whereas the straight line cuts at 247·59.

Similarly, an arc of radius 327·15, centre H, cuts 245E at

17.5 Intersection of Chained Rays

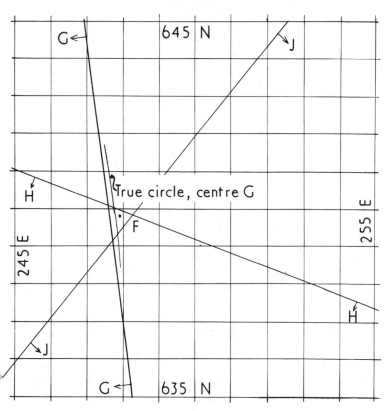

641·07N and 255E at 637·38N; and one of radius 288·75, centre J, cuts 635N at 244·22E and 645N at 252·57N. Since the radii are larger, these will approximate still more closely to straight lines. A programme for a hand calculator, which speeds the work considerably, is given in table 17.2.

Plotting these to scale 1/50, the triangle of error is appreciably larger than for angular measurements, as might be expected. Selecting by eye a point whose distances from the arcs centred on G are proportional to 134, 327, and 272, or roughly 1:2½:2, the likely position for F is at about 247·9E, 639·8N.

Again, the one-metre square 247–248E, 639–640N, could be examined to a larger scale, and the point F could be chosen so that the distance from each side of the triangle of error would be

Table 17.2 Intersection of Arc with Co-ordinate Line, Using Calculator

Data: Length GF = 134·05 metres.
    Coordinates of G: 114·75 E; 622·75 N.
Required: The E. coordinates at which an arc of radius 134·05
    metres with centre G cuts the lines 635 N and 645 N.

Programme	Data	Results	Notes
Figs.	134·05		Length GF.
x². STO 1. -.			
Figs. x².	12·25		635 N. - N. coord. of G
=. F. √x. +.			
Figs. F. STO 2.	114·75		E. coord. of G
=.		248·24	E. coord. of intersection with 635 N.
RCL 1. -.			
Figs. x².	22·25		645 N. - N. coord. of G
=. F. √x. +.			
F. RCL 2. =.		246·94	E. coord. of intersection with 645 N.

proportional to the radius of the corresponding arc, thus making the percentage adjustment the same for each line; but having regard to the inherent possible inaccuracy of the measurements, the extra work would not seem worth while.

17.9 *Balancing a Chained Quadrilateral.* A chained network is almost always 'balanced' by eye: there is no standardised simple method of doing it by calculation. Nevertheless, the particular case of a quadrilateral with both diagonals measured can be treated fairly easily, and may occasionally be useful, as for example in preparation for an excavation. The corresponding problem with measured angles is discussed in Para. 20.6. It is important to remember that 'balancing' does not eliminate errors (still less mistakes); it merely distributes them so that the network becomes geometrically possible (see Para. 19.2).

   The quadrilateral to be balanced is BEJF. The data are set out in table 17.3, together with the main calculations involved, and the necessary graphical work is shown in Figure 17.6. To allow comparison with the 'true' lengths and co-ordinates, the 'measured' lengths have been reduced proportionately so that their total is the same as that for the 'true' lengths; even so, the 'errors' included are larger than would be acceptable if the work were important enough to justify the work of balancing.

   The principle involved is simple. The measurements are geometri-

Table 17.3 Balancing Chained Quadrilateral

Data:	Line	Length	0.5 % strain
	BE	197.5	+ 0.99
	BF	251.8	+ 1.26
	BJ	348.3	- 1.74
	EF	333.7	- 1.67
	EJ	232.8	+ 1.16
	FJ	288.3	+ 1.44

Coordinates of J: 470.0 E; 455.0 N.
Bearing of JF: 309.7294°
whence
Coordinates of F: 248.277 E;
639.271 N.

Programme	For FE and FB.			For JE and JB		
	Data	Results	Notes	Data	Results	Notes
Figs. x^2. STO 1. -.	333.7		Length FE	232.8		Length JE
Figs. x^2. =. F. $\sqrt{x}$. +.	19.729		659 N - N(F)	109.00		579 E - E(J)
Figs. F. STO 2.	248.277		E(F)	455.00		N(J)
=.		581.39	FE cuts 659N		660.71	JE cuts 579E
RCL 1. -. Figs. x^2. =. F. $\sqrt{x}$. +.	22.729		662 N - N(F)	112.00		582 E - E(J)
F. RCL 2. =.		581 20	FE cuts 662N		659.09	JE cuts 582E
Figs. x^2. STO 1. -.	251.8		Length FB	348.3		Length JB
Figs. x^1. =. F. $\sqrt{x}$. +. F. RCL 2.	160.729		800 N - N(F)	-30.00		440 E - E(J)
=. RCL 1. -.		442.10	FB cuts 800N		802.01	JB cuts 440E
Figs. x^2. =. F. $\sqrt{x}$. +.	163.729		803 N - N(F)	-27.00		443 E - E(J)
F. RCL 2. =.		439.58	FB cuts 803N		802.25	JB cuts 443E

Point	Coords. before strain	Coords. after 0.5% strain	Coords. after 0.19%
B	E: 440.39 N: 802.04	442.96 800.52	441.37 801.46
E	E: 581.37 N: 659.43	578.46 662.31	580.26 660.52
F	E: 248.28 N: 639.27	247.17 640.19	247.86 639.62

cally incompatible, so we strain them (that is, increase or decrease them) all in the same proportion so that they can be fitted together. To find what strain is needed, one of the lines, BE in this case, is left out, and the network solved. The gap BE is found, in this case, to be longer than the line BE which should close it. A small strain is then imposed on all the lines, and the gap and line BE again compared. From this it is easy to work out the strain which would make the fit exact.

The calculations, essentially the same as those in table 17.2, are set out in table 17.3, the squares examined being 440–443E, 800–803N for B and 579–582E, 659–662N for E. In practice rather

17.6 Balancing a Chained Quadrilateral

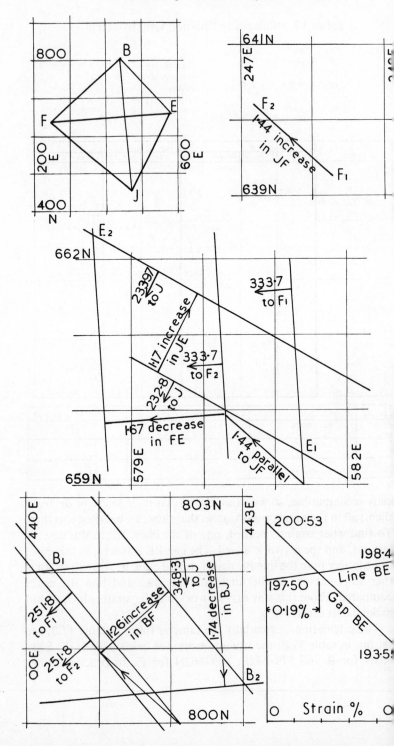

larger squares would probably be more convenient. The resulting co-ordinates (of B_1 and E_1 in the diagram) give a gap of 200·53 m, as against the measured length for BE of 197·5 m, a difference of about 1·5 per cent. So a strain of 0·5 per cent in each line, chosen so as to decrease the gap, seems likely to be of about the right magnitude.

The necessary changes in most of the lines are obvious, and a rough plot giving JF a large change in length shows that an increase in that line will decrease the gap BE, so the effect of increasing JF, BF, and EJ, and of decreasing BJ and EF, all by 0·5 per cent, is examined.

All the remaining work can be done graphically, and although at first glance the diagrams look complicated they are in fact simple if considered step by step.

The radius JE is supposed to have been increased by 1·17 m, so the new straight line, which approximates to the short length of arc through E_2, will be 1·17 m from the line through E_1 and parallel to it. Similarly, the new 'arc' through B_2 will be 1·74 m nearer J.

Two steps are needed to find the new positions of the 'arcs' centred on F. The line JF is to be increased, so F_2 moves 1·44 m away from J, in a direction parallel to JF. If the radii FB and FE were not altered, the new arcs would be represented by lines parallel to the original 'arcs' but distant from them by 1·44 m *measured parallel to JF*; these intermediate lines are shown on the diagram. In fact though, FE has decreased in length, so to get the correct position of the new 'arc' the line must be moved a further 1·67 m towards F. The intersection of this 'arc' with the new 'arc' centred on J gives E_2, the new position of E. BF has increased by 1·26 m, and a similar construction gives B_2.

The co-ordinates of B_2, E_2, and F_2 can all be read directly from the large-scale plots. The gap B_2E_2 proves to be 193·55 m, while the line BE, if increased by 0·5 per cent, becomes 198·49 m. Plotting these shows that the gap and line will be equal when the strain is 0·19 per cent. The corresponding co-ordinates can be found graphically, for example by dividing the line E_1E_2 in the ratio 19 to 50; but it is just as easy to calculate them. Thus, with no strain E(B) is 440·39, and with 0·5 per cent strain it is 442·96, an increase of 2·57; so 0·19 per cent will correspond to an increase of 0·98, making the value of E(B) after 'balancing' the network 441·37. As a final check, the lengths corresponding to the final co-ordinates should be worked out, to make sure that the strain in each line is acceptably close to 0·19 per cent.

17.10 *Resection: The Three-point Problem.* Sometimes, especially perhaps during a 'salvage' excavation, it may be very useful indeed to be able to fix the position of a point by observations from it to stations which are visible but inaccessible. Suppose that F is the required point, and G and H are known stations; then if the angle GFH is known, it defines a circle, passing through G and H, on which F must lie. Similarly, if J is another known station, angle HFJ defines another such circle through H and J, and F will be where the two circles cut.

In practice, this construction is not used, or only in a very modified form, but it makes one very important point clear: the problem cannot be solved if F lies on (or very near) the circle which passes through G, H, and J. Since this cannot easily be detected in the field, a fourth station should always be observed if at all possible. Ideally, one station should be distant, and two close; provided the station co-ordinates are known relative to the site grid, they need not lie within the area represented by the plan.

There are several different methods of solution, all rather laborious; the semi-graphical method described here is the least so.

The data are set out in table 17.4.

Initially, the approximate co-ordinates of F are found by drawing rays at the appropriate angles on a sheet of tracing-paper. Stations A, G, H and J are plotted on a separate drawing to a suitable scale, and the tracing is moved over it until the rays pass through the relevant points. The position of F can then be pricked through. For some purposes, as for example when working on a chain survey on which A, G, H and J are shown, this solution is adequate, but if the co-ordinates of F are needed accurately more calculations are needed. We will assume that by this 'tracing-paper' method they have been found to be about 250E, 640N. As previously, a suitable square is examined. In this case 248–252E, 638–642N seem appropriate; as the diagram becomes rather crowded, a large scale is desirable, and the original plot was drawn to 1/25.

The longest ray is HF, so the uncertainty in the co-ordinates of F will have least effect on the bearing of that line. As a first approximation that is found to be 20·2093°, from which the corresponding bearings of AF, GF, and JF can be found. The intersections of those rays with the grid lines which form the sides of the square can then be worked out. The results are set out in table 17.4, but the calculations are not given in detail as the method

Table 17.4 Resection

Data: Coordinates   A 169·10 E; 779·25 N.
                    G 114·75 E; 622·75 N.
                    H 136·75 E; 332·35 N.
                    J 470·00 E; 455·00 N.

     Angles   AFG 67·8833°
              GFH 62·8967°
              HFJ 70·0967°

Required: Coordinates of F.

   A calculator has been used for convenience, but the same method is applicable with logarithms.

First approximation: F taken as at 250 E; 640 N.
Tan (Bg. HF) = (250·00 - 136·75) ÷ (640·00 - 332·35)
             = 0·368113
Whence Bg. HF = 20·2093°
From this the bearings of the other lines can be found, and thus their intersections with the relevant grid lines.

| Line | Bearing | E. coords. of intersections with | | |
		638 N	642 N	640 N
AF	150·9893°	247·43	245·21	246·32
HF	20·2093°	249·26	250·74	

| Line | Bearing | N. coords. of intersections with | | |
		248 E	252 E	250 E
GF	83·1060°	638·86	639·34	
JF	310·1126°	642·02	638·65	

Second approximation: F taken as at 248 E; 640 N.
Tan (Bg. HF) = (248·00 - 136·75) ÷ (640·00 - 332·35)
Whence Bg. HF = 19·8806°

| Line | Bearing | E. coords. of intersections with | | |
		638 N	642 N	640 N
AF	150·6606°	248·49	246·25	247·37
HF	19·8806°	247·28	248·72	

| Line | Bearing | N. coords. of intersections with | | |
		248 E	252 E	250 E
GF	82·7773°	639·64	640·14	
JF	309·7839°	639·86	636·53	638·20

has already been described in Para. 17.7. In arranging the table, space is left in case more values are needed; thus, the line AF cuts 642N inconveniently far west of the square being examined, so the intercept with 640N is found by interpolation.

When plotting these (Figure 17.7, indicated by suffix 1) it is helpful to use coloured (fine) ball-point pens, as the number of lines involved can lead to confusion; in the diagram different styles of line are used. Examination of this first plot suggests that 248·0E, 640·0N would be a rather better approximation for F. This gives the second set of approximations in the table (suffix 2 on plot).

Now consider the rays from A and G. The intersections AG_1 and

17.7 Resection

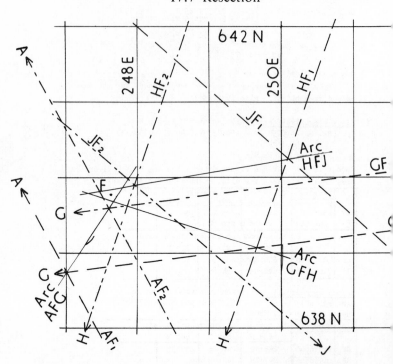

AG$_2$ both correspond to points on the circle through A and G, o
some point of which F must lie; so the line joining those point
represents accurately at this scale, a short length of th
circumference of that circle. Similar reasoning applies to all othe
intersections. If the angles observed from F had all been exactl
right, the three circles, and therefore the three equivalent straigh
lines would all meet in a point, but since the angles contain error
the lines form a small triangle. A first estimate for the co-ordinate
of F is found by bisecting the angles of the triangle of error, givin
247·65E, 639·77N (the 'true' values are 247·70, 639·75).

As always, a final check should be made, by working out th
bearings corresponding to this point. The calculated angles prov
to be: AFG, 67·9113° (0·0230° too big); GFH, 62·8655° (0·0312
too small); and HFJ, 70·1105° (0·0138° too big). If thes
discrepancies are considered unacceptably large, the calculation
can be repeated, using the co-ordinates 247·65E, 639·77N as a thir

pproximation to the co-ordinates of F and examining square 247-48 E, 639–640 N at a larger scale. This should get rid of naccuracies caused by representing the arcs by straight lines, but he effect of errors in angular measurements will remain.

18 Miscellaneous Calculations

18.1 Drawing a Grid; 18.2 Tracing a Gridded Plan; 18.3 Plotting Intermediate Points on Chain Lines; 18.4 Rotation of Co-ordinate Axes; 18.5 Linkage to National Grid; 18.6 True Bearing from National Grid; 18.7 Calculation of Areas; 18.8 Calculation of Volumes.

18.1 *Drawing a Grid*. If stations are to be plotted using their co ordinates, the accuracy of the background grid is important. Eve for a chain survey a grid is useful, if the plan is large, for th original drawing can then be done on cartridge paper and th dimensional changes corrected, when tracing, as described i Para. 18.2.

The grid must be constructed by drawing a rectangle of the fu size required and then dividing it; it must not be built up fror smaller squares. The construction is essentially the same as fo setting out a rectangle with a chain (Para. 7.5). It is illustrated i Figure 18.1, where the inaccuracies have been exaggerated; bu working with a set square of ordinary size the verticals are alway liable to be slightly wrong.

As an example, suppose that we wish to draw a rectangle ABCL 100 cm long and 80 cm high. Only the construction for C will b given; that for D is exactly similar.

AB is drawn with the straight-edge, and lines at right angles t AB are marked off at B (and A) with the set square. These lines ar produced to make BC_1 (and AD_1) 80 cm. Since the set square probably of only 15 or 20 cm side, BC_1 and AD_1 will not be exactl perpendicular to AB, but they will nearly be so, and therefore C_1D will be parallel to AB and at the required distance from it.

If ABC were exactly 90°, then AC_1 would equal $\sqrt{100^2 + 80}$ = 128·06 cm.

Draw the straight line AX aiming to pass through C_1. It does no matter if you miss by a short distance, which may easily happen a AX is rather longer than the (assumed) metre straight-edge. Mak AX the required 128·06 cm and draw XC perpendicular to AX_1 cut the line D_1C_1 at C. In practice, the length XC will be relative very small, so this is almost exactly equivalent to drawing an arc c

18.1   Drawing a Rectangular Grid

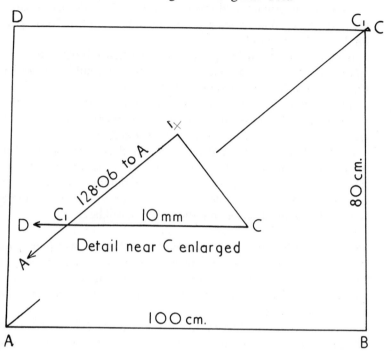

Detail near C enlarged

radius 128·06 cm with centre A. D is then fixed by the same method, and finally both diagonals and all four sides are checked.

To give an idea of the accuracy which may be expected, suppose that a very imperfect set square has been used, so that C_1 came 10 mm to the left of C (as in the diagram). Then if all the other works were done with complete accuracy, the line DC would be 0·06 mm too close to AB, and 0·12 mm too long; such errors would be imperceptible.

Provided the rectangle is not unduly long and narrow any proportions can be used. Other things being equal, a 3–4–5 triangle is to be preferred, since the calculation needed to fix the diagonal is then very simple.

18.2 *Tracing a Gridded Plan.* If the pencil draft of a large plan has been drawn on cartridge paper it will often prove to have altered slightly in its overall dimensions before it is ready for tracing. This can easily be corrected when the tracing is made; it is assumed that that will be on dimensionally stable material.

Suppose the original grid was in squares of 20 cm side (the same method applies to any sized grid). Draw in pencil a true 20 cm grid on the tracing material.

Now consider a single square; for convenience, points in it are specified by their co-ordinates relative to the south-west corner (0,0); thus (20,10) is the middle of the east side.

Superimpose (0,0) on the tracing and on the draft and trace the detail within a 10 cm square centred on that point. Then move the tracing so that the (0,10) points on tracing and draft coincide, and trace the adjacent detail; and so on moving the co-ordinates which are made to coincide by 10 cm at a time until the whole draft has been traced. The discrepancies at the boundaries of the 10 cm squares will be inappreciable. There is of course no need to adhere to the measurements given, but the principle will be clear.

18.3 *Plotting Intermediate Points on Chain Lines.* Large plans can sometimes be plotted more conveniently on several small sheets rather than on one very large one. A chain line may then join two stations which are on different sheets; but points on the line can easily be determined.

As an example, consider the line BE; B is at 441·2E, 801·1N, E at 580·3E, 659·9N. The measured chainage from B to E is 197·8 (as compared to the true distance between those co-ordinates which is 198·21), so small adjustments will need to be made when plotting detail (see Para. 6.4).

The midpoint is easily fixed, at $(441·2 + 580·3) \div 2 = 510·75$ and $(810·1 + 659·9) \div 2 = 730·5N$, and its chainage will be $197·8 \div 2 = 98·9$. The quarter-points can be obtained similarly, lying midway between the ends and the midpoint, and hence if desired the eighth-points. Often no more is needed, but sometimes the intersection with a specified grid-line is useful. Suppose that 500E is the line at which two sheets join. Call the intersection of BE with 500E the point P.

The easting of BP is $500 - 441·2 = 58·8$ m, while that of BE is 139·1 m. The southing of BE is 141·2 m, so the southing of BP is $141·2 \times 58·8 \div 139·1 = 59·688$. Since B is at 801·1N, P is at $801·1 - 59·688 = 741·421N$. Similarly the chainage of P, measured from B, is $197·8 \times 58·8 \div 139·1 = 83·61$ m.

As a check, it is advisable to plot also the half- and quarter-points to make sure that they lie on BP, PE.

18.4 *Rotation of Co-ordinate Axes.* Occasionally, it may be desirable to alter the co-ordinate axes; the most usual reason, to relate your survey to the National Grid, is discussed in the next section.

Suppose you have a point P, with co-ordinates x, y in your co-ordinates, and that your y-axis has a bearing z relative to true N. Then the straightforward formulae are

$$E = x \cos z + y \sin z$$
$$N = -x \sin z + y \cos z$$

If the origins are different, the E and N co-ordinates of the (x,y) origin must be added.

Calculation by logarithms is laborious. A programme for a calculator is given in table 18.1, and will be described in some detail as it is a good illustration of the use of the Polar keys.

The calculation is supposed to be the first of a sequence of points (Q, S, etc), so the N co-ordinate of the (x, y) origin is stored in the second memory; if only a single point were involved it could be entered later (see below). Unfortunately, with two memories, no store is available for the corresponding E co-ordinate, and the full figures will have to be keyed in for each calculation. The bearing of the y-axis relative to the N-axis is then stored in memory 1; for a single calculation, this also could be entered later.

Now the main calculation starts. The y co-ordinate of Q is entered, and by using the F. and x/y. keys is transferred to the (invisible) y register. The x co-ordinate is then entered, and pressing the P. key yields the Polar co-ordinate of the point Q, that is, the length OQ. The F. and x/y keys transfer that to the y register, replacing the y co-ordinate, and yield the bearing of OQ relative to the y axis. The sequence (. +. RCL 1. and). brings the bearing of the y axis out of memory 1 and adds it to the last figure, giving the true bearing of OQ. If this were a single calculation, the figures for the bearing of OQ relative to the y axis could be entered instead of RCL 1. Since you are using the Polar keys, take care not to forget the brackets.

Since you have the length OQ in the y register and the true bearing in the visible x register, the R. key gives the Northing of

Table 18.1 Rotation of Axes, Using Calculator with Polar Keys

Data: Q at x = 103·4 y = 217·6
      S at x = 127·6 y = 303·4
Origin for (x,y) axes at 442·1 E 206·2 N.
Bearing of y-axis, 28·24° E. of N.
Required: E and N coordinates of Q and S.

Programme	Data	Results	Notes
(a) Figs.	206·2		N. coord. of 0.
(a) F. STO 2.			
Figs. STO 1.	28·24		Bearing of y-axis
Figs.	217·6		y (for Q)
F. x/y			
Figs.	103·4		x (for Q)
P.		(240·9177)	(length 0Q)
F. x/y.		(25·4163)	(Bearing of 0Q from y-axis)
(. +. RCL 1.).		(53·6563)	(Bearing of 0Q from N.)
R.		(142·7744)	(Northing of 0Q)
(a) (. +. F.			
(a) RCL 2.).		348·9744	N. coord. of Q
F. x/y.		(194·0535)	(Easting of 0Q)
(a) (.+.Figs.	442·1		E. coord. of 0.
(a)).		636·1535	E. coord. of Q
Programme repeats:			
Figs.	303·4		y (for S)
F. x/y.			
Figs.	127·6		x (for S)
P.		(329·1403)	(length 0S)
F. x/y.		(22·8100)	(Bearing of 0S from y-axis)
(. +. RCL 1.).		(51·0500)	(Bearing of 0S from N.)
R.		(206·9113)	(Northing of 0S)
(a) (. +. F.			
(a) RCL 2.).		413·1113	N. coord. of S
F. x/y.		(255·9707)	(Easting of 0S)
(a) (.+.Figs.	442·1		E. coord. of 0.
(a)).		698·0707	E. coord. of S

(a)...(a): These are not needed if the two coordinate systems have the same origin.

OQ, and (by using brackets) the N co-ordinate of the origin can be recalled, or entered direct, and added. That gives the N co-ordinate of Q. The F. and x/y. keys then give the Easting of OQ, and adding the E co-ordinte of the origin gives the E co-ordinate of Q.

18.5 *Linkage to National Grid.* Save in exceptional cases, the Grid, unlike ordnance datum for levels, cannot be fixed precisely on the ground, so there is no real advantage in showing it on a plan if the scale much exceeds 1/2,500. Some people do not realise this

Table 18.2 Linking Surveys to National Grid

Data:	National Grid		Survey	
	E	N	x	y
A	(1)021	208	129·90	1·10
B	980	358	124·25	156·15
C	(1)063	416	217·75	194·14
D	901	213	13·90	33·95

Points A and C are in square 59 80, B and D in 58 80.

	National Grid Coord. Diffs.			Survey Coord. Diffs.			Diff. in
Line	E	N	Bearing	x	y	Bearing	Bearings
AB	−41	+150	344·7126	− 5·65	+155·05	357·9131	13·2005
AC	+42	+208	11·4158	+87·85	+193·04	24·4697	13·0539
AD	−120	+5	272·3859	−116·00	+32·85	285·8116	13·4257
BC	+83	+58	55·0543	+93·50	+37·99	67·8876	12·8333
BD	−79	−145	208·5828	−110·35	−122·20	222·0829	13·5001
CD	−162	−203	218·5909	−203·85	−160·19	231·8389	13·2480
						Average:	13·2102

Coordinates of points relative to Survey origin, after rotating axes 13·2102 degrees anticlockwise:

	E	N	Differences from National Grid E	N
A	126·211	30·756	894·789	177·244
B	85·278	180·412	894·722	177·588
C	167·622	238·764	895·378	177·236
D	5·774	36·228	895·226	176·772
	Averages:		895·029	177·210

Hence the coordinates of the points relative to the National Grid are:

	E	N
A	59 021·24	80 207·97
B	58 980·31	80 357·62
C	59 062·65	80 415·97
D	58 900·80	80 213·44

though, and the result can look impressive. Table 18.2 sets out in summary the method which can be used.

Four points are supposed to be identified on the national grid and on your survey (but see further comments below). Their grid co-ordinates are known to the nearest metre (0·4 mm on the 1/2,500 map); perhaps an estimate to half a metre could be made, but the method is unaffected.

These four points define six lines, and the bearings of these are worked out relative to the national grid and to the survey grid. If the national grid co-ordinates were exact, the difference for any pair of bearings would give the angle between the survey and the national grids, but in fact there is a range of uncertainty, so an average is taken.

The axes of the survey grid are then rotated (as in Table 18.1, but without moving the origin), and the differences between these new co-ordinates and the national grid co-ordinates found and averaged. From these, the co-ordinates of the points relative to the national grid are found by addition, and the grid can easily be superimposed on the plan.

Four points is a convenient number; two, at least, are essential. With more than four, the number of lines increases rapidly; six points define fifteen lines. In such circumstances it would be reasonable to select the longest half dozen or so.

If your survey can be linked to an OS Trigonometrical Station, then in principle you should be able to make an exact connection with the grid; but the policy of the Ordnance Survey over revealing such information varies, and in any case, save in the unlikely event that such accuracy is really essential, it would be difficult to justify taking up an inevitably overworked Officer's time with such an enquiry.

The scale of the OS maps does in fact vary slightly as you move from east to west across the country, owing to the projection used; but the variation is not appreciable, so if you find the 'metres' of your plan differ from those of the 1/2,500 map, your survey is wrong.

18.6 *True Bearing from National Grid.* If the accurate direction of true north is needed, as for example in examining the possible function of a stone alignment, it can be found either by astronomical observations or from the National Grid. The former is difficult, and will not be discussed here. The latter is, in principle, simple, but also requires tiresome calculations if accuracy better than about 01' or 02' is needed. In that case, reference should be made to *Projection Tables for the Transverse Mercator Projection of Great Britain* (Ordnance Survey, published by HMSO, 1950), which give all the necessary information. In any case, three difficulties arise.

(a) Assume that the required direction is found by estimating the relative bearing of two points, located by their grid references on the 1/2,500 map; then both positions are liable to an uncertainty of at least 0·5 m (0·2 mm on the map), giving a total uncertainty of a metre at least, which requires a line of sight 3·5 km long to give the bearing relative to the grid correct to within 01'. With the 1/10,000 map, owing to its great generalisation, the corresponding distance may be as much as 70 km. This applies whatever method is used to convert grid bearing to true bearing.

(b) As will be apparent to any user of 'one-inch' or 1/50,000 maps, grid north may diverge by as much as 3° from true north, and the amount alters according to longitude. On the 1/50,000 maps the value is given, to the nearest minute, for each corner, so the required correction can easily be interpolated for the point at which the observation is made; but the accuracy will only be to about one minute. If greater precision is needed the 'Convergence' must be calculated using the *Projection Tables*.

(c) A third, less obvious, source of error arises because the map has to represent a spherical surface on a plane. Straight lines on the ground may therefore appear slightly sinuous on the map. Even for a 100 km sight the divergence is seldom as much as 01·5 minutes, but for really accurate work it also should be calculated from the Projection Tables. The effect is zero for an east-west grid line, greatest for one running north-south.

Fortunately, for most purposes, an accuracy within two minutes is good enough; it will at least allow a decision as to whether an alignment is likely to be of astronomical significance. Nevertheless, when stating a significant bearing obtained only by measurements on the 1/2,500 map and interpolation from the 1/50,000, the basis for the calculation should be given, so that anyone who wishes to do so can appreciate what accuracy is to be expected.

18.7 *Calculation of Areas.* In describing an enclosure, the area usually needs to be stated. For many purposes, a rough value is good enough, and can be found by sketching by eye the outline of a simple figure which appears to be of about the same area. In Figure 18.2, part of the outline of the sketched oval is shown, as well as the estimated equivalent trapezium. For the oval, the area is given by

$\frac{\pi}{4} \times$ length $\times$ breadth (the same will apply to a D-shaped figure),

and for the trapezium, the mean of the lengths of the two parallel sides $\times$ the distance between them. The results are given in table 18.3. Even when a more accurate estimate is to be made, a rough estimate of this kind should always be worked out as a check.

If the area is needed more precisely, the figure is divided up into strips of equal width; there will usually be a small segment unaccounted for at each end; these will be considered later.

18.2 Estimation of Areas

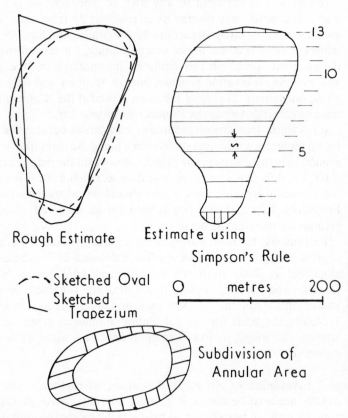

Rough Estimate

Estimate using
Simpson's Rule

- - - Sketched Oval   O   metres   200
⌐ Sketched
    Trapezium

Subdivision of
Annular Area

Suppose the strips are all of width S, and the sides, taken in order, measure a, b, c, d, . . . m, n, p. Two formulae (out of many) are commonly used.

The simplest is the Trapezoidal Rule. Each strip is treated as a trapezium, so their areas are s(a + b) ÷ 2, s(b + c) ÷ 2 and so on. The total area thus becomes

$$s(\frac{a}{2} + b + c \ldots + m + n + \frac{p}{2}).$$

If the outline is convex, a little is lost in each strip. The number used may be odd or even.

Table 18.3 Estimating Areas

Rough Estimates:

Equivalent Oval (sketched): $257 \times 146 \times \pi/4$
=29470 square metres
= 2·95 hectares.

Equivalent Trapezium: $224 \times \dfrac{173 + 74}{2}$
= 2·77 ha.

Estimate using Simpson's Rule:
One-third of Spacing times (Sum of ends + 4 x Sum of 'evens'
                                        + 2 x Sum of 'odds')

Section	Ends	Evens	Odds
1	50		
2		53	
3			62
4		77	
5			106
6		128	
7			142
8		152	
9			158
10		161	
11			156
12		139	624 x 2 = 1248
13	90	710	x 4 = 2840
	140		140

Spacing: 20 m.x ⅓ x $\overline{4228}$ = 2·82 ha.
N. Segment: 90 x 6 x 2/3   = 0·04 ha.
S. Segment: 50 x 16 x 2/3   = 0·05 ha.

TOTAL   2·91 ha.

Simpson's Rule is more accurate. The value found is exact, providing the boundary curves are cubics. The strips are considered

in pairs, and the areas are $\dfrac{s}{3}(a + 4b + c)$, $\dfrac{s}{3}(c + 4d + e)$, etc, so that

the total is $\dfrac{s}{3}(a + 4b + 2c + 4d + \ldots + 2m + 4n + p)$

or $\dfrac{s}{3}$(sum of first and last measurements plus

$4 \times$ sum of even measurements plus $2 \times$ sum of odd measurements excluding first and last). As will be seen in table 18.3, this lends itself to a simple arrangement for calculation.

To apply Simpson's Rule, the number of strips must be even, so that the number of measurements is odd; but if for any reason the number of strips is odd, one can be treated as a trapezium, Simpson's Rule being used for the rest. It is often convenient to take a simple measurement for the spacing (20 m in Figure 18.2), and to treat separately the little segments left over. Simpson's Rule, for these, gives the formula Area = base × height × ⅔.

For an area such as the water surface in a moat (see Figure 18.2),

to calculate the total and the internal areas and to take the difference
is not very accurate, for each will include an error, and these will be
combined and may be quite large relative to the much smaller area
of the 'moat'. A better result is obtained by dividing it up into
several lengths for which the areas can be calculated by Simpson's
Rule, the wedge-shaped pieces joining them being worked out
separately treating each as built up from a triangle plus a segment.
The wedges, of course, need not be right-angled.

Areas can also be found using a planimeter. This ingenious
application of the calculus comprises two arms pivoted together,
one supported on a pivot, the other carrying a pointer. Near their
junction a small wheel measures, by its rotation, the area traced out
by the pointer. There are two objections to this instrument, apart
from its cost. To get an accurate result requires very great care in
following the perimeter *exactly*, and movement must be slow and
careful to ensure that the small wheel rotates as it should, and does
not slip. Also, unless you use the device frequently, it will take you
far longer to remember how to apply it than to work out the
required area numerically. Nevertheless, if you have a lot of areas
to measure, and do not require great accuracy, a planimeter may be
useful.

18.8 *Calculation of Volumes.* Except for very simple cases,
volumes are more laborious to calculate than areas. Moreover,
there is no approximate check comparable to sketching the
apparent equivalent oval. For a mound circular in plan and having
a profile which is symmetrically parabolic, the volume is half the
height times the area of the base, and this can be extended fairly
accurately to any low oval mound.

Accurate calculations, though essentially simple, can be
laborious. Save for one special case, considered later, the method is
to take equally spaced parallel sections, work out their areas, and
then work out the volume either using the Trapezoidal or
Simpson's Rule; the latter is very much to be preferred if a fair
degree of accuracy is needed.

The sections can be parallel to any plane, but will usually be
either vertical or horizontal. The former, which would be the
method of choice for a length of rampart, is so obvious as to need
no explanation. The latter, which is to be preferred for mounds of
limited extent, can involve some minor difficulties, so an example is
given. The volume of material is to be estimated, given a contoured

18.3 Estimation of Volumes

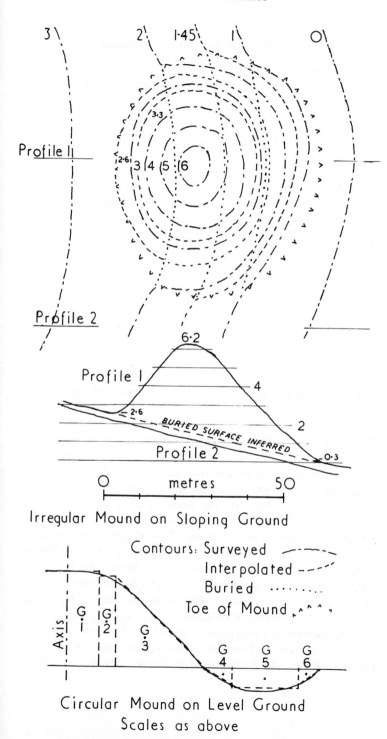

Irregular Mound on Sloping Ground

Contours: Surveyed — · — · —
Interpolated – – – –
Buried · · · · · · · ·
Toe of Mound ︿ ︿ ︿

Circular Mound on Level Ground
Scales as above

Table 18.4 Estimating Volumes

(a) <u>Contoured Mound</u>.

Contour Level	Area enclosed	Vertical Spacing	Volume (cu. m.)
0·3	0		
1·45	809·6	1·15	1883·0
2·6	1673·8		
2·6	1673·8		
3·3	1068·1	0·7	1548·7
4·0	691·2		
4·0	691·2		
5·0	296·9	1·0	650·7
6·0	73·4		
6·0	73·4		7·3
6·2	0		

(volume of 'cap' equals half area of base times height)

	4089·7

Volume of Mound: 4090 cubic metres.

(b) <u>Circular Mound on Level Ground</u>.

Radius from Axis to C.G.	Width	Height	Area times Radius
4·5	9·0	5·0	202·5
11·25	4·5	4·8	243·0
21·83	25·0	4·8 (triangle)	1309·8
			1755·3
		x 2π =	11028·9
43·5	7·5	0·8 (triangle)	130·5
55·0	18·0	1·05	1039·5
66·0	6·0	0·8 (triangle)	158·4
			1328·4
		x 2π =	8346·6

Estimated volumes in cubic metres: <u>Mound, 11030</u>;
<u>Ditch, 8350</u>.

plan of a mound resting on sloping ground (Figure 18.3 and table 18.4).

The first step is to draw a profile of the mound. By drawing one or more further profiles adjacent to its base, the probable contours of the natural ground surface beneath the mound can be drawn.

Examination of the profile indicates that at 2·6 m above site datum, the level of the toe on the upper side, there will be a discontinuity in the shape of the curve relating area enclosed to contour level, so that part of the mound needs to be examined separately. A fairly accurate result will be obtained by considering the areas enclosed by contours at 0·3 (the lowest part on the toe) 1·45, that is, $(2·6 + 0·3) \div 2$, and 2·6 (the upper edge), though a better result would be given by using 0·725 and 2·175 also. The 1·45 contour is interpolated on the mound and as one of the 'buried' contours. This encloses a crescentic space, corresponding to the made up material cut by a plane at level 1·45 above site datum. The area is found by using Simpson's Rule, and is 809·6 square metres. Value for 0·725 and 2·175 would be found similarly if required.

The 2.6 contour is also found by interpolation; it is an oval, corresponding to the surface of the mound, and is treated here as having the area of an ellipse of the same overall dimensions, as are all higher contours.

Above 2·6 m, and leaving aside the rounded summit above 6·0 m, there is a height of 3·4 m. This could be divided into an even number of parts, but it is less bother simply to interpolate the 3·3 contour midway between 2·6 and 4·0, and to work out that part and the part from 4·0 to 6·0 separately. The calculations are set out in table 18.4.

It will be observed that the check, height times area of base divided by two, gives a very much larger result, roughly 7,000 cubic metres. The reason for this is that the sides of the mound are concave in profile, not convex as assumed in the above formula.

If a bank, mound or ditch is truly circular in plan, and of uniform cross section, the volume is given by the cross-sectional area times the length of arc traced by its centre of gravity (not its mid point, unless the profile is symmetrical). The centre of gravity can be located by dividing the section into vertical strips, not necessarily all of the same width, and multiplying the area of each by its distance from some convenient zero line; the total is divided by the total area. Usually, though, a satisfactory approximation to the true profile can be built up out of rectangles and triangles, as in Figure 18.3, where G_1, G_2 etc. indicate the positions of their centres of gravity. The calculations necessary to find the volume are also given in table 18.4. The multiplication by 2π, to give the lengths of the arcs traced out by the centres of gravity, can be left until last. The only rule which has to be remembered is that the centre of gravity of a triangle is at one-third of its height; if for example, a strip has a steeply sloping top, it can be treated as made up from a triangle and a rectangle, each part being worked out separately.

The same approach is applicable to any bank or ditch of uniform profile: the volume is given by the cross-sectional area times the length of the line corresponding to the centre of gravity of the cross section. In practice, this seldom differs appreciably from the length of the centre-line.

If the cross section is not uniform, there is no simple exact solution, but provided it does not vary much, reasonable accuracy can be obtained by plotting the line corresponding in plan to the centre of gravity, taking cross sections equally spaced along that line, and finding the volume by Simpson's Rule.

19 The Traverse

19.1 *General.* One of the most useful applications of the theodolite is surveying by means of a traverse. This is essentially a series of straight lines, the direction of each being fixed by measurement of the angle it makes with the adjacent ones; its nature will become obvious from the examples which follow. A traverse may be 'closed' in which case it starts and finishes at the same station, or 'open'; an open traverse may link two known points, but need not necessarily do so.

Traversing is the only possible method for most underground surveying. On the surface, its main application is on wooded ground, as for example following the ramparts of an enclosure where the central area is planted. It is a wise precaution when traversing to supplement the theodolite observations with magnetic bearings: unless this is done a mistake can only be located by remeasuring all the angles. The check on the total of the internal angles (Para. 19.3) should always be made before leaving the site.

Although a polygon with a central station (Chapter 20) requires rather more angular measurements than a simple closed traverse, it is always preferable, for it allows a very much better distribution of any errors which occur, as well as reducing the risk of mistakes escaping unnoticed. The techniques of calculation for traverses and polygons with central stations include particular attention to methods of distributing errors, so the principles governing such distribution can usefully be discussed here.

19.2 *Distribution of Errors.* Some examples of this have already been given without discussion (Paras. 17.7–10), but the principles need to be explained in more detail.

The most important is to emphasise that distribution (also termed 'balancing') may only be applied to 'errors' (Para. 2.1).

'Mistakes' must be found and eliminated before any calculation is started. This can be understood from a simple example. Suppose you had three stations forming a triangle of which the true angles (if you could determine them) were 65° 12', 35° 14', and 79° 34'. Estimating your measured angles to 0·1', you might get these to be 65° 11·6', 35° 13·6' and 79° 33·3', adding up to 179° 58·5'. Since the real total *must* be 180° and you are equally likely to make an 'error' in each measurement, you would add 0·5' to each reading, giving 'adjusted' angles 65° 12·1', 35° 14·1', and 79° 33·8'. 'Adjusted' is a better term than 'corrected', for you have no way of knowing what is 'correct', you only know what the total angles of a triangle must be.

Suppose, though, that your records read 65° 11·6', 35°13·6', and 89° 33·3', adding up to 189° 58·5'. Obviously you have made a 'mistake', probably by misreading 10° in one of the angles. If you 'balance' them by deducting 3° 19·5' from each you finish up with all three angles badly wrong.

The first principle, then, is that the quantity you wish to distribute must be small enough to arise from 'errors' only. The distinction depends on the nature of the work being done, and unless defined by specific rules must be a matter of subjective judgement; for most archaeological work 01·5' closing error, or in bad conditions even 05', would be reasonable, but for a geodetic survey it would imply a 'mistake'.

The second principle is that all measurements of the same kind are equally liable to error, unless of course you have valid reasons to suppose one is worse than the others. So in the triangle just considered you adjust all angles equally, by 0·5'. The purist would maintain that you must not introduce any subjective element, but my own view is that if, say, the first two angles had been measured under ideal conditions and the third from a very windy hill top one might legitimately argue 'the last angle is likely to be much less accurate than the other two; let us allow it 3 units of "error", as against one each for them'. The unit then comes out to 1·5' ÷ 5 = 0·3', making the adjusted angles 65° 11·9', 35° 13·9', and 79° 34·2'.

For a linear measurement, the error which may occur is likely to depend on the length of the line; some assumption has to be made about this. One possibility is that the error may be expected to vary with the length; another, for which there is perhaps rather more theoretical justification, is that it should vary according to the square root of the length. To illustrate what these alternatives mean, imagine that you have five pegs, successive measurements between them being recorded as 100, 200, 300 and 400 m, but the total length being known from other evidence to be 1001 m. Then according to the first assumption, the best values for the adjusted lengths would be 100·1, 200·2, 300·3 and 400·4 m, but according to the second 100·16, 200·23, 300·28 and 400·33 m.

Without additional evidence, there is no way of deciding which set of adjusted measurements is the better. I have discussed them at some length in order to emphasise this, for the object of distributing errors is simply to ensure that at every stage you are dealing with a geometrically possible problem and that you have got the errors evenly distributed. It is reasonable to hope that by doing this you will be getting a fairly good approximation to whatever the 'true' shape of the network may be. Bearing in mind that the errors are by definition relatively small, then in the type of survey considered here you can legitimately depart a little from the theoretically ideal method of balancing them in order to simplify your calculations. This argument would not be valid for really precise work.

Essentially then, the method followed is that the calculations fall into successive stages, at each of which the errors which cause geometrical impossibilities, such as a triangle with angles not totalling 180°, are distributed as evenly as possible according to some simple rule. These adjustments are then incorporated in the data and forgotten, and the adjusted measurements are used in all subsequent calculations, being subjected to further adjustment if necessary.

19.3 *Closed Traverse using Logarithms.* Because of the importance of the traverse as a survey method, a full solution is given both by the use of logarithms (in this section) and using the hand calculator (in the next). The principles are exactly the same, but the arrangement differs.

The first step should be to draw out a table (as table 19.1), preferably on a wide sheet of paper, though if necessary, as here, the table can be arranged in two parts, separating the 'Departure' to 'Co-ordinates' from the rest. The data, underlined in table 19.1, are then entered. Note that the entries run anticlockwise.

The next step before doing anything else is to draw out carefully, to any convenient small scale, an outline of the traverse, using a protractor for the angles (Figure 19.1). This will detect any

Table 19.1 Closed Traverse, Using Logarithms

Data underlined.

Station	Line	Angle	Adjusted	True Bearing	Reduced Bearing	Length
	JF			309° 43.8'		
F		132° 59.6'	59.0'			
	FG			262° 42.8'	S 82° 42.8' W	134.05
G		92° 57.3'	56.6'			
	GH			175° 39.4'	S 04° 20.6' E	290.95
H		110° 06.5'	05.8'			
	HN			105° 45.2'	S 74° 14.8' E	357.35
N		71° 38.5'	37.8'			
	NJ			357° 23.0'	N 02° 37.0' W	219.90
J		132° 21.5'	20.8'			
	JF			309° 43.8' ✓	N 50° 16.2' W	288.75
Total		540° 03.4'	00.0'			

Station and Line	Departures E	W	Latitudes N	S	Adjustments E	W	N	S	Coordinates E	N
F									247.70	639.75
FG	—	132.967	—	17.002	—	+.175	—	+.022		
G									114.558	622.726
GH	22.034	—	—	290.114	+.012	—	—	+.153		
H									136.604	332.459
HN	343.928	—	—	97.019	-.452	—	—	-.128		
N									480.080	235.568
NJ	—	10.039	219.671	—	—	-.013	-.289	—		
J									470.054	454.950
JF	—	222.067	184.561	—	—	+.292	+.243	—		
F									247.695	639.754 ✓
Totals	365.962	365.073	404.232	404.135						

Diffs. E - W = 0.889   N - S = 0.097

Calculations. Set out in full:

```
                 2.123 745  Dep. = 132.967                        1.343 103  Dep. =  22.034
log sin 82° 42.8'  9.996 478             log sin 04° 20.6'  8.879 285
FG log 134.05      2.127 267             GH log 290.95      2.463 818
log cos 82° 42.8'  9.103 235             log cos 04° 20.6'  9.998 751
                 1.230 502  Lat. =  17.002                        2.462 569  Lat. = 290.114
```

Usual arrangement; antilogarithms are entered directly in the table.

```
      2.536 467                1.001 700                2.346 485
l.s.  9.983 373      l.s.      8.659 475      l.s.      9.885 963
HN    2.553 094      NJ        2.342 225      JF        2.460 522
l.c.  9.433 764      l.c.      9.999 547      l.c.      9.805 617
      1.986 858                2.341 772                2.266 139
```

Distribution of Closing Error by Method 1.

Closing Error = 0.894 metres. Parallel through station J, JX = 340 metres.
So all except GH are adjusted in the ratio 0.447 to 340; JF and FG are
increased, HN and NJ are decreased.

For GH, the length GX (204 m.) has to be increased, while XH (87 m.) has to
be decreased. So although GH is 291 metres long, the corresponding Departure and
Latitude are only increased as if it were 117 metres; that is, they are increased
in the ratio $\frac{117}{291} \times \frac{0.447}{340}$.

19.1 Closed Traverse

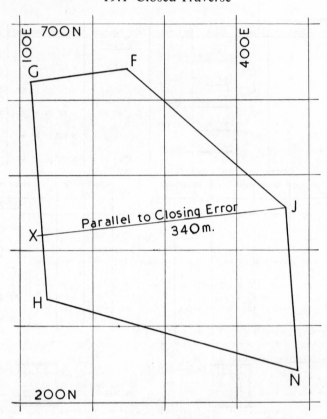

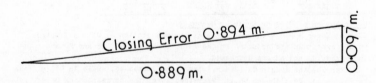

gross mistakes, and is useful subsequently.

The sum of the internal angles is then checked. If there are n sides, the total must be (n − 2) × 180°. In the example there are five sides and H can be joined to J and F, showing that the angles must add up to (5 − 2) × 180° = 540°. In fact, the angles as measured total 03·4 minutes too much, so we have to deduct 0·7 minutes from four of them and 0·6 from one; as the effect of 0·1 minute is insignificant, it does not matter which. The total of the adjusted angles is checked.

The true bearings are then worked out. That of JF is given. The next is found by adding the internal angle at F and subtracting 180°; if , as at N, the total is less than 180°, that amount is added. If you have inadvertently arranged your data in clockwise order, the internal angle has to be subtracted, which most people find slightly more difficult to do mentally.

From the true bearings, the reduced bearings are found; the quadrant in which a line lies is obvious from the small-scale plot.

The next step, which is the most laborious part of the work, is to calculate the departures and latitudes (as Para. 16.8). These calculations should be arranged systematically and before any logarithms are looked up the quantities needed should be indicated. In the table these have been shown in full, as for example, "FG 134·05" and "log sin 82° 42·8' '', "log cos 82° 42·8' '' but in practice it is usually sufficient to write simply 'FG' 'ls' and 'lc', and to look up the required lengths and angles in the table above. You will find it advisable to put a / through the unadjusted 'minutes' figure, to reduce the risk of using that when looking up the logarithms, instead of the 'adjusted' value. Also, unless you are quite exceptionally good at avoiding mistakes, you should make the first entries for the logarithms in pencil, and check through the whole set a second time. This sounds horribly laborious, but in total will save time, for the effect of an unnoticed mistake is cumulative.

Then go through the Departure and Latitude columns, first putting a / in those you will not be using and then copying the figures automatically into the others.

Since it is a closed polygon, the total Eastings must equal the total Westings, and similarly for Northings and Southings. In fact, the Eastings add up to 365·962 m, and the Westings to 365·073, a difference of 0·889 which has to be distributed. There are several ways in which this can be done, two of which will be given here; remember that you are merely distributing the error evenly, not getting rid of it.

In method 1, the closing error is drawn to the largest convenient scale (Figure 19.1). From this its magnitude (0·894 m) and direction can be found. A line is drawn parallel to that direction and passing through a station chosen to give the longest possible line across the traverse. In this case it passes through J, cutting GH at X; this is slightly longer than a parallel line through H would have been.

The calculated circuit started at F and finished 0·889 m to the east and 0·097 m to the north, a total distance of 0·894 m, but the same closing error would have been found if the calculations had started at J. It follows that if all the lengths JF, FG, and GX were increased in the proportion 0·447 ÷ JX, and XH, HN and NJ decreased similarly, the closing error would be eliminated. By making JX the longest possible line, the adjustments are kept as small as possible. In practice, since the work is graphical, a small residual closing error remains.

The second method, set out in table 19.2, distributes the error in Departures in proportion to their magnitude, and similarly for the Latitudes. For both methods, since the adjustments are small, a slide-rule gives sufficient accuracy.

Table 19.2 Closed Traverse: Adjustment of Closing Error by Method 2

Station and Line	Departures E	W	Latitudes N	S	Adjustments E	W	N	S	Coordinates E	N
F									247·70	639·7?
FG	—	132·967	—	17·002	—	+·162	—	+·002		
G									114·571	622·74
GH	22·034	—	—	290·114	-·027	—	—	+·035		
H									136·578	332·59
HN	343·928	—	—	97·019	-·418	—	—	+·011		
N									480·088	235·5
NJ	—	10·039	219·671	—	—	+·012	-·026	—		
J									470·037	455·2?
JF	—	222·067	184·561	—	—	+·270	-·022	—		
F									247·700	639·7?

Totals   Departures 365·962 365·073   Latitudes 404·232 404·135
Diffs.   E - W = 0·889   N - S = 0·097

In this method the Departures and Latitudes are dealt with separately. The sum of all the Departures is 731 metres, and the Eastings exceed the Westings by 0·889 metres. So all Eastings are decreased, and all Westings increased, in the proportion 0.889 to 731. Similarly, all Northings are decreased, and all Southings increased, in the proportion 0·097 to 808.

The theoretical merit of the first method is that it does not alter the bearings of the lines, and thus does not alter the angles between them; this is logical for a theodolite traverse, since the angles are measured much more accurately than the lengths. The second method is more automatic, but has the disadvantage that it alters the angles appreciably. For example, that at J becomes 132° 18·7' as against 132° 20·8' after adjustment. Since the whole closing error for the angles was only 3·4', the angle at J is unlikely to require 2' further adjustment. The second method is more appropriate when the angles are not very accurately known, as for example with magnetic bearings; but its convenience will sometimes outweigh its theoretical defects.

Both these methods apply when the angles, and hence the bearings of the lines, are known accurately. When the bearings are known much less accurately than the linear measurements, as for example in a traverse where nothing better than a prismatic compass is available for angular measurements, there is some justification for distributing the closing error in the Departures in proportion to the lengths of the Latitudes, and conversely. In practice though, the potential accuracy of such a survey is seldom great enough to justify the labour of calculation.

19.4 *Closed Traverse using Hand Calculator*. The data are the same as for the last section. The differences of a few millimetres between the results arise from different accuracies in 'rounding-off' the adjustments.

The programme (table 19.3) is rather more complicated than those given hitherto, because of the need first to get results and then to distribute the closing errors. The angles are supposed to have been balanced, and the true (adjusted) bearings worked out; but there is no need to set out the very simple programmes involved. Similarly, at the end of the work, no programme is given for calculating the adjustments needed to eliminate the closing error.

If space permits, separate columns can be used for the Results and Adjustments relating to Departures and for those relating to Latitudes; but if that is done, then before any calculations start dashes should be put in the spaces which will not be used. A few other points deserve note.

First, the programmes are repetitive, so in the main programme only the six lines would need to be written out, on a separate sheet, and this would be moved down the page as required. Second, there is no need to 'reduce' the bearings; the calculator will give the correct figures if the 'true bearings' are entered. In calculating the adjustments, method 1 has been used. The entries cannot be made completely automatically, for it is necessary to note that for the sides of the polygon which have to be increased the adjustment is of the same sign as the Northing or Easting (and conversely), so 'inc' and 'dec' should be entered in the appropriate columns before the

Table 19.3 Closed Traverse, Using Calculator

Only the main programme is given. The angles are assumed to have been balanced, and the bearings worked out from them.

Programme	Data	Results	Adjustments	Coords.	Remarks
Figs. STO 1.	639·75				N(F)
Figs. F. STO 2.	247·70				E(F)
Figs. F. x/y.	134·05		inc.		FG
Figs.	262·7120				Bg(FG)
R.		(- 17·005)	(-·022)		N(FG)
(. +. RCL 1.). STO 1.		622·745	-·022	622·723	N(G)
F. x/y.		(-132·967)	(-·176)		E(FG)
(. +. F. RCL 2.).		114·733	-·176	114·557	E(G)
F: STO 2.					
Figs. F. x/y.	290·95		inc.		GH
Figs.	175·6557				Bg(GH)
R.		(-290·114)	(-·158)		N(GH)
(. +. RCL 1.). STO 1.		332·631	-·180	332·451	N(H)
F. x/y.		(22·040)	(+·012)		E(GH)
(. +. F. RCL 2.).		136·773	-·164	136·609	E(H)
F. STO 2.					
Figs. F. x/y.	357·35		dec.		HN
Figs.	105·7527				Bg(HN)
R.		(- 97·015)	(+·128)		N(HN)
(. +. RCL 1.). STO 1.		235·616	-·052	235·564	N(N)
F. x/y.		(343·929)	(-·455)		E(HN)
(. +. F. RCL 2.).		480·701	-·619	480·082	E(N)
F. STO 2.					
Figs. F. x/y.	219.90		dec.		NJ
Figs.	357·3830				Bg(NJ)
R.		(219·671)	(-·290)		N(NJ)
(. +. RCL 1.). STO 1.		455·286	-·342	454·944	N(J)
F. x/y.		(- 10·040)	(+·013)		E(NJ)
(. +. F. RCL 2.).		470·661	-·606	470·055	E(J)
F. STO 2.					
Figs. F. x/y.	288.75		inc.		JF
Figs.	309·7300				Bg(JF)
R.		(184·561)	(+·244)		N(JF)
(. +. RCL 1.). STO 1.		639·847	+·098	639·749	N(F)
F. x/y.		(-222·068)	(-·294)		E(JF)
(. +. F. RCL 2.).		248·593	-·900	247·693	E(F)
F. STO 2.					
Figs.	639.75				N(F) at start
-. RCL 1. =.		- 0·097			N Closing Error
Figs.	247.70				E(F) at start
-. F. RCL 2. =.		- 0·893			E Closing Error

Note the repetitive character of the Programme. The abbreviations in the Remarks column are those given in Section 16.4.

The Adjustments are worked out by Method 1; there is no need to describe the appropriate Programme. "Inc. " or "dec." is first entered against the Line, to indicate whether it should be increased or decreased; that is, whether the sign of the adjustment is the same as that of the Departure or Latitude, or the opposite. The effect of the adjustments is cumulative. Thus the adjustments to the Northings of FG, GH, and HN are -·022, -·158, and +·128 respectively; the adjustment to the North Coordinate of N is the sum of these, -·052.

numerical values are worked out; these differ slightly from those in the previous section, for the reason explained above.

Note also that the effect of these corrections is cumulative, and note also that if the first entry is negative, as here, the $^+/-$ key must be used. As in the last section, a negligibly small residual closing error remains, because of the inherent slight inaccuracy in semi-graphical methods of distributing errors.

19.5 *Open Traverses*. An open traverse, strictly, is only linked to the main survey at one end. Particular care is needed in the field in such a case, for a small angular error can cause quite a large displacement in all the points beyond it, and there is no way of distributing, or even of detecting, any of the errors which are likely to occur. This is, therefore, a rather unsatisfactory type of survey, but is sometimes unavoidable, as for example in underground work.

More often, an 'open' traverse in fact closes on some fixed point at each end, with angles taken to some known direction. This is solved in exactly the same way as a closed traverse. The closing error is distributed by method 2; since the ends of the traverse are reliably fixed, the slight theoretical defect of that method is more than outweighed by its simplicity.

19.6 *Linked Traverses*. It is often convenient to use traverses which have one or more sides in common. Unfortunately there is no logically satisfactory way of distributing the closing errors without introducing the complications of the Theory of Least Squares.

The simplest method is to solve the complete outer circuit as a closed traverse, and to take the co-ordinates so found as established; the traverse links are then treated as open traverses running between known points. Thus in Figure 19.2 (assuming JK is not measured) there are the two linked traverses FGHNJ and FJNMKE. The traverse FGHNMKE would be solved first, and then NJF treated as a subsidiary traverse connecting N and F. If the two angles at N as measured do not add up to the adjusted value of angle HNF, each is adjusted by half the error in order to work out the initial bearing of NJ; and similarly at F.

If the second traverse had been divided into FJKE and JNMK, the simplest solution would be to find three pairs of co-ordinates for J, working from F, K, and N independently. J is then taken as being located at the average of these.

19.2 Linked Traverses

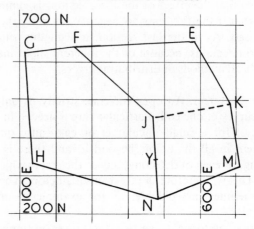

Both these methods give undue weight to the outer circuit, but this can be tolerated if the cross-links are fairly long. Suppose though, that there is only a single cross-link, as would occur if the two traverses linked were FGHNJ and JNMK. Clearly the direct measurement JN is likely to be rather more reliable than the distance between J and N calculated as part of the traverse FGHNMKJ. So where there is a single link, the least unsatisfactory treatment is to solve the two traverses separately, making the co-ordinates of the mid point of the link the same for both. The co-ordinates of the ends of the link are then averaged, the others being left unaltered.

There is no need to go into full detail, but with the example given the following results are obtained.

As already calculated (table 19.2) the co-ordinates of J are 470·055E, 454·944N; and for N, 480·082E, 235·564N. So if Y is the mid point, its co-ordinates are 475·069E, 345·252N.

Taking this as the starting point for YNMKJ, and retaining the same bearing (177° 23·0') for NJ gives the following co-ordinates, using data from Appendix III.

    N 480·092E, 235·343N
    M 711·936E, 330·421N
    K 684·865E, 494·744N
    J 470·046E, 455·163N

These values are accepted for M and K, but for N and J the

averages from the two traverses are used, giving

    J 470·050E, 455·054N

    N 480·087E, 235·453N

This involves accepting small changes in some of the measured angles. It may be worth while to emphasise, once again, that all such methods are merely intended to distribute the errors evenly throughout the network; they do not eliminate them.

20 The Polygonal Network

20.1 Use of the Network; 20.2 Numerical Examples: General
Discussion; 20.3 Reduction of Polygonal Network by Logarithms;
20.4 Reduction of Polygonal Network Using Calculator;
20.5 Different Applications of Single Polygonal Networks;
20.6 Balancing a Quadrilateral; 20.7 Two Linked Polygons;
20.8 Four Linked Polygons; 20.9 Derivation of Formula.

20.1 *Use of the Network*. Very few archaeological sites require the
elaboration of a theodolite survey to fix their plan; in a quarter of a
century, I have probably used the method, on average, less than
once a year, and about a third of those sites could have been done
entirely by chain survey, though less easily and less accurately.
Nevertheless, when the theodolite is needed it is very useful indeed.
The applicability of the traverse to wooded sites and to
underground work has already been discussed, but some types of
open site can also offer difficulties.

The main criterion in deciding whether or not to use a theodolite-
controlled network is the ease of chaining. On open ground, and
with the type of accuracy envisaged here, that will always be the
method of choice, even if several lines have to be measured which
pick up no detail and are required merely to fix the shape of the
network. The theodolite becomes of value on craggy sites where
direct measurements of some necessary lines may be difficult or
impossible, or in dealing with enclosures where substantial rampart
systems prevent any easy link across them. Nevertheless, since there
is perhaps some personal satisfaction in the feeling that a plan
is really accurate, the theodolite may sometimes be used to measure
angles when these are not essential; an obvious occasion would
be when the instrument is to be used as a tacheometer to provide
spot levels for contouring. As will be seen from the examples
below, the greater accuracy of angular measurements tends to
balance out the linear errors.

20.2 *Numerical Examples: General Discussion*. The typical basic
network for this type of work is a polygon, usually five- or six-
sided, with a central station. Geometrically this is a very satisfactory rigid arrangement, and it becomes even better when several

such polygons are linked together (Paras. 20.7, 20.8). Unhappily, the calculations involved in reducing the actual observations to the co-ordinates of the stations are laborious; but they are not inherently difficult, involving merely addition and subtraction and the use of tables or a calculator. Since a survey of this kind may well take two people a week or more in the field, it is surely unreasonable to grudge less than half a man-day spent on working out the results.

In the two sections which follow, complete solutions, including the calculation of co-ordinates, are given for a typical single polygon; partial solutions for interlocking polygons are given in Paras. 20.7 and 20.8. The single polygon is solved first using logarithms and second with a hand calculator, using identical data. The first solution, though rather longer, is more easily followed and will simplify the understanding of the second. Both provide a programme of work which is applicable to any problem of this kind.

The main difficulty in solving such a problem lies not in understanding what has to be done, but in doing it right. Each calculation involves well over 500 digits, and my own experience indicates that the chance of writing one down incorrectly is high. The calculations are designed to detect a mistake, but only when the work is finished. You are therefore very strongly advised to make all entries in pencil, and to follow the advice given as to checking, wearisome though it may be.

20.3 *Reduction of Polygonal Network by Logarithms.* All the angles of the network have been measured, as well as the chain lines corresponding to the circumference, but not the radial lines. The co-ordinates of station B are known, and the bearing of EB. These are entered in the appropriate tables below.

The first step, as when working out a traverse, is to draw the network carefully to a suitable scale (Figure 20.1). Squared paper may make a convenient background. As with any type of survey, this small-scale plot not only makes it easier to envisage what is being done, but will detect any large mistake. To simplify the notation imagine that you are looking outwards from the centre along each radial line and name the two angles at the circumference 'Right Hand' and 'Left Hand' (RH and LH); for example ∠AGF is ∠GR, ∠FGH is ∠GL.

Most of the laborious routine of calculation is made necessary by

20.1 Polygon Network

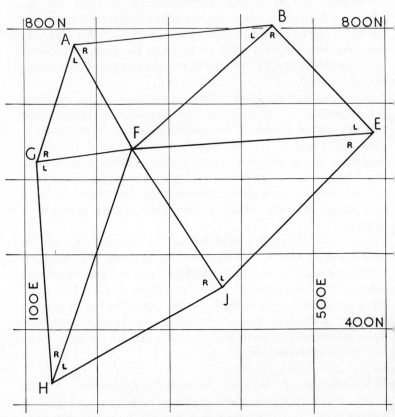

the presence of errors. As explained in Para. 19.2, the objective at each stage is to have a geometrically possible diagram as basis for your calculations. Only the relevant errors are distributed at each step and the figures which result are used in the next stage. Logically, this is rather unsatisfactory; why, for example, should the central angles, once balanced, be immune from further adjustment, in contrast to those at the circumference? The main reason is simply convenience for although a system of step by step calculation could be devised to give almost the same adjustment to every angle, the work involved (unless a computer were available) would be excessive, and the final result would be only a little more accurate, for the errors which have to be distributed are small.

The calculation should proceed by the following stages:

(i) After drawing the small-scale plan, draw out a table (as table 20.1), first setting out the whole scheme of calculation symbolically, then entering the known numerical values.

(ii) Next, the measured angles are adjusted to satisfy the elementary requirements of geometry. First, the angles of each triangle are brought up to total 180°. The measured angles of GFH, for example, add up to 180° 02·4', so each is reduced by 0·80', similarly for BFA each is increased by 0·23' or 0·24'. My own preference is to work to the absurd 'accuracy' of 0·01', rather than to worry about where to put an odd 0·1'; but this is purely a matter of individual choice.

When the triangles have been 'balanced', the total of the central angles will usually require further adjustment, to bring them to the necessary total of 360°. In this case, the sum is 0·17' too small, so five get an additional 0·03', one 0·02'. The central angles are given no further adjustment, but the other two angles of each triangle have to be decreased, by 0·01' or 0·02', to bring the totals back to 180° again.

When this stage has been reached, a / is drawn through each previous 'minutes' figure, to eliminate the risk of using it by mistake.

Although it is good practice to use this rather meticulous double adjustment of the angles, it would be acceptable to miss out the first stage, so that you start by balancing the central angles to give 360°, and then balance each triangle by adjusting only the other two angles.

(iii) You now have six geometrically possible triangles which fit together at their vertices to give a total of 360°, so at first glance you may hope that all the inconvenient demands of geometry are satisfied; but one remains.

If you start with an assumed length for one radial (say AF) and work all round the circuit using the $a/\sin A = b/\sin B$ formula until you get back to AF, you will find that the final value differs from that with which you started.

Suppose that it is smaller, and you have gone anticlockwise. Then the diagram (Figure 20.2) shows that this would occur if some right-hand angles were too large and the corresponding left-hand angles too small. Since we do not know where the errors are likely to be, we 'shift' the same adjustment from each RH angle to each LH angle, thus leaving the total for each triangle unaltered. This is

Table 20.1 Polygonal Network, Using Logarithms
(a) Adjustment of Sides and Angles

Angles: preliminary balancing.

Triangle	Left-hand Angles Measured	Adjusted 1	2	Central Angles Measured	Adjusted 1	2	Right-hand Angles Measured	Adjusted 1	2	Initial Total
GFH	92° 57·3'	56·50'	56·48'	62° 53·8'	53·00'	53·03'	24° 11·3'	10·50'	10·49'	180° 02·
HFJ	49° 58·1'	57·90'	57·89'	70° 05·8'	05·60'	05·63'	59° 56·7'	56·50'	56·48'	180° 00·
JFE	78° 33·3'	33·70'	33·68'	43° 11·8'	12·20'	12·23'	58° 13·7'	14·10'	14·09'	179° 58·
EFB	48° 53·8'	53·80'	53·79'	36° 20·8'	20·80'	20·83'	94° 45·4'	45·40'	45·38'	180° 00·
BFA	35° 13·9'	14·13'	14·12'	79° 34·5'	34·73'	34·75'	65° 10·9'	11·13'	11·12'	179° 59·
AFG	48° 33·6'	33·80'	33·79'	67° 53·3'	53·50'	53·53'	63° 32·5'	32·70'	32·68'	179° 59·

359 59·83'

Angles: calculation of Shift.

Triangle		Left-hand Angle	log. sin.	Diff. 01'		Right-hand Angle	log. sin.	Diff. 01'
GFH	GL̂	92° 56·48'	9·999 427	-006	HR̂	24° 10·49'	9·612 278	281
HFJ	HL̂	49° 57·89'	9·884 030	106	JR̂	59° 56·48'	9·937 274	073
JFE	JL̂	78° 33·68'	9·991 287	026	ER̂	58° 14·09'	9·929 528	078
EFB	EL̂	48° 53·79'	9·877 097	110	BR̂	94° 45·38'	9·998 502	-011
BFA	BL̂	35° 14·12'	9·761 128	179	AR̂	65° 11·12'	9·957 928	058
AFG	AL̂	48° 33·79'	9·874 879	112	GR̂	63° 32·68'	9·951 960	063
	Totals		9·387 848	527			9·387 470	542

Sum for L.H. Angles exceeds that for R.H. Angles by 378; so Shift required
equals 378 divided by 1069, equals 00·35' from L.H. to R.H. Angles.

Adjusted Angles and Bearings.

GH	175° 40·10'	(given)	S 04° 19·90' E
HR̂	24° 10·84'		
FH	199° 50·94'		S 19° 50·94' W
HL̂	49° 57·54'	- 180°	
HJ	69° 48·48'		N 69° 48·48' E
JR̂	59° 56·83'		
FJ	129° 45·31'		S 50° 14·69' E
JL̂	78° 33·33'	- 180°	
JE	28° 18·64'		N 28° 18·64' E
ER̂	58° 14·44'		
FE	86° 33·08'		N 86° 33·08' E
EL̂	48° 53·44'	+ 180°	
EB	315° 26·52'		N 44° 33·48' W
BR̂	94° 45·73'		
FB	50° 12·25'		N 50° 12·25' E
BL̂	35° 13·77'	+ 180°	
BA	265° 26·02'		S 85° 26·02' W
AR̂	65° 11·47'		
FA	330° 37·49'		N 29° 22·51' W
AL̂	48° 33·44'	- 180°	
AG	199° 10·93'		S 19° 10·93' W
GR̂	63° 33·03'		
FG	262° 43·96'		S 82° 43·96' W
GL̂	92° 56·13'	- 180°	
GH	175° 40·09'		

Calculation of Sides (GH taken as 290·95).

```
log FG  2·126 769
+ ls. HR 9·612 376
        2·514 387   ⟶              2·514 387
+ ls. GL̂ 9·999 430  - ls. GFH 9·949 431
  log FH 2·513 817     log GH  2·463 818
- ls. JR 9·937 299
        2·576 518                  2·576 518
+ ls. HL̂ 9·883 993  + ls. HFJ 9·973 244
  log FJ 2·460 511     log HJ  2·549 762
- ls. ER 9·929 555
        2·530 956   ⟶              2·530 956
+ ls. JL̂ 9·991 278  + ls. JFE 9·835 434
  log FE 2·522 234     log JE  2·366 390
- ls. BR 9·998 498
        2·523 736   ⟶              2·523 736
+ ls. EL̂ 9·877 058  + ls. EFB 9·772 818
  log FB 2·400 794     log EB  2·296 554
- ls. AR 9·957 948
        2·442 846                  2·442 846
+ ls. BL̂ 9·761 065  + ls. BFA 9·992 777
  log FA 2·203 911     log BA  2·435 623
- ls. GR 9·951 982
        2·251 929                  2·251 929
+ ls. AL̂ 9·874 840  + ls. AFG 9·966 835
  log FG 2·126 769     log AG  2·218 764
```

	Measured	Calculated as above
GH	290·95	290·950
HJ	355·45	354·619
JE	233·15	232·482
EB	197·80	197·950
BA	273·00	272·661
AG	165·65	165·487
Totals	1516·00	1514·149
logs	3·180 699	3·180 169 Diff. = 530

So 530 must be added to all the calculated log

Table 20.1 Polygonal Network, Using Logarithms
(b) Calculation of Co-ordinates

Traverse round circumference:

Line	Station	Departures E	Departures W	Latitudes N	Latitudes S	Coordinates E	Coordinates N
	G given					114·750	622·750
GH		22·002	—	—	290·473		
	H					136·752	332·277
HJ		333·231	—	122·552	—		
	J					469·983	454·829
JE		110·390	—	204·925	—		
	E					580·373	659·754
EB		—	139·057	141·219	—		
	B					441·316	800·973
BA		—	272·127	—	21·734		
	A					169·189	779·239
AG		—	54·441	—	156·490		
	G					114·748	622·749

Radial lines:

Line	Station	Departures E	Departures W	Latitudes N	Latitudes S	Coordinates E	Coordinates N
	G given					114·750	622·750
GF		132·981	—	16·958	—		
	F					247·731	639·708
FH		—	110·979	—	307·431		
	H					136·752	332·277
FJ		222·252	—	—	184·879		
	J					469·983	454·829
FE		332·642	—	20·046	—		
	E					580·373	659·754
FB		193·585	—	161·265	—		
	B					441·316	800·973
FA		—	78·542	139·531	—		
	A					169·189	779·239

Calculations:

```
        1·342 467           2·522 745           2·042 929           2·143 193
ls.     8·878 119     ls.   9·972 453     ls.   9·676 009     ls.   9·846 109
log GH  2·464 348     log HJ 2·550 292    log JE 2·366 920    log EB 2·297 084
lc.     9·998 758     lc.   9·538 029     lc.   9·944 675     lc.   9·852 810
        2·463 106           2·088 321           2·311 595           2·149 894

        2·434 772           1·735 925           2·123 790           2·045 241
ls.     9·998 619     ls.   9·516 631     ls.   9·996 497     ls.   9·530 894
log BA  2·436 153     log AG 2·219 294    log FG 2·127 293    log FH 2·514 347
lc.     8·900 985     lc.   9·975 192     lc.   9·102 087     lc.   9·973 401
        1·337 138           2·194 486           1·229 380           2·487 748

        2·346 845           2·521 977           2·286 872           1·895 103
ls.     9·885 804     ls.   9·999 213     ls.   9·885 548     ls.   9·690 662
log FJ  2·461 041     log FE 2·522 764    log FB 2·401 324    log FA 2·204 441
lc.     9·805 846     lc.   8·779 266     lc.   9·806 217     lc.   9·940 231
        2·266 887           1·302 030           2·207 541           2·144 672
```

20.2 Effect of Shifts in Circumferential Angles

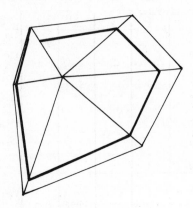

called 'the Method of Equal Shifts'.

To understand the method of calculation, write down the a/sin A = b/sin B equation for each triangle as follows, using logarithms.

log BF − log sin ∠AR = log AF − log sin ∠BL
log AF − log sin ∠GR = log GF − log sin ∠AL
log GF − log sin ∠HR = log HF − log sin ∠GL
log HF − log sin ∠JR = log JF − log sin ∠HL
log JF − log sin ∠ER = log EF − log sin ∠JL
log EF − log sin ∠BR = log BF − log sin ∠EL

∠AR and ∠AL are the 'right-hand' and 'left-hand' angles at A, and similarly throughout.

Adding, you will see that the 'log sines' sum is the same on each side of the equation. The geometrical requirement, therefore, is that the sum of the 'log sines' of the LH angles equals that of the RH angles.

Now enter the logarithms, to six figures, of the sines of the *balanced* angles, in the appropriate columns of table 19.3. For those not familiar with the convention, the use of 9 rather than 1 or 8 instead of 2 is merely for simplicity in addition; in this context there is no possibility of confusion. You also enter, in the Diff 01' column the amounts by which the last three figures of the 'log sines' increase if the angle is increased by 01'. Note that if the angle exceeds 90° as in ∠GL and ∠BR, the effect is negative, so ring these quantities to avoid confusion. Using wide paper, this and the previous part of the table can be combined.

Now, having laboriously looked up and noted twelve six-figure logarithms you will, if you are sensible, look them all up again. The reason for this barely tolerable penance is that if you do make a mistake at this stage you will not detect it until you have done a lot more calculation, all of which will be wasted.

Adding the columns, the sum of the 'log sines' for the LH angles proves to be 374 greater than that for the RH angles, and a shift of one minute from the LH to the RH angles will decrease the LH total by 527 and increase the RH by 542. The shift needed is therefore $374 \div 1069 = 0.35'$.

(iv) Now, assuming your arithmetic is right, you have a network of triangles which is geometrically consistent. You have now to calculate the sides, and from them the station co-ordinates, but there ought to be no more closing errors to distribute; if any greater than a few millimetres appear, a mistake has been made somewhere.

The bearings will be needed later, and if they are worked out at this stage they will give an automatic check on the accuracy of the list of adjusted angles. Note, when making out this part of the table, that the type of entry recurs every fourth line; so the easiest way of preparing it is to list first of all the circumferential lines, GH, HJ, etc. at the appropriate spacing, then the right-hand angles, ∠HR, ∠JR etc. and so on. The adjusted angles, and the given bearing of GH are then entered, and the calculation proceeds automatically.

(v) The lengths of the lines must now be worked out. Arrange a table, in symbolic form with space for logarithms, corresponding to the a/sin A = b/sin B formula applied round the circuit. It is desirable always to keep to the same arangement, with radial lines on the left, and circumferential lines on the right. If FG were known, then Log FG − log sin ∠GHF (abbreviated to l.s. ∠HR) + log sin ∠HGF = log FH; log FH − log sin ∠HJF + log sin ∠JHF = log FJ; and so on until FG is reached again. For the circumferential lines, log FG − l.s. ∠HR + log sin ∠GFH = log GH; log FH − l.s. ∠JR + l.s. HFJ = log HJ etc. Note again, that the type of quantity entered recurs regularly; this simplifies the preparation of the table.

When the symbolic framework for this calculation is complete, enter the log sines of the adjusted angles; but to calculate the lengths of the sides we need to assume some known lengths to start with.

As in the next section, we could start by assuming FG = 100 m, but for a reason given below it is better to get the lengths nearly right. Only the circumferential lines have been reliably measured, so we start with GH (any other measured line would serve), and the actual procedure of calculation is log GH − l.s. ∠GFH (= 2·514387) + l.s. ∠HR = log FG and log GH − l.s. ∠GFH + l.s. ∠GL = log FH, after which the calculation proceeds as before. Two points should be noted: first, that the 'radial-line' column starts with the line immediately before the measured circumferential line; and second that special care is needed to be sure that you do not *add* log GH and l.s. ∠GFH. Indeed, you would be well advised to check as you proceed that the measurements on your small-scale plan do agree reasonably well with the calculated logarithms. To do this is tiresome, but less so than finding a mistake after you have completed all the arithmetic. Assuming everything has been done correctly, the final value of log FG will agree very closely with the initial value; a small difference in the last figure is to be expected.

(vii) Unfortunately, the calculation had to be started using a single measurement. In this example, we have assumed that all the circumferential lines were measured with equal care, so they ought all to be taken into account, and their total is presumably more reliable proportionately than the length of GH only. The measured total is 1516 m, while that calculated from GH is 1514·149 m; the logarithms of these numbers differ by 0·000530, so that amount must be added to all the calculated logarithms of the lengths. As we started with a measured line, the adjustment is small and the addition can easily be done mentally.

(viii) The remaining work requires no special comment. The departure and latitude are calculated in the standard way for all lines, and set out in tabular form. Note that every station is fixed in two ways, as part of the traverse round the circumference and by radials from F. Do not yield to the temptation to rest content with one of these calculations, for the duplication provides a valuable final check on the accuracy of your work.

20.4 *Reduction of Polygonal Network Using Calculator* (Table 20.2). The principles involved are exactly the same as in the last section, to which reference should be made for explanation of the reasoning. What follows describes the differences in approach required with a calculator, although much of it is almost identical with table 20.1.

Stages (i) and (ii) are the same as when using logarithms, though the arrangement of the table is different and the angles are expressed as decimals of a degree.

Stage (iii), calculation of the required 'Shift', proceeds differently. Rather than looking up 'log sins', it is quicker to start with some assumed value for a radial line, and work round the circuit back to it. In this case FG is taken as 100 and the value on returning to it is 100·088. Examination of the programme shows that if the LH angles are too big the final result is too big; that is, a change in the last datum produces a similar change in the result, which is a fairly easy rule to remember. This assumes that you have worked anticlockwise. A second calculation is therefore made with a shift of 0·01° from LH to RH angles, giving a final result of 99·940 for FG. So the actual Shift needed will be 0·01 × 0·88 ÷ 0·148 = 0·00595° from LH to RH angles; this can be applied as 0·0059° and 0·0060° alternately.

For stages (iv) and (v), using the adjusted angles plus or minus the shift as appropriate, a similar programme gives all the lines starting with the assumption that FG is 100. As previously, the total of the lengths of the reliable measured lines is compared with the total as calculated, but as the necessary multiplication can be done rapidly by putting the required factor into a memory, there is no advantage now in getting the calculated lengths nearly right.

The remaining work, stage (viii), again requires little comment. The two sets of calculations, for the circuit and for the radial lines, are arranged for easy comparison of the results. Note that in working out the bearings, there is no need either to reduce them or to express them as positive angles.

The mathematically minded reader will observe that the method of calculating 'shifts' is not really identical with that used for logarithms, but the difference is completely negligible. He will also see that the tables could have been arranged rather more compactly: for example, the bearings could have been entered directly in the calculation of co-ordinates. This has not been attempted, because too elaborate a scheme can tend to cause mistakes.

20.5 *Different Applications of Single Polygonal Networks.* There are two modifications of the polygonal network which are sometimes useful. One is, paradoxically, to have the 'central' station outside the circuit (Figure 20.3). The RH and LH angles are assigned as before; the slight confusion at V and Y in the figure is easily resolved. In balancing the 'central' angles the numerical

Table 20.2 Polygonal Network, Using Calculator
(a) Adjustment of Sides and Angles

Except that decimals of a degree are used instead of minutes, the preliminary balancing of the angles proceeds exactly as in Table 20.1a. The balanced angles are used in the table below.

Calculation of Shift:

Programme	With angles as balanced Data	Results	After 0 01′ shift, LH to RH Data	Results	Notes
Figs. ÷ .	100·00		100·00		FG taken as 100
Figs. sin. x.	24·1747		24·1847		HR
Figs. sin.	92·9415		92·9315		GL
÷.		(243·867)		(243·774)	(FH)
Figs. sin. x.	59·9415		59·9515		JR
Figs. sin.	49·9647		49·9547		HL
÷.		(215·728)		(215·593)	(FJ)
Figs. sin. x.	58·2347		58·2447		ER
Figs. sin.	78·5615		78·5515		JL
÷		(248·695)		(248·504)	(FE)
Figs. sin. x.	94·7565		94·7665		BR
Figs. sin.	48·8964		48·8864		EL
÷.		(188·045)		(187·874)	(FB)
Figs. sin. x.	65·1853		65·1953		AR
Figs. sin.	35·2354		35·2254		BL
÷.		(119·526)		(119·378)	(FA)
Figs. sin. x.	63·5448		63·5548		GR
Figs. sin.	48·5630		48·5530		AL
=.		100·088		99·940	FG

Shift required = 0·00595. This has been included in the angles entered below.

Adjusted Angles and Bearings

Programme	Data	Results	Notes
Figs. STO 1.	180		
Figs. +.	175·6683		Bg(GH)
Figs.	24·1806		HR
+.		199·8489	Bg(FH)
			HL
Figs. -. RCL 1.	49·9587		
+.		69·8076	Bg(HJ)
			JR
Figs.	59·9475		
+.		129·7551	Bg(FJ)
			JL
Figs. -. RCL 1.	78·5556		
+.		28·3107	Bg(JE)
			ER
Figs.	58·2406		
+.		86·5513	Bg(FE)
			EL
Figs. -. RCL 1.	48·8904		
+.		-44·5583	Bg(EB)
			BR
Figs.	94·7625		
+.		50·2042	Bg(FB)
			BL
Figs. -. RCL 1.	35·2295		
+.		-94·5663	Bg(BA)
			AR
Figs.	65·1912		
+.		-29·3751	Bg(FA)
			AL
Figs. -. RCL 1.	48·5570		
+.		-160·8181	Bg(AG)
			GR
Figs.	63·5508		
+.		-97·2673	Bg(FG)
			GL
Figs. -. RCL 1.	92·9356		
=.		-184·3317	Bg(GH) ✓

Calculation of sides after Shift with FG taken as 100.

Programme	Data	Results	Notes
Figs. ÷.	100·00		'FG'
Figs. sin. x. STO 1.	24·1806		HR
Figs. sin.	62·8838		GPH
=.		217·298	GH
RCL 1. x. Figs. sin.	92·9356		GL
÷.		243·812	FH
Figs. sin. x. STO 1.	59·9475		JR
Figs. sin.	70·0938		HFJ
=.		264·849	HJ
RCL 1. x. Figs. sin.	49·9587		HL
÷		215·648	FJ
Figs. sin. x. STO 1.	58·2406		ER
Figs. sin.	43·2038		JFE
=.		173·630	JE
RCL 1. x. Figs. sin.	78·5556		JL
÷.		248·582	FE
Figs. sin. x. STO 1.	94·7625		BR
Figs. sin.	36·3471		EFB
=.		147·839	EB
RCL 1. x. Figs. sin.	48·8904		EL
÷		187·943	FB
Figs. sin. x. STO 1.	65·1912		AR
Figs. sin.	79·5793		BFA
=.		203·637	BA
RCL 1. x. Figs. sin.	35·2295		BL
÷.		119·438	PA
Figs. sin. x. STO 1.	63·5508		GR
Figs. sin.	67·8922		AFG
=.		123·593	AG
RCL 1. x. Figs. sin.	48·5570		AL
=.		100·000	FG ✓

Table 20.2 Polygonal Network, Using Calculator
(b) Calculation of Co-ordinates

Total for GH, HJ, JE, EB, BA, and AG, as measured = 1516·00
Total with FG taken as 100 = 1130·847
Ratio = 1·34059

The lengths used below in calculating the coordinates are therefore 1·34059 times the value found with FG taken as 100.

Traverse round circumference				Radial lines			
Programme	Data	Results	Notes	Programme	Data	Results	Notes
				Figs. STO 1.	622·75		N(G)
				Figs. F. STO 2.	114·75		E(G)
				Figs. F. x/y.	134·059		FG
				Figs. +/-.	-277·2673		Bg(GF)
				R.			
				(. +. RCL 1.).		639·708	N(F)
				STO 1.			
Figs. STO 1.	622·75		N(G)	F. x/y.			
Figs. F. STO 2.	114·75		E(G)	(+. F. RCL 2.).		247·732	E(F)
				F. STO 2.			
Figs. F. x/y.	291·307		GH	Figs. F. x/y.	326·851		FH
Figs.	175·6683		Bg(GH)	Figs.	199·8489		Bg(FH)
R.				R.			
(. +. RCL 1.).		332·275	N(H)	(. +. RCL 1.).		332·275	N(H)
STO 1. F. x/y.				F. x/y			
(. +. F. RCL 2.).		136·753	E(H)	(. +. F. RCL 2.).		136·753	E(H)
F. STO 2.							
Figs. F. x/y.	355·053		HJ	Figs. F. x/y.	289·095		FJ
Figs.	69·8076		Bg(HJ)	Figs.	129·7551		Bg(FJ)
R.				R.			
(. +. RCL 1.).		454·830	N(J)	(. +. RCL 1.).		454·830	N(J)
STO 1. F. x/y.				F. x/y.			
(. +. F. RCL 2.).		469·984	E(J)	(. +. F. RCL 2.).		469·984	E(J)
F. STO 2.							
Figs. F. x/y.	232·766		JE	Figs. F. x/y.	333·246		FE
Figs.	28·3107		Bg(JE)	Figs.	86·5513		Bg(FE)
R.				R.			
(. +. RCL 1.).		659·755	N(E)	(. +. RCL 1.).		659·755	N(E)
STO 1. F. x/y.				F. x/y.			
(. +. F. RCL 2.).		580·373	E(E)	(. +. F. RCL 2.).		580·375	E(E)
F. STO 2.							
Figs. F. x/y.	198·191		EB	Figs. F. x/y.	251·954		FB
Figs. +/-.	-44·5583		Bg(EB)	Figs.	50·2042		Bg(FB)
R.				R.			
(. +. RCL 1.).		800·973	N(B)	(. +. RCL 1.).		800·972	N(B)
STO 1. F. x/y.				F. x/y.			
(. +. F. RCL 2.).		441·315	E(B)	(. +. F. RCL 2.).		441·316	E(B)
F. STO 2.							
Figs. F. x/y.	272·993		BA	Figs. F. x/y.	160·117		FA
Figs. +/-.	-94·5663		Bg(BA)	Figs. +/-.	-29·3751		Bg(FA)
R.				R.			
(. +. RCL 1.).		779·240	N(A)	(. +. RCL 1.).		779·239	N(A)
STO 1. F. x/y.				F. x/y.			
(. +. F. RCL 2.).		169·189	E(A)	(. +. F. RCL 2.).		169·191	E(A)
F. STO 2.							
Figs. F. x/y.	165·687		AG				
Figs. +/-.	-160·8181		Bg(AG)				
R.							
(. +. RCL 1.).		622·752	N(G)				
F. x/y.							
(. +. F. RCL 2.).		114·749	E(G)				

20.3 Polygon with Centre outside Circuit

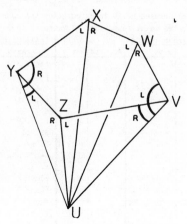

values of some (for example, ∠YUZ and ∠ZUV) will need to be increased by the average adjustment, and others (∠VUW, ∠WUX, ∠XUY) to be decreased.

The second application is when a closed traverse has a central feature (such as a church spire) which is visible but not accessible. The accuracy of the traverse can be greatly improved by including this feature in the points observed from each station of the circuit. The central angles can easily be found, as 180° less the two relevant angles at the circumference, and the calculation then follows the procedure for a polygon with a central station, with the gain in accuracy given by the use of angular rather than mainly linear measurements.

20.6 *Balancing a Quadrilateral.* The quadrilateral is important enough to deserve special mention. Besides being a convenient network for many types of structure, it is useful when the ground is generally irregular. A short base line, preferably one diagonal, is located on good ground and measured with particular care; then, again taking particular care with measurement of the angles, it can be extended to give an accurate length for the other diagonal which can be three or four times as long, with its ends so placed as to be part of the main network, although accurate direct measurement between them would be difficult. Another special case is the final check on accuracy in setting out a rectangle (Chapter 15).

Table 20.3 Quadrilateral with Angles Measured

Balancing Angles:

	Measured	Adjusted		Measured	Adjusted
B̂R	39·8033	39·8058	ĴR	45·5033	45·5058
ÊL	48·8967	48·8992	F̂L	43·1962?	43·1992
	88·7000	88·7050		88·7000	88·7050
ÊR	58·2283	58·2358	F̂R	36·3467	36·3442
ĴL	33·0517	33·0592	B̂L	54·9533	54·9508
	91·2800	91·2950		91·3000	91·2950

Measured sides:
BE = 197·80
EJ = 233·15
JF = 288·75
FB = 252·20

Average angle at X = 90° +/- 1·2950

Calculation of Shift:

Programme	With angles as balanced Data	Results	With 0·01′ shift, LH to RH Data	Results	Notes
Figs. ÷.	100 00		100·00		XB taken as 100
Figs. sin. x.	36·3442		36·3542		F̂R
Figs. sin.	54·9508		54·9408		B̂L
÷					gives XF
Figs. sin. x.	45·5058		45·5158		ĴR
Figs. sin.	43·1992		43·1892		F̂L
÷.					gives XJ
Figs. sin. x.	58·2358		58·2458		ÊR
Figs. sin.	33·0592		33·0492		ĴL
÷.					gives XE
Figs. sin. x.	39·8058		39·8158		B̂R
Figs. sin.	48·8992		48·8892		ÊL
=.		100·116		99·970	XB

So required Shift = 0·01′ x 116 ÷ 146 = 0·0079′

Calculation of sides after shift:

Programme	Data	Results with XB = 100	Final Results	Notes
Figs. ÷.	100·00		149·373	XB
Figs. sin. x. STO 1.	36·3521			F̂R
Figs. sin. F. STO 2.	88·7050			X̂
=.		168·663	251·938	BF
RCL 1. x. Figs. sin. ÷.	54·9429			B̂L
Figs. sin. x. STO 1.	45·5137			ĴR
F. RCL 2. =.		193·525	289·075	FJ
RCL 1. x. Figs. sin. ÷.	43·1913			F̂L
Figs..sin. x. STO 1.	58·2437			ÊR
F. RCL 2. =.		155·776	232·688	JE
RCL 1. x. Figs. sin. ÷.	33·0513			ĴL
Figs. sin. x. STO 1.	39·8137			B̂R
F. RCL 2. =.		132·687	198·199	EB
RCL 1. x. Figs. sin.	48·8913			ÊL
=.		100·0006 ✓		XB

Total excluding XB = 650·651 and Measured Total = 971·9.
So Ratio   1·49373

In a four-sided traverse also, when diagonal observations are possible, solution as a quadrilateral network will give a more accurate adjustment of the errors than the usual method; and it is sometimes possible, even in a polygonal traverse, to treat four stations as the corners of a quadrilateral.

The only difficulty which arises is how best to 'balance' the measured angles. One alternative is to treat the quadrilateral as a triangular 'polygon' (EBF in the example which follows) with an external 'centre' (J); but this is open to the objection that the angles at J receive different treatment from the others. The method set out in table 20.3 seems preferable. The calculations are only carried as far as the determination of the lengths of the lines.

Little comment is needed. The point X, the intersection of the two diagonals, is not marked on the ground, but is introduced as part of the calculations; there is no need to work out its co-ordinates. The procedure is to work out the four possible angles at X from the angles at the circumference, and to average the results. The right-hand and left-hand angles are then adjusted so that the triangles total 180°, and the calculation proceeds in the usual way. Note that since the sine of an angle is the same as the sine of 180° minus that angle, one of the calculator's memories can be used to save re-entering the central angle at each repetition.

20.7 *Two Linked Polygons.* For a large irregular site it is often impossible to find a single 'central' station from which all those on the perimeter can be observed. Such a site can be covered by two or more interlocking polygons; this arrangement gives a very good rigid network.

Two such polygons are shown in Figure 20.4, and the calculations, including the data (the measured angles) are set out in table 20.4; they are carried as far as determining the shifts needed. The first step, as always, is to 'balance' the triangles, essentially as in Para. 20.3, stage (ii). The first adjustments, 1, bring each triangle to 180°. The central angles, though, now total 0·0083° too much around E and 0·0030° too little around F. Two triangles, EFB and EFJ, are shared; for example, the angle EFB is a central angle for the polygon centred on F, but a right-hand angle for that centred on E. As there are still four triangles in each polygon which are not shared, the simplest way to distribute the central closing errors is to distribute them among those four. Thus the triangles EFB, EFJ, are now treated as fixed, and in the polygon centred on E, for

20.4 Two Polygons Linked

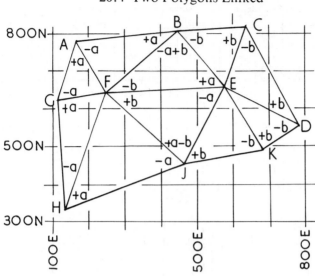

example, the 0·0083° is distributed among the other four central angles, reducing three of them by 0·0021° and one by 0·0020°; the ten-thousandth part of a degree is insignificant, and can be disposed of in any angle without affecting the results. The triangles no longer total 180°, so the right-hand and left-hand angles are all increased by 0·0010° or 0·0011° to eliminate the error. You could if you wished go two steps further, as explained in the next section, to get a rather more even distribution of the errors; but there seems no need to do so in this case.

These adjusted angles are used to calculate the shifts. As will be seen, various approaches which differ in detail are possible, but all depend on the same principle of 'equal shifts'.

The increase, for an increase of 0·01°, in the last three figures of a six-figure 'log sin', is given by 075·8 divided by the tangent of the angle; proof, if you want it, is given in Para. 20.9. So these increases can easily be tabulated; but if you have tables to hand it is quicker to use them as in Para. 20.8 Then assuming that in each polygon there is a shift from right-hand to left-hand angles as shown in Figure 20.4, the relative increase in the 'left-hand' sum of the log sins can be written down.

Each polygon is then solved, using the angles as balanced; the

Table 20.4 Two Polygons Linked

Angles: preliminary balancing.

Triangle	Left-hand Angles			Central Angles			Right-hand Angles			Initial
	Measured	Adjusted 1	2	Measured	Adjusted 1	2	Measured	Adjusted 1	2	Total
FEJ	43·1967	·2033	2033	58·2281	·2350	2350	78·5550	·5617	5617	179·98
JEK	51·2667	·2800	·2810	60·5483	·5616	·5595	68·1450	·1584	·1595	179·96
KED	88·9983	·9917	·9927	30·7717	·7650	·7630	60·2500	·2433	·2443	180·02
DEC	34·0700	·0783	·0794	97·9083	·9167	·9146	47·9967	·0050	·0060	179·97
CEB	65·2133	·2067	·2077	63·6400	·6333	·6312	51·1667	·1600	·1611	180·02
BEF	94·7567	·7567	7567	48·8967	·8967	8967	36·3467	·3466	3466	180·00
				360·0083						
EFB	48·8967	·8967	8967	36·3467	·3466	3466	94·7567	·7567	7567	180·00
BFA	35·2317	·2356	·2353	79·5750	·5788	·5795	65·1817	·1856	·1852	179·98
AFG	48·5600	·5633	·5629	67·8883	·8917	·8925	63·5417	·5450	·5446	179·99
GFH	92·9550	·9417	·9413	62·8967	·8833	·8840	24·1883	·1750	·1747	180·04
HFJ	49·9683	·9650	·9646	70·0967	·0933	·0941	59·9450	·9417	·9413	180·01
JFE	78·5550	·5617	5617	43·1967	·2033	2033	58·2283	·2350	2350	179·98
				359·9970						

Increase in 4th. to 6th. figure of log sin for increase of 0·01° = 075·8 ÷ tangent.

	L. H. Angles	inc	Shift		R. H. Angles	inc	Shift			L. H. Angles	inc	Shift		R. H. Angles	inc	Shi
FEJ	43·2033	81	+b		78·5617	15	+a -b		EFB	48·8967	66	+a		94·7567	-6	-a
JEK	51·2810	61	+b		68·1595	30	-b		BFA	35·2353	107	+a		65·1852	35	-a
KED	88·9927	1	+b		60·2443	43	-b		AFG	48·5629	67	+a		63·5446	38	-a
DEC	34·0794	112	+b		48·0060	68	-b		GFH	92·9413	-4	+a		24·1747	169	-a
CEB	65·2077	35	+b		51·1611	61	-b		HFJ	49·9646	64	+a		59·9413	44	-a
BEF	94·7567	-6	-a -b		36·3466	103	-b		JFE	78·5617	15	+a -b		58·2350	47	-a

Totals: + 6a + 284b   + 15a - 320b   + 315a - 15b   - 327a - 6b

Relative increase of 'left-hand' sums:
- 9a + 604b   + 642a - 9b

Calculation of Shifts:

Programme	Polygon centre E.			Polygon centre F.		
	Data	Results	Notes	Data	Results	Notes
Figs. ÷.	100·00		EF	100·00		FE
Figs. sin. x.	78·5617		JR	94·7567		BR
Figs. sin. ÷.	43·2033		FL	48·8967		EL
Figs. sin. x.	68·1595		KR	65·1852		AR
Figs. sin. ÷.	51·2810		JL	35·2353		BL
Figs. sin. x.	60·2443		DR	63·5446		GR
Figs. sin. ÷.	88·9927		KL	48·5629		AL
Figs. sin. x.	48·0060		CR	24·1747		HR
Figs. sin. ÷.	34·0794		DL	92·9413		GL
Figs. sin. x.	51·1611		BR	59·9413		JR
Figs. sin. ÷.	65·2077		CL	49·9646		HL
Figs. sin. x.	36·3466		FR	58·2350		ER
Figs. sin.	94·7567		BL	78·5617		JL
=.		99·9063	EF		100·0877	FE
Logarithms	1·999 593			2·000 381		
	= 2 - ·000 407					

So the required Shifts are given by the equations: 9a - 604b = -407

642a - 9b = -381

whence a = - ·58 = - ·0058; b = ·66 = ·0066°

programme is the same as in table 20.2, but for brevity the circumferential lines have not been included. Considering the polygon centred on F, if FE is taken as 100 to start with, its final value is 100·0877. The logarithm of this is 2·000 381, so the sum of the log sins for the left-hand angles exceeds that for the right-hand angles by 0·000 381; the slight difference from the 374 in table 20.1 arises because extra angles have been taken into account in the preliminary balancing. This 381 has to be disposed of by the combined effects of the shifts a and b. Similar reasoning applies to the polygon centred on E, though in that case the 'left-hand' sum is relatively 0·000 407 too small. The simultaneous equations given in table 20.4 can thus be written down and solved for a and b. The method has been described in detail, to clarify the next section, but in practice, with only two polygons, you will almost always get a very close approximation to the correct values by working out the shift for each polygon separately, without considering the effect of the other.

Once the shifts have been found, the procedure is essentially the same as for a single polygon. A little work is saved by starting the calculations for both polygons with the shared line EF.

Although a calculator has been used here, the required equations can also be found by summing log sins as in table 20.1; or a and b can each be made equal to 0·01° and the effects for each polygon found by the method used in table 20.2.

20.8 *Four Linked Polygons.* Any number of polygons can be linked together, and the method of solution remains essentially the same. An example, for four polygons, is shown in Figure 20.5, and the calculations, as far as finding the shifts, are set out in table 20.5. It is assumed for illustration that log tables and a calculator are available.

The advantage of this is that although most calculations can be done much more quickly with a calculator, the changes in the log sin of an angle can be read off directly from tables without any intervening calculation. Since the change varies slowly no interpolation is needed and the measured angles, taken to the nearest minute, can be used in entering the tables.

Having arranged the blank table for your calculations, and ringed the shared triangles, you convert the measured angles into decimals of a degree and enter them in the section for preliminary balancing, and at the same time list them to the nearest minute in

Table 20.5 Four Polygons Linked
(a) Balancing Angles

Preliminary balancing:

Triangle	Left-hand Angles Measured	Adjusted 1	3 & 5	Central Angles Measured	1	Adjusted 2	3 & 4	Right-hand Angles Measured	Adjusted 1	3 & 5	Initial Total
BFA	35·2317	·2356	·2355	79·5750	·5788	·5793	·5790	65·1817	·1856	·1855	179·98
AFG	48·5600	·5633	·5632	67·8888	·8917	·8922	·8920	63·5417	·5450	·5448	179·99
GFH	92·9550	·9417	·9416	62·8967	·8833	·8838	·8835	24·1883	·1750	·1749	180·04
HFJ	49·9683	·9650	·9693	70·0967	·0933	·0938	·0935	59·9450	·9417	·9372	180·01
JFE	78·5550	·5617	·5597	43·1967	·2033	·2038	·2052	58·2283	·2350	·2351	179·98
EFB	48·8967	·8967	·8942	36·7467	·6466	·5471	·3468	94·7567	·7567	·7590	180·00

Central angles total: after 1st. adjustment 359·9970; after 3rd. adjustment 360·0

Triangle											
BEP	94·7567	·7567	·7590	48·8967	·8967	·8953	·8942	36·3467	·3466	·3468	180·000
FEJ	43·1967	·2033	·2052	58·2283	·2350	·2336	·2351	78·5550	·5617	·5597	179·98
JEK	51·2667	·2800	·2796	60·5483	·5616	·5602	·5634	68·1450	·1584	·1570	179·96
KED	88·9983	·9917	·9863	30·7717	·7650	·7636	·7624	60·2500	·2433	·2513	180·02
DEC	34·0700	·0783	·0796	97·9083	·9167	·9153	·9141	47·9967	·0050	·0063	179·97.
CEB	65·2133	·2067	·2079	63·8400	·6333	·6320	·6308	51·2667	·1600	·1613	180·02

Central angles total: after 1st. adjustment 360·0083; after 3rd. adjustment 360·00

Triangle											
EJF	58·2283	·2350	·2351	78·5550	·5617	·5583	·5597	43·1967	·2033	·2052	179·98
FJH	70·0967	·0933	·0935	59·9450	·9417	·9383	·9372	35·9550	·9630	·9693	180·01
HJN	35·9550	·9517	·9540	72·4133	·4100	·4065	·4054	71·6417	·6383	·6406	180·01
NJM	70·3083	·3128	·3150	60·1583	·1628	·1594	·1583	49·5200	·5244	·5267	179·98
MJK	53·4150	·4228	·4328	37·6567	·6644	·6610	·6598	88·9050	·9128	·9074	179·97
KJE	68·1450	·1584	·1570	51·2667	·2800	·2765	·2796	60·5483	·5616	·5634	179·96

Central angles total: after 1st. adjustment 360·0206; after 3rd. adjustment 360·00

Triangle											
EKJ	60·5483	·5616	·5634	68·1450	·1584	·1538	·1570	51·2667	·2800	·2796	179·96
JKM	37·6567	·6644	·6598	88·9050	·9128	·9082	·9074	53·4150	·4228	·4328	179·97
MKL	55·3933	·3833	·3860	50·2800	·2700	·2655	·2647	74·3567	·3467	·3493	180·03
LKD	48·6650	·6717	·6744	63·6833	·6900	·6854	·6846	67·6317	·6383	·6410	179·98
DKE	60·2500	·2433	·2513	88·9983	·8917	·9871	·9863	30·7717	·7650	·7624	180·02

Central angles total: after 1st. adjustment 360·0229; after 3rd. adjustment 360·00

Increase in 4th. to 6th. figure of log sin for increase of one minute, from tables.
Angles are entered to nearest minute.

	L. H. Angles	inc	Shifts	R. H. Angles	inc	Shifts
BFA	35°14	179	+a	65°11	058	-a
AFG	48°34	112	+a	63°32	063	-a
GFH	92°57	(-06)	+a	24°11	281	-a
HFJ	49°58	106	+a -c	59°57	073	-a
JFE	78°33	026	+a-b	58°14	078	-a +c
EFB	48°54	110	+a	94°45	(-11)	-a+b

527a - 26b - 106c   -542a - 11b + 78c

Relative increase of 'left-hand' sums:

1069a - 15b - 184c

	L. H. Angles	inc	Shifts	R. H. Angles	inc	Shift
BEP	94°45	(-11)	-a+b	36°21	172	-b
FEJ	43°12	135	+b-c	78°33	026	+a-b
JEK	51°16	101	+b -d	68°09	051	-b+c
KED	89°00	002	+b	60°15	072	-b
DEC	34°04	187	+b	48°00	114	-b
CEB	65°13	058	+b	51°10	102	-b

11a + 472b - 135c - 101d   26a - 537b + 51c + …

Relative increase of 'left-hand' sums:

- 15a + 1009b - 186c - 173d

	L. H. Angles	inc	Shifts	R. H. Angles	inc	Shifts
EJF	58°14	078	-a +c	43°12	135	+b-c
FJH	70°06	046	+c	49°58	106	+a -c
HJN	35°57	174	+c	71°38	042	-c
NJM	70°19	045	+c	49°31	108	-c
MJK	53°25	094	+c-d	88°54	002	-c
KJE	68°09	051	b+c	60°33	071	-c+d

- 78a - 51b + 488c - 94d   106a + 135b - 464c +71d

Relative increase of 'left-hand' sums:

- 184a - 186b + 952c - 165d

	L. H. Angles	inc	Shifts	R. H. Angles	inc	Shift
EKJ	60°33	071	-c+d	51°16	101	+b
JKM	37°39	164	+d	53°25	094	+c
MKL	55°24	087	+d	74°21	035	
LKD	48°40	111	+d	67°38	052	
DKE	60°15	072	-b +d	30°46	212	

- 72b - 71c + 505d   101b + 94c - 494d

Relative increase of 'left-hand' sums:

- 173b - 165c + 999d

Table 20.5 Four Polygons Linked
(b) Calculation of Shifts

Programme	Data		Data		Data		Data	
Figs. ÷.	100·00	FE	100·00	EF	100·00	JK	100·00	KJ
Figs. sin. x.	94·7590	BR	78·5597	JR	60·5634	ER	53·4328	MR
Figs. sin. ÷.	48·8942	EL	43·2052	FL	68·1570	KL	37·6598	JL
Figs. sin. x.	65·1855	AR	68·1570	KR	43·2052	FR	74·3493	IR
Figs. sin. ÷.	35·2355	BL	51·2796	JL	58·2351	EL	55·3860	ML
Figs. sin. x.	63·5448	GR	60·2513	DR	49·9693	HR	67·6410	DR
Figs. sin. ÷.	48·5632	AL	88·9863	KL	70·0935	FL	48·6744	LL
Figs. sin. x.	24·1749	HR	48·0063	CR	71·6406	NR	30·7624	ER
Figs. sin. ÷.	92·9416	GL	34·0796	DL	35·9540	HL	60·2513	DL
Figs. sin. x.	59·9372	JR	51·1613	BR	49·5267	MR	51·2796	JR
Figs. sin. ÷.	49·9693	HL	65·2079	CL	70·3150	NL	60·5634	EL
Figs. sin. x.	58·2351	ER	36·3468	FR	88·9074	KR	100·0338	KJ
Figs. sin.	78·5597	JL	94·7590	BL	53·4328	ML	—	
=.	100·0941	FE	99·9047	EF	99·9703	JK		

Logarithms 2·000 409   1·999 575   1·999 881   2·000 147

= 2-·000 425   = 2-·000 119

So the Shifts are given by the equations

$$1069a - 15b - 184c \qquad\qquad = -409$$
$$-15a + 1009b - 186c - 173d = +425$$
$$-184a - 186b + 952c - 165d = +119$$
$$\qquad\quad -173b - 165c + 999d = -147$$

which can be re-written as

$$a = \qquad\quad 0·014b + 0·172c \qquad\qquad -0·383$$
$$b = 0·015a \qquad\quad + 0·184c + 0·171d + 0·419$$
$$c = 0·193a + 0·195b \qquad\quad + 0·173d + 0·127$$
$$d = \qquad\quad 0·173b + 0·165c \qquad\qquad -0·147$$

Step-by-step solution:

		a	b	c	d	Total Change	Approx. Value	
Coefficients and first approx.	a	—	+ 0·014	+ 0·172	—	—	- 0·383	a
	b	+ 0·015	—	+ 0·184	+ 0·171	—	+ 0·421	b
	c	+ 0·193	+ 0·195	—	+ 0·173	—	+ 0·125	c
	d	—	+ 0·173	+ 0·165	—	—	- 0·147	d
First change, caused by first approx.	a	—	+ 0·006	+ 0·022	—	+ 0·028	- 0·355	a
	b	- 0·006	—	+ 0·023	- 0·025	- 0·008	+ 0·413	b
	c	- 0·074	+ 0·082	—	- 0·025	- 0·017	+ 0·108	c
	d	—	+ 0·073	+ 0·021	—	+ 0·094	- 0·053	d
Second change, caused by first change.	a	—	neg.	- 0·003	—	- 0·003	- 0·358	a
	b	neg.	—	- 0·003	+ 0·016	+ 0·013	+ 0·426	b
	c	+ 0·005	- 0·002	—	+ 0·016	+ 0·019	+ 0·127	c
	d	—	- 0·001	- 0·003	—	- 0·004	- 0·057	d
Third change, caused by second change	a	—	neg.	+ 0·003	—	+ 0·003	- 0·355	a
	b	neg.	—	+ 0·003	- 0·001	+ 0·002	+ 0·428	b
	c	- 0·001	+ 0·002	—	- 0·001	neg.	+ 0·127	c
	d	—	+ 0·002	+ 0·003	—	+ 0·005	- 0·052	d

The final values should be checked by substitution in the original equations. To the second decimal place the Shifts can be taken as:

a = - 0·35'; b = + 0·43'; c = + 0·13'; d = - 0·05'.

20.5 Four Polygons Linked

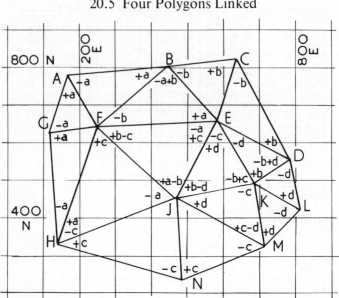

the section for calculating the effect of shift (table 20.5a). The change in log sin per minute change in angle is then filled in, after which the tables can be put aside.

The next step is to give the angles their preliminary balancing. To exemplify method, this has been taken through five stages, but to stop at the third would often be legitimate; it may perhaps give undue weight to the measured angles in the shared triangles.

The method is essentially the same as that given previously; illustrated figures are mostly taken from the polygon centred on K. Although the description of the procedure sounds complicated it will be found simple and automatic if followed step by step.

(i) Adjustment 1 brings each triangle to a total of 180°. Thus in triangle EKJ, which is 0·0400° too small, each angle is increased by 0·0133° or 0·0134°. The odd one ten-thousandth of a degree is insignificant, and can be disposed of in any angle without affecting the results.

(ii) When this has been done, the central angles no longer add up to 360°. Since three of the angles round K, for example, are shared, to treat those as fixed would involve a disproportionately large adjustment to the remaining two. So the central angles are *all* given a second adjustment, − 0·0045° or 46 round K, and similarly for the other polygons.

(iii) The arbitrary decision is now taken to give one more adjustment, 3, to the two triangles EFJ and EJK which are shared between three polygons, and then to keep their angles fixed. Taking the *central* angles in these triangles as having the values found after the second adjustment, those for EJK add up to 179·9905°, so each is increased by 0·0031° or 32. These, the third adjusted angles, are entered in the appropriate columns, ringed and henceforth left unaltered. Triangle EFJ is treated similarly.

(iv) The central angles for each polygon are then added up again, replacing the second adjustment for the shared triangles by the ringed figures. Angle EKJ, for example, has increased from 0·1538° to 0·1570°, so the total around K is 0·0032° too great; each of the remaining four central angles is therefore reduced by 0·0008°. This is the fourth adjustment, and applies only to the central angles, but the resulting figures must be entered in the appropriate columns for the other shared triangles. Thus JKM is a Central Angle at K, and has the value 88·9074° after the fourth adjustment; but it is also a right-hand angle in the polygon centred on J, so ·9074 is entered in that column. Similarly, the fourth adjusted value 35·6598 for the central angle MJK is entered as a left-hand angle for the triangle centred on K. All these angles are underlined; they are given no further adjustments.

(v) Finally, keeping these angles fixed, the triangles are once again balanced. For triangles such as JKM, shared by two polygons, only one angle remains available for adjustment, but unless some mistake has been incorporated in the calculations this fifth adjustment will be small.

Each polygon is then solved, using the same programme as in the last section; to save space, no separate column has been provided for 'Results'. The simultaneous equations for the shifts can then be written down.

The solution of four simultaneous equations by normal methods is laborious, but fortunately these are of a type which can be solved step by step. Each unknown is much the most important quantity in one equation, so as a first approximation the rest can be neglected. Each first approximation can then be substituted in the equations, and will produce a change in the approximate values. Then inserting these first changes in the equations a second change is found, and so on. As will be seen from the table, further changes soon become negligible. The final approximate values are substituted in the original equations, to make sure that they are in fact sufficiently accurate solutions.

20.9 *Derivation of Formula.* For the sake of completeness, and for the benefit of those not willing to take it on trust, the derivation of the formula used in Para. 20.7 is given here.

$$\text{The first differential of } \log_e \sin x \; = \frac{1}{\sin x}\frac{d}{dx}(\sin x)$$
$$= \frac{\cos x}{\sin x}$$
$$= \frac{1}{\tan x}$$

But this is the change of the logarithm to base *e* for a change in angle of 1 Radian.

$$\log_{10} \sin x = 0\cdot4343 \log_e \sin x$$

$$\text{and } 0\cdot01° = \frac{\pi}{100 \times 180}\text{Radians}$$

So change in $\log_{10} \sin x$ for one-hundredth of a degree change in

$$\text{angle} = \frac{0\cdot4343 \times \pi}{18,000 \tan x}$$
$$= \frac{0\cdot000\,075\,8}{\tan x}$$

Part VI
MISCELLANEOUS TECHNIQUES

21 Plotting from Oblique Aerial Photographs

21.1 *Introduction.* All archaeologists are familiar with the overwhelming mass of information, much of it new, yielded by aerial photography, but most of these photographs have of necessity been taken obliquely and without the exact records of height and other details needed for stereogrammetric plotting (Para. 22.1). Nevertheless, subject to two conditions which are very often satisfied, a reliable plan can be drawn using such a photograph, without the need for any complicated apparatus.

Two methods have been described by I. Scollar (*Aerial Reconnaissance for Archaeology*, ed. D. R. Wilson, CBA 1975, pp. 52–9) and a supplementary alternative has been given by R. Palmer (*Journal of Archaeological Science*, vol. 3 (1976), pp. 391–4). These authors have also given computer programmes (Scollar, *Aerial Reconnaissance* and *World Archaeology*, vol. 10 (1978), pp. 71–87; Palmer, *JAS* vol. 4 (1977), pp. 283–90) but these fall outside the scope of this book. Other methods which do not require a computer are described below.

One condition which must be satisfied is that four points, identifiable on the photograph, must also be identifiable on an accurate plan; usually a 1/2,500 map will provide these, but they can of course be surveyed. The points should lie at the corners of an (imaginary) quadrilateral which encloses most of the features to be plotted.

The second condition is more restrictive. The ground photographed *must* be a plane surface, not necessarily horizontal but flat. Fortunately, most crop-mark sites, for which these methods are particularly useful, occur on such terrain. The principles are equally applicable to a flat wall, and can therefore often be used to draw the elevations of a building, but generally there are simpler ways of doing this. Theoretically, given enough landmarks, a curved ground surface could be replaced by several intersecting planes, each of which would be treated separately; where these overlap the lines plotted would diverge and would be 'smoothed in' by eye. In practice, save in exceptionally simple cases, this seems unlikely to be a useful approach.

In any plot of this kind, one rule must be absolutely invariable: a copy of the original print must be kept entirely free from any marking. If you do not keep to this rule, you will discover that you have been carefully transferring to the plan a pencil mark you made a few days ago; or worse still you will not discover it, and the mark will be recorded as a genuine feature. The ideal is to have a good glossy enlargement to be kept virginal, and a matte enlargement on which to work; but if only one print is available the relevant detail should be very carefully replotted as a working drawing.

In the figures relating to the examples which follow, the upper part of the diagram relates to the photograph, the lower to the map. All are based on a genuine site, though details have been simplified.

21.2 *The Network Method (The 'Möbius' Network).* This, first published by Scollar, is easy and versatile. It is the method of choice for simple sites, unless great accuracy is needed. Straight lines photograph as straight lines (accurately enough, with the type of camera used for this work). So if you imagine a network of straight lines joining up features on the ground (or on the map), a corresponding network can be drawn on the aerial photograph; the angles and lengths will be different, but every line will be identifiable. So will every intersection, and these can be joined up to give secondary lines, and so on almost indefinitely. Using this method, the more identifiable points you have the better, so you may find it worth while to measure in features such as trees or gate posts which are recognisable on the photograph but which do not appear on the map.

In the example (Figure 21.1), six points are used, all being the junctions of field boundaries except D which is a ruined wind-pump. Consider the large subrectangular enclosure. Suppose ae and bd intersect at 1, be and cf at 2, ab and ef at 3, ac and df at 4, and ac and be at 5. Then secondary lines can be drawn: b to 4 cuts ad at 6, 2 to 1 cuts ad at 7 and df at 8. The tertiary lines, 5–6, 6–8, 8–c, and d–2, frame the enclosure; more lines can be drawn if

21.1 Oblique Aerial Photographs: Network Method

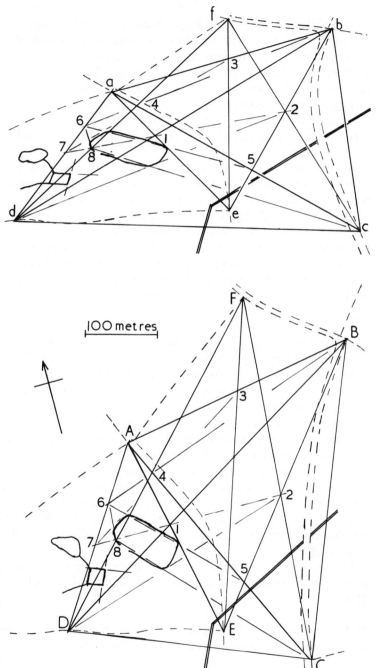

100 metres

desired. All the corresponding lines can be drawn on the map, and the true outline of the enclosure can be sketched in quite accurately.

In addition to its simplicity, this method has a particular merit when several different photographs are available, for the same network can be established on all of them. All other approaches involve separate treatment of each photograph. In fact, even where other methods are used, it is very well worth while to mark the main network on the plan and photographs, as a guide to the reliability of the results.

Two points may be noted at this stage, though they are applicable throughout what follows. The first is obvious: any or all methods described here can be used in conjunction.

The second is equally so, when stated: if the photographs are being used as a guide for excavation, any of these constructions can be carried out on the ground; there is no need to transfer the information to a plan, as an intermediate stage. One precaution is advisable: the poles used should be distinguished by different coloured flags (or rags) to avoid confusion between different alignments.

21.3 *The Paper Strip Method*. This also is described by Scollar, who gives references to earlier publications.

Suppose that we wish to fix the position of the bend in the parch-mark caused by the Roman Road (X in Figure 21.2). This can be done provided that we can draw lines BX and DX on the map corresponding to bx and dx on the photograph. For simplicity only two lines have been drawn on the diagram, but in practice three should always be used; a small triangle of error will result.

To draw the line BX, a strip of paper is placed on the photograph, and the points a, d, c, x, marked where the rays ba, bd, bc, and bx cross its edge. The strip is then transferred to the map and moved so that a lies on BA, d on BD, and c on BC; then the line BX, through x on the strip, corresponds to bx on the photograph.

The method is very simple, though rather laborious if many points have to be located. A proof of its validity is outlined in Para. 21.5.

21.4 *Palmer's Method*. Imagine that the ground carries two or more pairs of widely spaced parallel lines. In an oblique

21.2 Oblique Aerial Photographs: Paper Strip Method

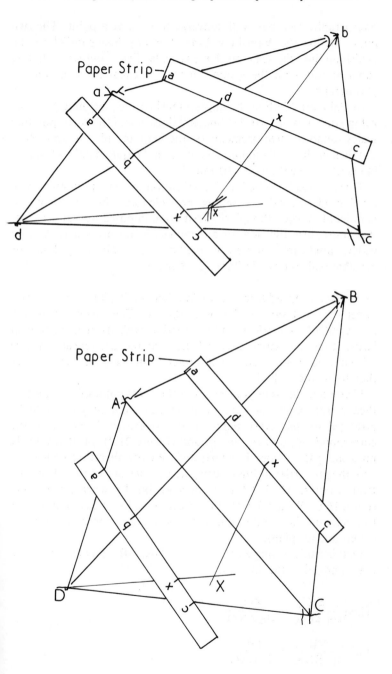

photograph, each pair will converge to meet at a point. The two points define the Vanishing Line. For any line parallel to the vanishing line, the scale on that particular line is uniform; that is, equal divisions on the ground appear as equal divisions on the photograph.

In Palmer's Method, having established the vanishing line (see below) one or more parallel lines are drawn, and the corresponding scales found by measurements on the map and photograph. Rays can then be drawn from known points, and required points fixed by intersection (see Paras. 21.10 and 11).

This method is limited in its application, for except in areas with much modern detail it is seldom possible to establish two pairs of parallel lines, even though the restriction imposed by Palmer, that they must form the sides of a rectangle, is not necessary. A more widely applicable numerical method of establishing lines of constant scale is given in Paras. 21.8 and 9.

21.5 *Theory*. In addition to their other merits, the network and paper strip methods involve no arithmetic. The two which follow are essentially numerical, and this section explains their theoretical basis. It can be skipped, for all the formulae are repeated where relevant; but some readers will prefer to understand them, rather than to use them blindly.

If you imagine that your eye is at the focal point of the camera, then a transparent positive print held in front of you could be arranged so that every point on it was exactly in line with the corresponding point on the ground (Figure 21.3), or alternatively on a map; the theory is unaffected. We are therefore concerned with the properties of lines cutting across 'pencils' of rays diverging from a point. All that follows depends on the 'a/sin A' formula (Para. 16.6). With a few obvious exceptions, lower case letters refer to points on the photograph, capitals to corresponding points on the ground (or plan).

First consider a single pencil of rays OA, OB, and OX, all in one plane and cut by the line axb.

$$\text{Then } \frac{AX}{\sin AOX} = \frac{OA}{\sin AXO}$$

$$\text{and } \frac{XB}{\sin BOX} = \frac{OB}{\sin BXO}$$

21.3 Oblique Aerial Photographs: Theory

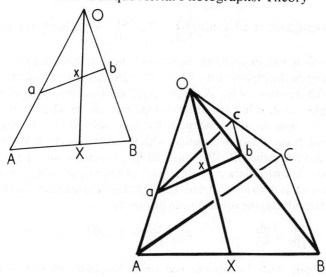

Since AXO = 180° − BXO, sin AXO = sin BXO

So $\dfrac{AX}{XB} = \dfrac{OA}{OB}\dfrac{\sin AOX}{\sin BOX}$

Similarly $\dfrac{ax}{xb} = \dfrac{Oa \sin aOx}{Ob \sin bOx}$

For any given lines AB, ab, $\dfrac{OA}{Oa}.\dfrac{Ob}{OB}$ is constant; so these equations can be written

$$\dfrac{AX}{XB} = R_{AB}\dfrac{ax}{xb}$$

where R_{AB} is constant. This holds for any position of X, whether between the points AB or outside them.

The same reasoning shows that provided the lines Aa, Bb, and Xx all converge, not necessarily at the focal point of the camera, then the same relationship must hold. This is the theoretical basis of the paper strip method.

Now suppose that O forms the vertex and ABC the base of an unsymmetrical pyramid. The vertices of a smaller triangle a, b, and c lie on OA, OB, and OC respectively. Then

$$R_{AB}.R_{BC}.R_{CA} = \frac{OA.Ob}{Oa.OB}.\frac{OB.Oc}{Ob.OC}.\frac{OC.Oa}{Oc.OA} = 1$$

Although the relationship $\frac{AX}{XB} = R_{AB}.\frac{ax}{xb}$ is probably the mos

convenient way of defining the ratio of measurements on the map
to those on the photograph, we usually need AX in terms of ax, ab
and AB (or conversely). A simple graphical construction is shown
in Figure 21.4; it has the disadvantage that except when $R = 1$ a
separate diagram has to be made for each point. Lines of lengths
DB and db are drawn at an angle, with B and b coincident. We wish
to make the ratio DP : PB equal to R_{DB} times the ratio dp : pb
which is known. Mark p on db, and make d_1p equal to $R_{DB} \times dp$.
Then if pP is drawn parallel to d_1D, P is the required point on DB.

Alternatively, the equation can be rewritten as

$$R_{DB} \times \frac{PB}{DP} = \frac{pb}{dp} \quad \text{or} \quad R_{DB}\left(\frac{DB}{DP} - 1\right) = \frac{db}{dp} - 1$$

which can easily be worked out either longhand or with a cal
culator. A suitable programme would be: enter figures for db; ÷
enter dp; —; 1; ÷; enter R_{DB}; (or: x: enter R_{BD};) +; 1; ÷; enter DB
=; take reciprocal. If several such calculations are to be made for the
same pair of lines, then assuming that only two memories are available
whichever of the three quantities DB, db, and R_{DB} has fewest digit
is entered each time it is needed; the other two can be stored.

21.4 Graphical Construction for Ratios

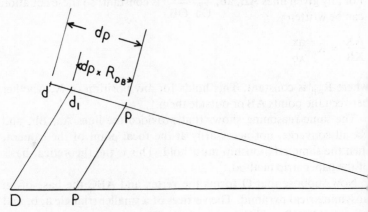

21.6 *Applications of Equations.* There are several different ways of using these equations, but basically they reduce to two: direct comparison of distances, and establishing lines of constant scale: these are described in the following sections. The necessary measurements can be made with any closely graduated scale. Although not essential, it is advisable to use the same scale for measuring the photograph and the map; this obviates the risk of finding that you have used, say, the 'map' scale on the photograph. In all the calculations which follow, the original measurements were taken with a 1/2,500 metric scale. Usually there is no need to give more than the number, but when necessary dimensions on the photograph (top in the diagrams) are stated in 'units' and on the map in 'metres'.

21.7 *Direct Comparison of Distances.* Suppose that we wish to fix the north-east corner of the small square crop-mark (Figure 21.1). This can be done by finding the intersection of its sides, produced, with lines DB and DF; so we require the relation between measurements on those lines and on db and df, on the photograph. There are several corresponding points on these pairs of lines. The measurements to them, and quantities derived from those measurements, are set out in table 21.1 and are plotted in Figure 21.5.

Provided no great accuracy is needed, the simplest method is to draw a smooth curve relating the known measurements on the map to those on the photograph. A better result is obtained by plotting $\frac{XD}{XB}$ against $\frac{xd}{xb}$; or by plotting their logarithms. The first plot should give a straight line passing through the origin and having slope R_{DB}. The second should give a straight line at 45° to the axes, and the value of $\frac{XD}{XB}$ when $\log. \frac{xd}{xb} = 0$ gives R_{DB}. The results obtained are also set out in table 21.1.

One warning must be given. The value of R is very susceptible to small errors in measurement, and while this will not have much effect on the positions of points fixed by this method provided they lie between the ends of the line, the inaccuracy increases rapidly outside those limits.

21.8 *Lines of Constant Scale: Theory.* The advantages of lines of constant scale (that is, lines parallel to the vanishing line) were pointed out by Palmer (Para. 21.4). This method differs from his

21.5 Oblique Aerial Photographs: Direct Comparison of Distances

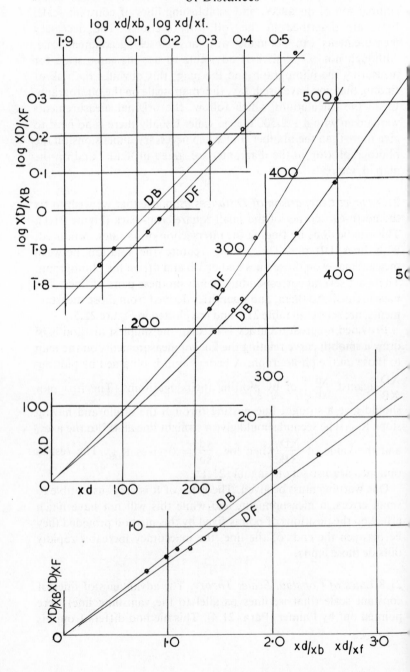

Table 21.1 Oblique Aerial Photographs: Direct Comparison of Distances

Line DB	cut by	D	AE	AC	Fence	FE	FC	B
Measurements:	Photo (xd)	0	226	253	265	342	396	510
	Map (XD)	0	198	227	240	327	395	547
	Photo (xb)	510	284	257	245	168	114	0
	Map (XB)	547	349	320	307	220	152	0
Ratios: Photo	xd/xb	0	0·7958	0·9844	1·0816	2·0357	3·4737	∞
Map	XD/XB	0	0·5673	0·7094	0·7818	1·4864	2·5987	∞
Logarithms:	xd/xb	− ∞	$\bar{1}$·9008	$\bar{1}$·9932	0·0341	0·3087	0·5408	+ ∞
	XD/XB	− ∞	$\bar{1}$·7538	$\bar{1}$·8509	$\bar{1}$·8931	0·1721	0·4148	+ ∞

Line DF	cut by	D	AE	AC	Fence	AB	F
Measurements:	Photo (xd)	0	221	231	239	287	403
	Map (XD)	0	227	241	251	321	516
	Photo (xf)	403	182	172	164	116	0
	Map (XF)	516	289	275	265	195	0
Ratios: Photo	xd/xf	0	1·2143	1·3430	1·4573	2·4741	∞
Map	XD/XF	0	0·7855	0·8764	0·9472	1·6462	∞
Logarithms:	xd/xf	∞	0·0843	0·1281	0·1635	0·3934	+ ∞
	XD/XF	∞	$\bar{1}$·8951	$\bar{1}$·9427	$\bar{1}$·9764	0·2164	+ ∞

Plotting Ratios gives: $R_{DB} = 0\cdot735$ $R_{DF} = 0\cdot662$

Plotting Logarithms gives: $R_{DB} = 0\cdot733$ $R_{DF} = 0\cdot652$

From calculation, Table 24: $R_{DB} = 0\cdot7209$

Intersects to locate N.E. corner of small square enclosure (to nearest metre).

	E. side	N. side		E. side	N. side
From d, on db	85	126	From d, on df	114	96
Hence from D on DB: reading off curve	70	105	Hence from D on DF: reading off curve	105	90
$R_{DB} = 0\cdot735$ or $0\cdot733$	70	106	$R_{DF} = 0\cdot662$	108	89
$R_{DB} = 0\cdot721$	69	105	$R_{DF} = 0\cdot652$	106	88

approach in that the lines are established by calculation. The only requirement, apart from flat ground, is that four points, at the corners of a fairly large quadrilateral, shall be identifiable on the map and on the photograph. There is no need to identify two pairs of parallel lines, and the method is applicable to nearly vertical views in which the vanishing line is inconveniently far from the print. In principle, the accuracy of this method is only limited by the precision of measurement possible on the photograph.

In Figure 21.6, suppose AM and am are a corresponding pair of lines of constant scale; stated another way, R_{AM} is unity. Since $R_{AB} \times R_{BM} \times R_{MA} = 1$ (Para. 21.5),

$$R_{MB} = R_{AB}$$

Also $R_{AB} = R_{AX} \times R_{XB}$ or $R_{AX} \div R_{BX}$

Keep in mind throughout what follows that $R_{AX} = 1/R_{XA}$

Hence if AX, BX, CX, and DX, and the corresponding lengths on the photograph are found, the values of R can be calculated for

21.6 Oblique Aerial Photographs: Lines of Constant Scale

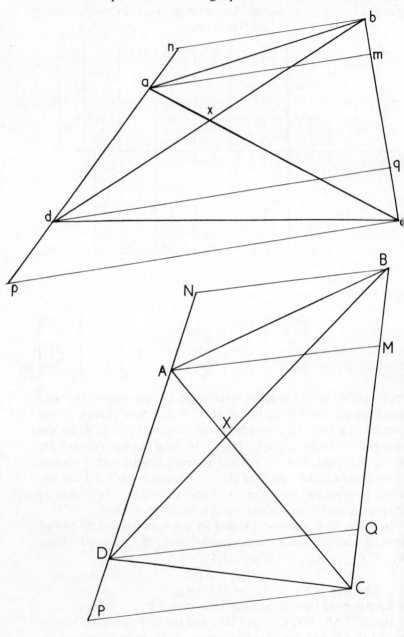

all the lines in the diagram. The necessary lengths can be determined by measurement, or more accurately by calculation.

Expressions for BM and bm can be found as follows:

$$\frac{BC}{CM} = R_{BM} \times \frac{bc}{cm} \qquad \text{or rearranging} \quad R_{BM} \times \frac{CM}{BC} = \frac{cm}{bc}$$

$$\text{and similarly} \quad R_{CM} \times \frac{BM}{BC} = \frac{bm}{bc}$$

Adding: $R_{BM} \times \dfrac{CM}{BC} + R_{CM} \times \dfrac{BM}{BC} = \dfrac{cm + bm}{bc} = 1$

Now writing $CM = BC - BM$ this gives

$$\frac{BM}{BC} = \frac{R_{BM} - 1}{R_{BM} - R_{CM}} \qquad = \frac{R_{BX} - R_{AX}}{R_{BX} - R_{CX}}$$

for $R_{BM} = R_{BA} = R_{BX} \times R_{XA}$

and $R_{CM} = R_{CA} = R_{CX} \times R_{XA}$

This expression may be described verbally as giving the distance from B at which a line of constant scale (through A) cuts the line BC. The order in which the angles of the quadrilateral are named in this sentence is the same as that in which they occur in the right-hand side of the equation; this simplifies writing down the expressions for AN, CQ, and DP.

A similar argument, starting with $R_{MB} \times \dfrac{cm}{bc} = \dfrac{CM}{BC}$ leads to the corresponding expression

$$\frac{bm}{bc} = \frac{R_{XB} - R_{XA}}{R_{XB} - R_{XC}}$$

These equations can be rearranged in many different ways, and even more ingenious programmes can be devised for use with a calculator; but the following scheme seems to introduce the least risk of mistakes:

$$BM = -\frac{R_{AX} - R_{BX}}{R_{BX} - R_{CX}} BC \qquad bm = -\frac{R_{CX}}{R_{AX}}\cdot\frac{R_{AX} - R_{BX}}{R_{BX} - R_{CX}} bc$$

$$CQ = -\frac{R_{CX} - R_{DX}}{R_{BX} - R_{CX}} BC \qquad cq = -\frac{R_{BX}}{R_{DX}}\cdot\frac{R_{CX} - R_{DX}}{R_{BX} - R_{CX}} bc$$

$$AN = -\frac{R_{AX} - R_{BX}}{R_{DX} - R_{AX}}AD \qquad an = -\frac{R_{DX}}{R_{BX}}\cdot\frac{R_{AX} - R_{BX}}{R_{DX} - R_{AX}}ad$$

$$DP = -\frac{R_{CX} - R_{DX}}{R_{DX} - R_{AX}}AD \qquad dp = -\frac{R_{AX}}{R_{CX}}\cdot\frac{R_{CX} - R_{DX}}{R_{DX} - R_{AX}}ad$$

The factors $(R_{AX} - R_{BX})$, $\dfrac{R_{AX}}{R_{CX}}$ etc. are worked out and listed as intermediate steps in the calculation.

21.9 *Determining Lines of Constant Scale.* Logically, to use several pairs of corresponding points rather than only four ought to give more reliable results, but in practice R is so sensitive to small errors in measurement that to get consistent values is difficult; three values along the sides of a triangle, which ought to give a product of unity, very seldom do so when calculated by the method described in Para. 21.7. By contrast, exact agreement is possible for the angles and sides of a quadrilateral.

If moderate accuracy is acceptable, the lengths ax, AX, etc. from which the other quantities are found can be measured. Table 21.2 gives the relevant calculations. If however, the greatest possible precision is desired, the lengths must be calculated, as in table 21.3; inevitably much more work is involved. Both tables refer to Figure 21.6. The calculations start from the co-ordinates, relative to arbitrary axes, of the angles of the quadrilateral; this obviates the need to 'balance' the sides and diagonals.

Owing to the sensitivity of R, mentioned above, the lines of constant scale as found in table 21.2 diverge quite considerably from their true positions given by table 21.3. Fortunately though, the errors are almost self-compensating. The first example in the next section is at worst only just over a 'unit' away from its true position when drawn out using the table 21.2 figures.

21.10 *Transferring Site Grid to Photograph.* Once the lines of constant scale have been determined, any point can be fixed from two or more intersecting lines. This example and the next will serve to illustrate the method. In both, the calculated results from table 21.3 are used (and see Figure 21.7).

The most usual requirement is to transfer detail from the photograph to the map, but sometimes it is desired to represent a true rectangle, such as a site grid, on the photograph. The principles involved are the same. The rectangle is supposed to

Table 21.2 Oblique Aerial Photographs: Lines of Constant Scale, by Measurement

All measurements are in "metres" on a 1/2500 scale.

Map		Photograph			
AX	115	ax	93	$R_{AX} = \dfrac{AC}{CX}\dfrac{cx}{ac} = 1 \cdot 0869$	
BX	318	bx	254	$R_{BX} = \dfrac{BD}{DX}\dfrac{dx}{bd} = 1 \cdot 1967$	
CX	267	cx	294	$R_{CX} = \dfrac{CA}{AX}\dfrac{ax}{ca} = 0 \cdot 7982$	
DX	229	dx	255	$R_{DX} = \dfrac{DB}{BX}\dfrac{bx}{db} = 0 \cdot 8584$	
BC	428	bc	272		
AD	263	ad	222		

Factors needed in calculations:

$R_{AX} - R_{BX} = - 0 \cdot 1098$ $R_{BX} - R_{CX} = + 0 \cdot 3985$ $\dfrac{R_{CX}}{R_{AX}} = 0 \cdot 7344$

$R_{CX} - R_{DX} = - 0 \cdot 0602$ $R_{DX} - R_{AX} = - 0 \cdot 2285$ $\dfrac{R_{DX}}{R_{BX}} = 0 \cdot 7173$

Intercepts on BC and AD.

$BM = - \dfrac{R_{AX} - R_{BX}}{R_{BX} - R_{CX}} BC = + 117 \cdot 9$ $bm = - \dfrac{R_{CX}}{R_{AX}}\dfrac{R_{AX} - R_{BX}}{R_{BX} - R_{CX}} bc = + 55 \cdot 0$

$CQ = - \dfrac{R_{CX} - R_{DX}}{R_{BX} - R_{CX}} BC = + 64 \cdot 6$ $cq = - \dfrac{R_{BX}}{R_{DX}}\dfrac{R_{CX} - R_{DX}}{R_{BX} - R_{CX}} bc = + 57 \cdot 3$

$AN = - \dfrac{R_{AX} - R_{BX}}{R_{DX} - R_{AX}} AD = - 126 \cdot 4$ $an = - \dfrac{R_{DX}}{R_{BX}}\dfrac{R_{AX} - R_{BX}}{R_{DX} - R_{AX}} ad = - 76 \cdot 5$

$DP = - \dfrac{R_{CX} - R_{DX}}{R_{DX} - R_{AX}} AD = - 69 \cdot 3$ $dp = - \dfrac{R_{AX}}{R_{CX}}\dfrac{R_{CX} - R_{DX}}{R_{DX} - R_{AX}} ad = - 79 \cdot 6$

Hence by measurement

	AM 289	BN 262	CP 361	DQ 345
	am 312	bn 254	cp 532	dq 474
Scales in units on photo. to 100m. on map	107·96	96·95	147·37	137·39

measure 200 by 150 m, located as shown. The line of the west side cuts AM at U, DQ at V. AU measures 31 m, and 100 m on AM corresponds to 106·5 units on am; so au is 34 units. Similarly DV measures 92 m, the scale is 135·6 units to 100 m, and dv therefore equals 127 units. The line of the east side is fixed in the same way.

The north and south sides cut the lines of constant scale inconveniently far off the map, and this is true even for the diagonals. One method of fixing the angles, and probably the simplest, is to bisect the sides (Figure 21.7) and preferably to extend them for half a length in each direction. The corresponding diagonals can easily be drawn. Thus the lines which cut at Y intersect AM 30 m to the left of A and 114 to the right, and DQ at 178 m to the right of D and 20 to the left; so using the scales as above the corresponding lines fixing y on the photograph cut am at 32 and 122 units from a and dq at 241 and 27 units from d. Plotting

Table 21.3 Oblique Aerial Photographs: Lines of Constant Scale, by Calculation

All lengths in 'metres' on 1/2500 scale; angles in degrees and decimals.
Coordinates from arbitrary axes:

	Map x	Map y		Photograph x	Photograph y
A	278	299	a	240	401
B	579	438	b	540	493
C	532	12	c	586	225
D	195	48	d	106	225

	Coord. difference x	y	Length	Bearing		Coord. difference x	y	Length	Bearing
AB	301	139	331·545	65·2128	ab	300	92	313·790	72·9510
AC	254	- 287	383·256	138·4906	ac	346	- 176	388·191	116·9611
AD	- 83	- 251	264·367	- 161·7021	ad	- 134	- 176	221·206	- 142·7157
BC	- 47	- 426	428·585	- 173·7041	bc	46	- 268	271·919	170·2606
BD	- 384	- 390	547·317	- 135·4441	bd	- 434	- 268	510·078	- 121·6958
CD	- 337	36	338·917	- 83·9025	cd	- 480	0	480·000	270·0000

In triangle ABX	In triangle abx	In triangle CDX	In triangle cdx
$\hat{A}$ = 73·2778	$\hat{a}$ = 44·0101	$\hat{C}$ = 42·3931	$\hat{c}$ = 26·9611
$\hat{B}$ = 20·6569	$\hat{b}$ = 14·6468	$\hat{D}$ = 51·5416	$\hat{d}$ = 31·6958
$\hat{X}$ = 86·0653	$\hat{x}$ = 121·3431	$\hat{X}$ = 86·0653	$\hat{x}$ = 121·3431
AB = 331·545	ab = 313·790	CD = 338·917	cd = 480·000

So using the a/sine A formula:

AX = 117·236	ax = 92·902	CX = 266·019	cx = 295·289
BX = 318·275	bx = 255·269	DX = 229·042	dx = 254·810

Hence, substituting in the expressions given in Table 23:

R_{AX} = 1·09592	R_{BX} = 1·19372	R_{CX} = 0·78236	R_{DX} = 0·86059
BM = 101·895	CQ = 81·506	AN = 109·867	DP = 87·883
bm = 46·151	cq = 71·729	an = 66·276	dp = 103·007

Calculations for scales. From now on, measurement would usually be adequate.

Programme	Triangle ABM Data, etc.	Triangle CDQ Data, etc.	Triangle ABN Data, etc.	Triangle CDP Data, etc.
Figs.	331·545 AB	338·917 CD	331·545 AB	338·917 CD
F. x/y.				
Figs.	58·9169 $\hat{B}$	90·1984 $\hat{C}$	46·9149 $\hat{A}$	102·2004 $\hat{D}$
R. (. -.				
Figs.	101·895 BM	81·506 CQ	109·867 AN	87·883 DP
). F. x/y.				
P.	292·270 AM	348·854 DQ	268·755 BN	367·665 CP
F. x/y.	76·2890 $\hat{M}$	103·7097 $\hat{Q}$	64·2862 $\hat{N}$	115·7114 $\hat{P}$ External angles

	Triangle abm	Triangle cdq	Triangle abn	Triangle cdp
Figs.	313·790 ab	480·000 cd	313·790 ab	480·000 cd
F. x/y.				
Figs.	82·6904 $\hat{b}$	80·2606 $\hat{c}$	35·6667 $\hat{a}$	127·2843 $\hat{d}$
R. (. -.				
Figs.	46·151 bm	71·729 cq	66·276 an	103·007 dp
). F. x/y.				
P.	311·302 am	473·177 dq	262·803 bn	548·555 cp
F. x/y.	91·1462 $\hat{m}$	88·8531 $\hat{q}$	44·1223 $\hat{n}$	135·8767 $\hat{p}$ External angles

Units on photo. to 100 metres on map

AM: 106·51   DQ: 135·64   BN: 97·79   CP: 149·20

If desired, the bearings can be worked out from the results given above.
Relative to the y-axes they are

AM: 82·5849°   DQ: 82·5862°   NB: 82·5841°   PC: 82·5865°
am: 81·4068°   dq: 81·4075°   nb: 81·4066°   pc: 81·4076°

showing that the four in each set are almost exactly parallel, as they should be

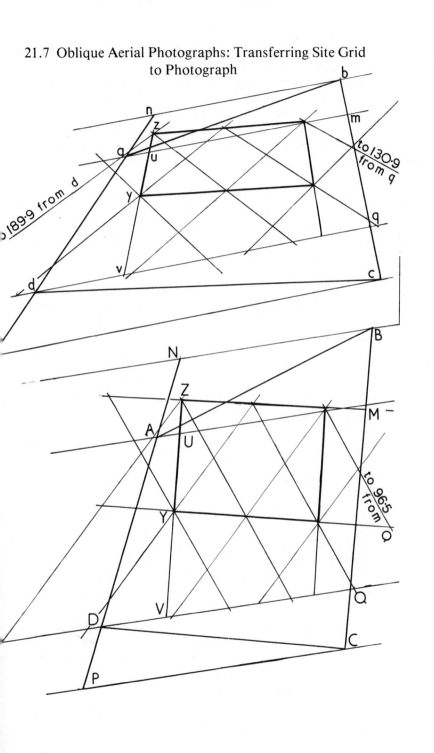

all eight diagonal lines and the east and west sides provides some check against mistakes.

For that reason a graphical solution is always desirable, but if greater accuracy is needed lengths measured along the sides, such as vy, can be calculated. Just as $R_{MB} = R_{AB}$ (Para. 21.8) so $R_{VU} = R_{VA} = R_{DA} = R_{DX}.R_{XA}$, so if the lengths VY, YU, UZ, and vu are known, yu and uz can be found; these calculations are also set out in table 21.3.

21.11 *Transferring Detail from Photograph.* When detail is to be transferred from the photograph to the map, any grid can be chosen. The most convenient arrangement is to impose a square grid on the photograph, with its lines at 45° to the lines of constant scale. In Figure 21.8 this has been done, with diagonals of 50 units. The corresponding spacing along AM is then 50 ÷ 106·5, that is 46·9 m, and along DQ 50 ÷ 135·6 = 36·9 m. The intersections with dq start at 3 and 14 units from d, corresponding to 2 and 10 m from D. The resulting grids can be repeatedly subdivided, as explained in Para. 26.7.

The advantage of imposing the square grid on the photograph rather than on the map is that the same grid, drawn on transparent material, can be used for all photographs, which can then be kept unmarked. The lines of constant scale are established on a separate drawing on which the grid is superimposed. The co-ordinates of the corners of the original quadrilateral are then noted, and the transparent grid can then be located relative to the photograph.

21.12 *Comparison of Methods.* Recapitulation may be useful. First, remember that no simple method is applicable unless the ground is flat. Subject to that condition, the network method is the simplest and most versatile when nothing more is needed than a good representative sketch-plan. The direct comparison of distances, using merely a smooth curve to relate measurements on photograph and map, will often be a helpful supplement to the network. Palmer's Method requires data which are often not available.

If rather greater accuracy is required, then direct comparison of distances, using one of the methods of finding R, is suitable if only a few points are to be fixed. If there is a lot of detail, a grid can be superimposed on photograph and map as in Para. 21.11, using measurements in the initial calculations.

21.8 Oblique Aerial Photographs: Transferring Detail from Photograph to Plan

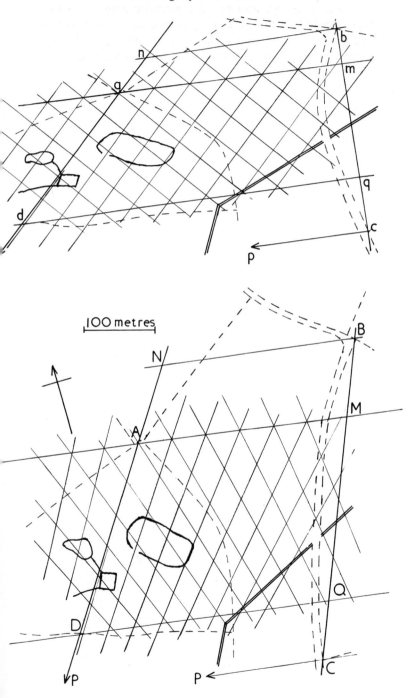

Finally, if the greatest possible precision is to be obtained, the grids should be established using calculated distances throughout, and points of special importance should be fixed either by intersection or by calculation; but if the features are visible a ground survey is always preferable.

22 Other Applications of Photography

22.1 *Photogrammetry.* A site with well-defined features, and not obscured by vegetation, can be accurately planned, with contours, from aerial photographs. These are observed stereoscopically, and at the same time twin pointers, one visible in each eyepiece, are adjusted to coincide with features visible on the photographs. The principle is thus simple enough, but the stereoplotter which applies it is a complicated and expensive device, and the necessary photographs have to be taken under carefully controlled and recorded conditions of height and tilt. The actual production of a plan by this method is therefore outside the scope of this book; but it is often worth while to examine the possibility of applying it to a major site.

22.2 *Conditions Justifying its Use.* As will be seen, quite a lot of work has to be done in the field even when the main plan is done by this method. Whether judged in terms of time or of cost, photogrammetry is not always the method of choice.

So many factors will influence your decision that only general guidelines can be suggested. These are summarised below, followed by considerations which justify them or may suggest some modification.

As a rough guide, photogrammetry is only likely to be worth while if contours are needed, whatever the nature of the site. If that condition is satisfied, sites of less than 3 hectares can usually be done more economically with chain and tacheometer, whereas for larger areas photogrammetry is to be preferred; but the critical area is not sharply defined.

The following factors have to be taken into account. First of all, arrangements have to be made with the company who will do the photography and plotting, preferably by personal discussion, which may well take a day unless their offices are close at hand. Next, the necessary ground control work will take about one other day, for two surveyors. Finally, when the photogrammetric plan has been received, at least another day's work in the field by archaeologists will be necessary, more if it is a site with much complex detail (see below). Photogrammetry, therefore, is unlikely to be advantageous from any standpoint if the survey can be done by chain and theodolite in three days or less. If the monetary cost is considered, this three days needs to be considerably increased, for the price of a photogrammetric survey is normally made up of a fairly large basic charge and a relatively small addition depending on the area covered. No exact figures can be given, but the basic charge could well be the equivalent of a fortnight's field expenses. The decision needed here is whether the time saved is worth the extra expense. In this context also, the financial arrangements of the organisation (if any) for which you work may be relevant; for example, photogrammetry may be preferable though more expensive because it is charged under a different subhead in the accounts, or because it sounds so scientific that it impresses those responsible for the allocation of funds.

Reverting to the nature of the site to be surveyed, accessibility is obviously important, but so also is the character of the remains. Massive grass-covered banks and ditches can be plotted direct from the photographs, and require very little checking. On the other hand hut-platforms may well not show up at all, and will then have to be surveyed on the ground; so nearly as much work will be needed as for a complete chain survey. Similarly, the lines of facing which can often be detected in a ruined stone wall will have to be recorded by ground survey. In fact, on dry-stone built structures of the kind common in the Highland Zone almost as much chaining will be needed as if the whole survey were done by that method; the advantage of photogrammetry is that contours are provided automatically.

22.3 *Organising a Photogrammetric Survey*. The first step is to find an organisation which will take the photographs and do the plotting; advice may be sought from the Geography or Civil Engineering Departments of a University or Technical College. If circumstances permit it is worth while to shop around. Cheaper rates can sometimes be arranged by accepting some delays so that your photography can be done during the same flight as other work, or by having several sites in the same region done at the same time.

The firm will need to know *precisely* what you wish to have surveyed, so you should provide at least 'six-inch' or 1/10,000 maps with the outline of the area marked; 1/2,500 maps are much better. You must also specify the scale required. Personal discussion with the firm's representatives is very desirable.

If the site to be surveyed is under your control, you should arrange at this stage where the ground control points are to be located. Each should be marked on the ground with a peg at the centre of a white-painted cross, so that they are clearly visible in the photographs. To be able to do this is very unusual, and normally these points have to be located at features visible on the photographs (see below).

The next stage is for the firm to take the necessary photographs and send duplicates to you; one print should preferably be matte to receive annotation. On one set of prints, unless ground control has already been marked, the firm will have indicated the points between which they require measurement and those where they wish for levels. Usually they will need two measured base lines and a ring of spot levels enclosing the site; rather surprisingly, they do not generally ask for a summit level when the plan represents a hill.

The control points for base line measurements will be sharply defined, such as gate or fence posts, corners of electricity pylons, or even one corner of an angular boulder. For levelling, less precision is needed; the centre of a gateway, for example, would be adequate. If for some reason the exact point specified is not accessible, another near by will be suitable, provided of course it is identifiable on the photographs; there is no need to consult the firm before using such an alternative. You will now measure the base lines and take the ring of spot levels, making sure of all the necessary checks.
I hope that it will never be useful for you to know that a gross mistake in chaining a base line may be indicated, when the site is being plotted, by what appears to be a mistake in levelling; but if a levelling mistake should be suspected, check the base line measurements before setting out to relevel the complete circuit.

At this stage you must also decide what points you will need in order to survey the detail. Posts or well defined angular boulders are to be preferred, but if nothing better is available the inter-section of two sheep-tracks or anything which defines a recog-nisable and sufficiently permanent feature can be used. These points should be ringed on the matte print and listed, and will be plotted by the firm on the plan.

The annotated matte prints, as well as the data concerning base lines and spot levels, are all returned to the firm, who will prepare the plan, and send it to you. They should be asked to show top and toe of scarps and ramparts, for these do not appear clearly from contours. Obtain also at least two photoprints, one to take into the field and one for plotting detail. The main original plan should be kept unmarked.

Detail is then surveyed in the ordinary way, using the points chosen earlier. The results are plotted on one of the photoprints.

To make the final plan for publication, the chosen points are traced in pencil from the main plan, and using these the detail is copied from the photoprint. The contours and other features are then traced from the main plan.

22.4 *Triangulation from Photographic Pairs.* If the optical properties of a camera are known, a photograph provides, among other information, a permanent record of numerous angular measurements, but for the field archaeologist the advantages of such a camera, or its adaptation to a 'photo-theodolite', would not justify its high cost.

Nevertheless, on occasion a series of paired photographs taken with an ordinary hand camera may offer a convenient time-saving alternative to more conventional methods of surveying. An obvious application is to record a feature such as a ditch exposed in a working quarry face.

The photographs are taken from two fixed points (for example, fence-posts) which will form the ends of the base line. Their distance apart must be known. They need not be at the same height above Ordnance Datum, but the camera must not be tilted.

In addition to the feature to be recorded, each photograph must include at least one, and preferably two or three, permanent sharply defined landmarks, not necessarily the same for both views. The bearings of these landmarks relative to the base line must be determined, preferably with a theodolite though the average of three or four careful prismatic compass observations could be acceptable in an emergency.

The camera can be calibrated by photographing a range of five evenly spaced poles, set upright at (say) 100 m from the camera and on a line perpendicular to that joining the middle pole to the camera; but this is not essential.

22.1 Triangulation from Pairs of Photographs

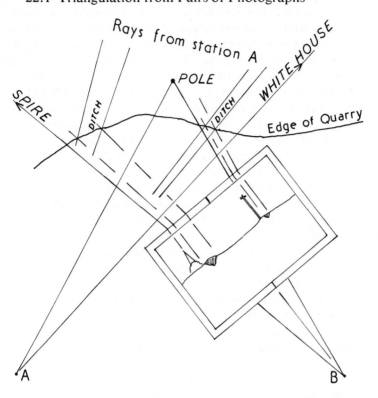

Few modern hand cameras take large negatives, so enlargements will be needed. It is very desirable that all should be to exactly the same magnification and they must not be trimmed or masked, so that the actual edges of the negative appear on the enlargement.

As an example, (Figure 22.1) assume observations are being made on ditches exposed in a quarry face. Two fence-posts, A and B, are taken as ends of the base line. The 'landmarks' visible in photographs are the gable of a (distinctive) white house from A only, a church spire from B only and pole (for electricity cables) from both. Suppose that the rays from A have been drawn, and we are dealing with the photograph taken from B, which is represented greatly simplified in the figure. The vertical axis of the photograph is drawn; it corresponds accurately enough to the line half way between the edges of the photographic image. Also , all the relevant points — the spire, edges of ditches, and pole — must be projected upwards perpendicularly to the edge of the photograph. Work is simplified if these points and the axial line are transferred to a sheet of tracing paper, either directly or by measurement; if measured, the scale can be increased.

The print or tracing is then slid over the plan until the points corresponding to the spire and pole lie on the relevant rays, and the axial line produced passes through B. The rays corresponding to the ditch edges can then be drawn, and their intersections with the rays from A fix the required points on the plan.

Up to a total of about half a dozen, the more 'landmarks' the better; but even if only one is available the method can still be used, with rather less accuracy, provided the camera has been calibrated as described above. The difference in bearing between the axial line and the spire (say) is known from the calibration, so the direction of the axial line can be drawn on the plan.

23 The Plane Table

23.1 General Remarks: 23.2 Description; 23.3 Use.

23.1 *General Remarks*. The plane table has a respectable ancestry, and many good-looking plans have been prepared by means of it, but it has serious disadvantages, especially for fieldwork in this country; I would most strongly advise against its use. Nevertheless, as there is a risk that you may find yourself persuaded or compelled to work with one, some account of it must be given.

The advantages claimed are that the method of use is simple and easily understood, and that since the plan is drawn directly in the field time is saved and possible mistakes in booking are avoided. Although I have never had an opportunity to compare a chain and a plane-table survey made on the same site, I think it is probably true that the *total* time required to produce a pencil draft ready for tracing is rather shorter by the latter method.

The counterbalancing disadvantages make a longer list: the instrument is cumbrous to transport, though perhaps not much more so than a theodolite; slight rain, and anything more than a moderate wind, make it unusable; the size of the plan is limited to the size of the board; although the *total* time required to produce the pencil draft may possibly be less, the time spent *in the field* will be longer than would be required for a chain or theodolite survey; to produce a clean and legible plan working in the open air is far more difficult than to do so indoors; and to balance errors is difficult and adds considerably to the work involved. Even the supposed advantage, that the plan develops before the surveyor's eyes while he is on the site, is open to the objection that this offers an almost irresistible temptation to sketch in detail by eye instead of measuring it, thus perhaps establishing on the plan a subjective and possibly mistaken interpretation of the remains. Finally, although the method is certainly simple, it is no simpler than chain surveying, and it is very much more difficult to adapt to single-handed work.

To sum up, a beginner should avoid the plane table; its use will establish faulty techniques, and he will have difficulty in extending his work to large sites. An experienced user of the instrument can produce satisfactory plans, and will no doubt be reluctant to change his methods, though for fieldwork in Britain he would be well advised to do so.

23.2 *Description* (Figure 23.1). The table itself is essentially a drawing-board, from about 40 cm square up to 80 by 60 cm, fitted with a spindle so that it can be rotated about a vertical axis and clamped as desired. In the simplest instruments the spindle rotates in a socket in the tripod head, but usually there is a set of levelling screws, or similar device, as for a theodolite or level.

Observations are made with an alidade or sight-rule. In its simplest form this is a ruler, 40 to 60 cm long depending on the size of the board, fitted with a sight at each end; one, corresponding to

23.1 Plane Table: Essential Features

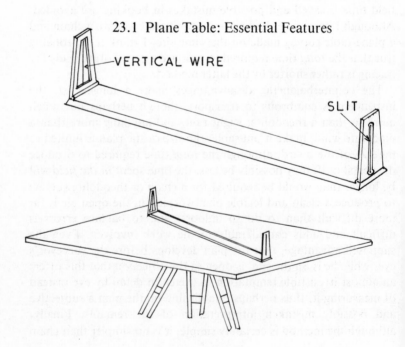

VERTICAL WIRE

SLIT

the eyepiece, is a narrow vertical slot, the other a wider slot with a wire stretched vertically along it. These give the line of sight, which must be parallel to the edge of the ruler. The ruler may be graduated with any convenient scale, or a separate scale can be used.

The sight-rule can be modified by fitting a telescope and vertical circle of the kind used on any theodolite, from the simplest up to the complications of a self-reducing instrument, with a corresponding increase in the versatility of the equipment. Levels and distances can then be found as with a tacheometer. The cost is comparable to that of a similar theodolite, as also is the inconvenience of transport, to which must be added the need to carry the table itself. Moreover, the sight-rule is not attached to the table, and the risk of several hundred pounds worth of instrumentation falling to the ground is appreciable.

The sight-rule usually carries a spirit-level, axis parallel to that of the ruler, which is used in setting up the plane table; a second spirit-level, with its axis at right angles to the above, is an advantage. The spirit-level can, however, be separate. The method of levelling is the same as for a level or theodolite.

The final essential is a compass, to orient the board approximately. The prismatic compass can be used, but greater accuracy is obtained with a trough compass, in which the needle, about 15 cm long, is contained in a narrow box with sides parallel to the meridian when the needle is pointing to zero; but the compass should invariably be used only to fix a rough orientation.

For large-scale work, a plumbing fork may be useful. This consists of two long arms, nearly parallel, joined rigidly together by a short rod. The free end of the upper arm rests on the table, and vertically beneath it the lower arm carries a plumb-line. Usually, with the scales employed, the relative position of points on the table and on the ground can be estimated accurately enough without the need for this device.

As a drawing surface, paper is not satisfactory for outdoor work unless the weather is reliably fine and dry; a non-absorbent synthetic material is to be preferred. It will usually need to be fixed to the board with drafting-tape sealing the edges completely; some boards have a clamping device. If paper is used it should preferably be damped before being fixed in position, and left to dry for a day. Then, provided it has not torn the fixing loose, it will have a taut smooth surface.

23.2 Use of Plane Table

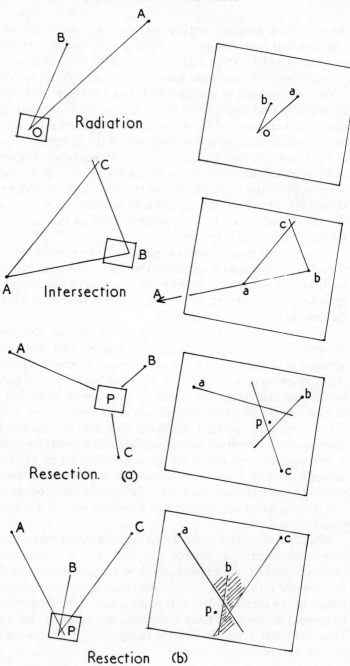

Radiation

Intersection

Resection. (a)

Resection (b)

23.3 *Use.* As with all other methods except photogrammetry, the preparation of a plan consists essentially of locating isolated points, which are then joined up to give the outline of the feature to be represented. With a plane table the required points can be fixed in three different ways (Figure 23.2); these methods can of course be combined. In what follows, capital letters refer to points on the ground, lower case to corresponding points on the plan.

(a) *Radiation.* The board is set up at some chosen point, O say, and oriented, either by sighting to a known point or magnetically. Then the direction OA can be sighted and the corresponding distance measured, so that the direction oa and the position of a can be marked on the plan. The distance can be taped, or if the scale is so small that the inaccuracy is unimportant it can be found tacheometrically.

(b) *Intersection.* Two points A and B are taken as the ends of a base line; they can be deliberately laid out as such or can be points fixed earlier in the survey.

The board is set up with a over A, and oriented so that ab is sighted along AB. By sighting the alidade towards C, ac can be drawn. Repetition of the same procedure at B gives bc, which fixes C. As always, the triangles should be 'well-conditioned'.

(c) *Resection: The Three-Point Problem.* The plane table is set up at P so that three (or more) known points (a, b, c) are visible. The problem is to fix p on the plan corresponding to the position of the plane-table. The solution for accurate surveying has already been described (Para. 17.10), and the same essential condition holds: the plane-table must not lie on (or too near to) the circle passing through the three known points.

The simplest solution is by systematic trial and error. Initially, the board is oriented as accurately as possible with the compass. Rays are then drawn through a, b, and c, towards A, B, and C; they will form a triangle of error near the correct position of p. A better position for p is then selected, according to the following rules:

If p lies within the triangle a b c it also lies within the triangle of error; its distances from the rays through a, b, c are proportional to the lengths pa, pb, pc.

If p lies outside the triangle a b c (which is not such a good arrangement for fixing the required point), a further rule is needed. Imagine yourself standing at a, b, c in turn looking towards p; then the correct position for p is either to the left of all three rays or to the right of all three, so it cannot lie in any part hatched in the

diagram. The other rule shows that it lies in roughly the position
shown (Figure 23.2, bottom), for it must be nearer to the ray
through b than to either of the others.

Having estimated a better position for p, the alidade is laid
along the line joining p to the most distant of the three points, and
the board reoriented. Rays are then drawn through the other two
points. If there is still a triangle of error, the procedure is repeated.

This method is useful for adding detail to an existing map,
especially when the scale is small enough to justify sketching most
of the detail. In suitable weather conditions the results should be
more accurate than can be obtained with a prismatic compass.

24 Underground Surveying

24.1 *General Remarks.* Unlike the rest of this book, this chapter is second-hand; for it has been my good fortune never to have had to survey an underground structure. Nevertheless, some notes will be useful, in case you are unlucky enough to have to undertake such a job.

Apart from the difficulties caused by darkness and often extremely unpleasant physical conditions, the arrangement of the survey itself offers problems. In general triangulation is impossible, and detail has to be based entirely on traverses (Chapter 19), often linked only at one end to the network used for an associated surface survey. Moreover, the link may well be *via* a vertical shaft, probably less than two metres in diameter, which gives a very short base by which to connect the surface and underground surveys.

24.2 *Degree of Accuracy needed.* Even moderate accuracy is much more difficult to attain in underground work than on the surface, so the first thing to consider is how much precision may reasonably be sacrificed, especially as regards angular measurement. A degree corresponds to 1·75 m in 100, so for a system of short tunnels which do not need to be related to surface features an accuracy of half a degree might be acceptable, assuming that no 'ritual' function is suspected. By contrast, much greater accuracy would be needed in dealing with an extensive system formerly served by vertical shafts which are now blocked and invisible from above but which need to be located precisely relative to surface features. Two widely separated links with the surface, on the other hand, allow the errors in the underground work to be balanced (Paras. 19.3–5), and thus again justify rather less accuracy. No general rule can be given, but fortunately most artificial features in Britain, other than mine-works, are fairly short.

24.3 *Methods of Measurement*. For linear measurement, the chain remains the method of choice, provided the floor of the tunnel is dry. If, as all too often, it is deeply concealed by water and liquid mud, the tape is preferable, for it can be pulled tight and kept above water level. Unless an extra helper is available to hold it, some device will be needed for anchorage. Probably the simplest is a deep wooden box, with a hook on one edge to anchor the tape and rope handles for carrying. This can be filled with stones on the site. Indeed, it would probably be worth while to make a 'nesting' pair of such boxes, so as to free both surveyors for detail measurements. A strong bulldog clip will be useful to hold the case end of the tape.

Tacheometric measurements are hardly accurate enough for this sort of work.

Offsets can be measured either with another tape, a pole or half-pole, or a folding rule, whichever is the most convenient.

For angular measurement, a theodolite gives the best accuracy, though it may prove rather unmanageable in difficult conditions. Apart from provision for illumination (Para. 24.4) it should preferably carry a magnetic compass, which will give appreciably more accurate readings than a prismatic compass. This is desirable, for in order to reduce the risk of mistakes and of cumulative errors *all* sights in underground surveying should have the magnetic bearing recorded.

Since many sites are small, though, prismatic compass observations are often adequate. The sights should be taken in both directions, preferably about half a dozen times each way, and averaged.

24.4 *Illumination*. In addition to lights to see where you are going, and to book your records, others are needed to illuminate the instruments and stations.

As station marks, a candle or a small electric hand torch can be used, but a white-painted board with a black X is better; the light is shone on to the board; cross-hairs can be more easily seen against an illuminated white background. The board can be provided with props, or can be suspended.

If you are doing a lot of underground work, it will be worth while to get a theodolite fitted with a device to illuminate the cross-hairs, but for occasional use these can be made visible by shining a torch obliquely into the object-glass.

If you are working with a prismatic compass, remember that the section of the graduated circle which you read is that beneath the prism.

24.5 *Marking Stations*. If the floor of the cave or tunnel is earth, or even bare rock, stations can be marked with a peg or spike, but often this will be impossible. If the roof is sound, a spike can be driven into it, if possible with a hooked head so that a marker can be hung from it. Alternatively, a reference point can be marked, with paint, crayon, or a spike, on the wall of the passage, the actual station being recorded as a specified distance perpendicular from the wall at that point. If the passage is not too wide, spikes can be driven into each side of the passage, slightly projecting, and the station established on a piece of wood cut to fit between them. If, as may be convenient, the wood is movable, care must be taken always to replace it the same way round, unless the mark is exactly central.

24.6 *Plumbing Down a Shaft* (Figure 24.1). Occasionally, you may need to relate the underground and surface surveys more accurately than magnetic observations permit, and the only possible link is by plumbing down a single narrow shaft. Two plumb-lines, 1 and 2, corresponding to points P and Q in the survey, are suspended from fixed supports just above the top of the shaft, the line PQ pointing roughly along the line of the underground tunnel. The upper ends of the lines are stationary, and can be tied into the surface survey without difficulty. Observation of the lower end gives an extremely thin and ill-conditioned triangle, but if PQ and QX are known (the theodolite being set up at X) then PQ sin QPX = QX sin PXQ. The angle QPX, giving the direction of PX relative to PQ and hence to the surface features, is thus found accurately.

Unfortunately, the plumb-lines are unlikely to be exactly stationary. The movement of the plumb-bobs can be damped by putting them in pails full of water. Alternatively, and rather more accurately, a horizontal scale readable through the theodolite can be fixed behind each plumb-line. Several successive readings of the plumb-line against the scale are taken for the limits of the swing and averaged (note that the last reading *must* be on the same side as the first, so there will be one more reading on that side). The mid point between the two averages gives the exact plumb. For example, if successive readings on the scale in centimetres, are 3·5, 22·1, 3·7, 21·8, 3·8, 21·7, 4·1, 21·5, 4·3 (alternately to left and

24.1 Plumbing down a Shaft

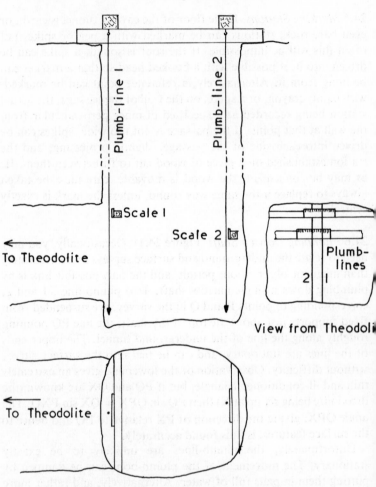

right), the mean value of the five left-hand values is 3·88, and of the four right-hand values 21·78. So the true vertical reading would be 12·83.

24.7 *Levelling*. Apart from illuminating the staff and cross-hairs, no special precautions are needed in underground levelling. If the staff is held inverted, to fix the level of the roof, the reading should not only be marked −, but should be ringed to reduce the risk of a mistake when working out levels. For rough work, especially on small sites, a clinometer is often adequate.

Bench marks or change-points at the top and bottom of a shaft can usually be located so that they can be related directly by taping vertically.

Part VII

RECONNAISSANCE AND ROUGH SURVEYS

25 The Ordnance Survey and Reconnaissance

25.1 Introduction; 25.2 The Ordnance Survey; 25.3 The Current Standard Maps; 25.4 Obsolescent Large-scale Maps; 25.5 The Prismatic Compass; 25.6 Reconnaissance; 25.7 Example.

25.1 *Introduction*. Among the most important objectives of field archaeology are the discovery, identification, and location of previously unrecorded structures. The first two are not specifically problems for a surveyor. Discovery results from a combination of luck and experience, and will be assisted by a study of the two books mentioned in Para. 28.4; these also form the best brief introduction to identification of remains. Experience supplemented by critical comment from fellow archaeologists is also necessary, and after many years of work mistakes are still possible. Nevertheless, however accurate the identification may be, it is not of much use if the position of the site is wrongly given, whereas if the location is correct the identification can always be checked, provided the structure still exists.

This chapter is concerned with simple methods for fixing the positions of sites on the ground (the complementary problem, of making rough plans, is discussed in the next). Much useful reconnaissance can be done with nothing more than a 1/25,000 map, but the addition of a prismatic compass to your equipment will be found very helpful indeed, especially in wild or mountainous country; it is also a valuable safeguard against getting lost in mist.

25.2 *The Ordnance Survey*. British archaeologists are exceptionally fortunate; wherever they may choose to work in this country, an accurate large-scale map is available, with most known field-monuments marked upon it. They owe this good fortune to the Ordnance Survey.

The indebtedness of British archaeologists to that body cannot be exaggerated. Not only did the Survey provide, in their old six-inch to the mile maps, what was probably the finest *complete* large scale coverage of any country in Western Europe if not in the world, they marked, as a regular practice, all known antiquities. The general accuracy of all this information was maintained by the Archaeology Division (now, 1979, being disbanded) who also prepared the incomparable series of Period Maps. Only the current standard scales will be discussed in detail here, but reference should be made to an extremely valuable booklet *The Historians Guide to Ordnance Survey Maps* (published for the Standing Conference for Local History by the National Council of Social Service, 1964) which describes all maps at a scale of one-inch to the mile or larger, *with dates of the various editions* and other information (by J. B. Harley), and includes a section on the Period Maps (by C. W. Phillips).

25.3 *The Current Standard Maps.* These are as follows:

The 1/50,000 superseding the former 'one-inch'. This is useful for finding one's way about the countryside and for visiting known sites, but is on too small a scale for original fieldwork.

The 1/25,000 or 'Two-and-a-half-inch' (*sc.* to the mile). This is now the basic map for fieldwork. All field boundaries are shown, though somewhat generalised, and 10 m corresponds to 0·4 mm on the map, so eight-figure grid references are possible.

The 1/50,000 and 1/25,000 both give details of magnetic variation.

The 1/10,000 map is nominally the successor to the 'six-inch', but is excessively generalised. It shows no more detail than the 1/25,000. Except that it is rather easier to read, it offers the fieldworker nothing to counterbalance the extra cost and bulk (see also below, in 25.4).

All the above maps are intended to cover the whole country.

The 1/2,500 (or 25-inch). This is an accurate and detailed map, covering all cultivated or built-up areas, but not moor or waste land. Spot levels are shown, but no contours. Most features are shown exactly, but earthworks may be somewhat generalised. For some areas the new edition (on national grid lines) has not yet replaced the older County sheets.

For some major towns and cities, maps are available at 1/1,250; they are essentially an enlargement of the 1/2,500 maps.

25.4 *Obsolescent Large-scale Maps.* The older large-scale maps, on county sheet lines, remain of value to fieldworkers and are often available for reference in libraries or in the offices of County Authorities. They are now irreplaceable reference documents, and should be treasured as such, especially in the case of the 'six-inch'.

Details of the history of these maps are given in the *Historians Guide* mentioned above (Para. 25.2), as well as lists of those towns for which very large scale plans are available, at 1/500, five feet, and ten feet to the mile; these may be useful for the study of town defences or industrial remains. As regards the 'six-inch' and '25-inch', some matters of particular interest to fieldworkers deserve mention.

The Ordnance Survey does not enforce copyright on maps published more than 50 years ago (see *Current Archaeology*, vol. V no. 53 (November 1975), p. 190) so copies of these can be used as a basis for maps or plans without charge; it is courteous to acknowledge the use of such material. The 'gridded' six-inch county sheets state the exact co-ordinates of their corners, so the National Grid cɛn easily be superimposed on the older sheets, and on the '25-inch' sheets, each of which coincides with a quarter of a 'six-inch' sheet.

All except the very latest of the county-sheet series indicate bench marks, and these are now again being shown on the 1/10,000 maps. At one stage they were omitted, and a fee was charged for the information. For most practical purposes, the bench marks on the County sheets are adequate. Note, though, that the older editions work from a different datum.

If you are working in open moorland or similar country the absence of landmarks will often cause inconvenience. You may then find it worth while to transfer to your field maps details which are shown on the County sheet series of 'six-inch' maps but which are now omitted, such as sheep-folds or ruined buildings. Among the less obvious of such reference points are bench marks. These are not always easy to find, but as a general guide, in the sort of country considered they will be cut on a fairly conspicuous outcrop or immovable boulder and will be visible to someone looking in the direction of the 'arrow' symbol. Some appear on the oldest editions but are not repeated on the later maps.

From the point of view of the fieldworker, the 1/10,000 map which has replaced the 'six-inch' is very unsatisfactory indeed. It is highly generalised, so that for example a small church of typical irregular outline may be shown as a simple rectangle, touching the side of a road even though there is in fact a space between them. Roads and lanes tend to be shown as of constant width, the variations which are often informative being suppressed. The conventional signs are very coarse; that for rocky ground, for example, can be misinterpreted as a group of oval sheep-folds.

Criticisms of this kind could be multiplied. Nevertheless, having regard to the extremely high quality of most of their work, the Ordnance Survey staff are unlikely to be directly to blame for this distressing (and one hopes temporary) collapse in standards; one may reasonably suspect that they, as well as the users of their maps, are victims of an external directive which they were not allowed to disregard.

25.5 *The Prismatic Compass.* Although this is not a precise measuring instrument, it gives results which are accurate enough for reconnaissance. With its use, points can almost always be located on the map within about 10 m, that is, closely enough to establish an eight-figure grid reference. The standard prismatic compass (Figure 25.1) comprises a graduated compass-card in a

25.1 Prismatic Compass: Diagram of Main Feautres

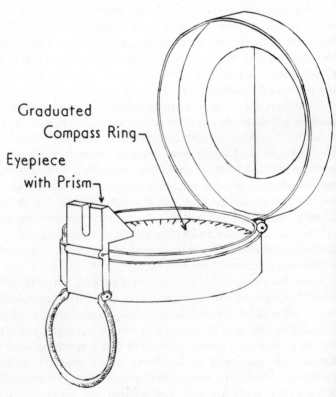

Graduated
    Compass Ring⌐
  Eyepiece
    with Prism⌐

glass-topped box about 6 cm in diameter, fitted with a prism so arranged that the graduated circle can be observed through a lens at the same time as a view forwards through a sighting-line. The prism usually moves on a slide so that it can be focused on the graduations, and there is a ring to fit over your thumb. The cheapest type, with 'dry' suspension, has a small button with which the oscillation of the needle can be damped, but the small extra cost of a 'liquid' suspension is well worth while, as in it the oscillations are eliminated almost at once. Larger types are available, including models which can be used on a tripod, but these sacrifice the great advantage of portability.

Get accustomed to using the compass with your non-writing hand, thus leaving your writing hand free to take notes without having repeatedly to disengage your thumb. Also, to avoid the risk of dropping the compass when in use, attach it to your clothes or to the carrying-case by a loop of string through the ring.

25.6 *Reconnaissance.* Pacing and the prismatic compass together are adequate for almost all reconnaissance work. You should try to establish the length of your normal walking pace under various conditions; it is unlikely to be the same, for example, when you are climbing a steep heather-covered slope as when you are crossing a level pasture. Nevertheless, even when you have a fairly good idea of the length of your pace, you should always try to start and finish at a known point, as this reduces the effect of any uncertainty.

It is impossible to cover every contingency, but the examples discussed below will suggest methods of approach. In general, obviously, the nearer the known landmarks, the greater the precision with which a point can be located; and since all observations are rather rough, at least one redundant measurement should be made, preferably two. Usually your objective will be merely to fix the national grid reference of some features, but in some circumstances you may need to publish, or to put on permanent record in some archive, the actual measurements you made. In the first case discussed, for example, x might be the find-spot of some relic; excavation might be desirable, and the point could be located more precisely on the ground from a record of the actual pacing than from a statement of the grid reference. Another possible example is that of an obscure site in open country which may be located on the ground, by reference to some obvious feature not shown on the map, more easily than from the grid alone.

Probably the simplest case is when the feature (x here and subsequently) stands in a field with defined angles ABCD (Figure 25.2a). If P is lined in with x and C, x can be located quite accurately by pacing AP, PD, PX and XC. If the distances involved are small, fewer measurements may be adequate; even if your assumed pace differs by as much as 0·2 m from its real value, 50 paces will be only 10 m wrong.

An alternative way of fixing x would be by taking prismatic compass sights from x to A, B, C, and D (Figure 25.2b), and correcting them for the magnetic variation by means of the information given on the 1/50,000 or 1/25,000 map. Theoretically, of course, two sights are adequate, but as errors are almost certain

25.2 Reconnaissance: Methods of Fixing Points

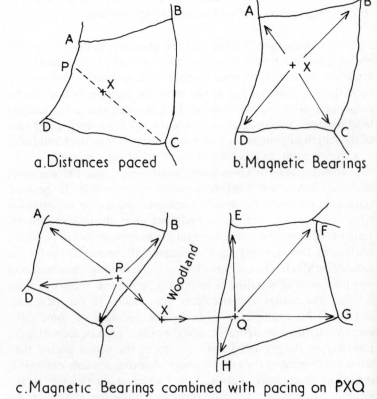

a. Distances paced

b. Magnetic Bearings

c. Magnetic Bearings combined with pacing on PXQ

to occur a third is taken, and if x on the map is placed in the resulting triangle of error, the accuracy should be improved. Provided the triangle of error *is* small, the fourth sight is not needed; but some time you will almost certainly make a mistake such as misreading 5°. With three sights, one wrong, the triangle will be large, and you will have no way of deciding which of the three vertices is the right one; but the fourth sight will almost always make it clear.

Obviously other ways, combining the use of pacing and compass bearings, can be devised; bearings and paced distances of AX and of XC would be one such way.

Owing to the lie of the ground or to the presence of vegetation direct sights between X and three known points may not be possible. In such a case intermediate 'stations' P, Q etc. can be used (Figure 25.2c), not themselves of any significance but capable of being fixed by observations to known points and themselves linked to X either by compass bearings alone or by bearings and paced distances. Since these more elaborate arrangements increase the risk of mistakes, and since the fact that they are necessary usually implies a shortage of landmarks, particular care is needed to make sure that all measurements are correct.

Finally, the use of the compass and pacing during search needs to be mentioned. Open moorland, and to a lesser extent woodland, often conceals undiscovered remains. In searching for these it is useful to record your course as a paced traverse. Marks, such as heaps of stones, crayon crosses on conspicuous rocks, or blazes on trees, can be left and recorded at suitable points; it is helpful if they can be numbered. These can be picked up by intersecting lines, but loops should be avoided, and each traverse should keep fairly near to a fixed bearing if possible, and should start and finish at points defined on the map. Rather than trying to reduce the traverse to some standard scale it is simpler to plot it to some arbitrary scale, for example 10 paces to a centimetre, and then, using the known grid references of start and finish to superimpose the national grid. The grid references of features discovered can then be read off (see next section).

That is often all that is needed, but if the area is likely to be revisited by you or by a colleague the course followed should be plotted on a record map and on a field map, so that duplication of of work can be avoided and the actual intensity of search is known.

25.3 Reconnaissance Survey

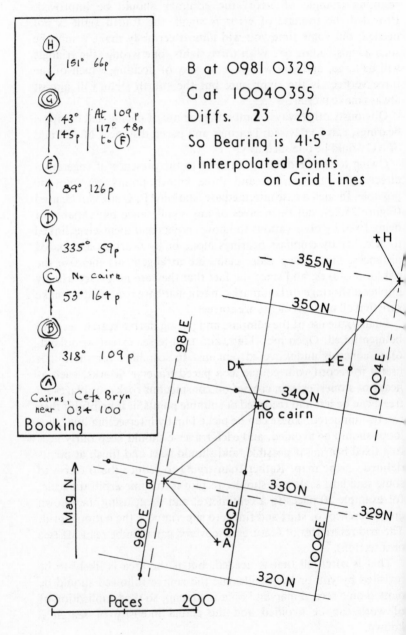

Booking

Cairns, Cefn Bryn
near 034 100

(A)
↑ 318° 109p
(B)
↑ 53° 164p
(C) N. cairn
↑ 335° 59p
(D)
↑ 89° 126p
(E)
↑ 43° 145p | At 109 p
              117° 48p
              to (F)
(G)
↓ 151° 66p
(H)

B at 0981 0329
G at 10040355
Diffs.   23   26
So Bearing is 41·5°
∘ Interpolated Points
   on Grid Lines

25.7 *Example.* Assume that a reconnaissance survey is made of a
group of cairns, two of which (B and G) appear on the OS map.
The booking appears as a simple linear diagram (Figure 25.3); the
description of each cairn is noted separately, and apart from the co-
ordinates of B and G need not be repeated here.

The first cairn found (A) is unrecorded. The magnetic bearing to
B is 318°, and the distance 109 paces. From B no other cairn except
G is visible, so you set off in about that direction, but after 164 paces
(that is, at point C) you notice another cairn D on your left; the
bearing is 335°, and the distance 59 paces. Thence it is 89° bearing
and 126 paces to E. From E you set out towards G, bearing 43°, but
at 109 paces you notice that you are passing a cairn (F) on your
right. Rather than make a dog-leg in the traverse, you decide to
take this by measurement from the line EG. *Before doing anything
else* you note 'At 109 p.' in the margin (it is surprisingly easy to
forget a number, or to forget to write it down, if you attempt to
carry it in your head while you do something else). Next mark your
position temporarily (for example by dumping your coat) at 109 p.
on EG, and then take the bearing and distance to F. Return to the
temporary mark and continue pacing to G. As you are leaving the
site you find another cairn H, and locate it by bearing and distance
back to G.

Plotting can conveniently be done on ordinary ruled paper, the
lines being taken as corresponding to a fixed magnetic bearing.
This is usually 0° or 90°, but need not be; in the example given 45°
might have been preferable, as BG runs roughly NE. Measurements
are plotted as booked, with no attempt to convert paces to metres
or to correct for magnetic variation. The traverse is drawn with a
protractor (not by calculation) and using any convenient scale. For
eight-figure grid references 5 paces to 1 mm is about the smallest
which is likely to be satisfactory; the original plot reproduced in
Figure 25.3 was at 1 pace to 1 m on a 1/2,500 metric scale.

The grid co-ordinates of B and G are known (in this case 0981
0329 and 1004 0355 respectively), so G lies 1004 − 0981 = 23(0) m
to east of B and 0355 − 0329 = 26(0) m to north, whence the grid
bearing of BG can be found either graphically or by calculation. It
is 41·5°. Hence the grid lines corresponding to 0981 and 1004E,
0329 and 0355N can be drawn through B and G. It is then easy to
draw the lines for 0980, 0990, 1000E and for 0320, 0330, 0340,
0350N. This can be done either by calculation or more simply by
holding a suitable scale inclined to the grid lines; in Figure 25.3, the

ringed dots which fix the positions of the E grid lines correspond to 0, 20, 40, and 60 on a 1/1,250 metric scale held with graduations 1 and 24 at grid lines 981 and 1004. Having drawn the grid to the arbitrary scale used, the eight-figure grid references can be read off and if desired the line of the traverse can easily be transferred to the record map.

The main precaution in using a pace-and-prismatic traverse in this way is that the reference points (B and G here) should lie at or near the ends of the run, since corrections for magnetic bearing and length of pace depend on them. Points A, F and H are not so reliably fixed as the remainder, but your pace may reasonably be supposed not to have differed much when you were fixing them from its value on the run BCDEG. As a check, when the plotting is finished, you should work out the magnetic variation and pace length (9° and 1·22 paces to a metre in the example); if they are wildly improbable a mistake should be suspected. Accuracy can be improved, and the risk of mistakes reduced, by sighting both ways along each line and by repeating the pacing. In booking, you should always write down a measurement immediately you have taken it or if your pacing is interrupted; any distraction, such as sudden recognition of a 'new' cairn, can very easily make you fail to record some essential figure.

Traverses of this kind can intersect to form a network. Suppose that cairn D were included in a similar run between known points P and Q. The grid reference for D would first be found independently for both runs, and the average value would be treated as a new 'fixed point'.

Although results are rather more reliable if the 'fixed points' are actual features shown on the map, spots fixed merely by bearings to known sites can be used if necessary.

26 Rough Surveys

26.1 General Remarks; 26.2 'Improving' the Ordnance Survey;
26.3 Methods of Measurement; 26.4 The Main Outline; 26.5 Detail;
26.6 Controls; 26.7 Plotting; 26.8 Enlarging a Plan; 26.9 Profiles
with a Clinometer.

26.1 *General Remarks.* Lack of time may often prevent you from
making an accurate survey of a site, but even a rough plan is more
informative and valuable than a long verbal description, subject to
one absolutely essential requirement: the standard of accuracy
must be explicitly stated.

The following examples will make this clear; the techniques
involved are discussed in greater detail later. The plan of a hill-fort
taken without alteration from one of the older 1/2,500 maps will
usually be accurate in scale and general outline, but may well omit
details which are archaeologically important. To fix our ideas,
suppose that you find on inspection that there is a faint unrecorded
bank curving away from the main rampart to form a large annexe.
For publication, therefore, you could either use the copy of the
1/2,500 outline unaltered and supplemented with a description, or
'improve' it by sketching on the annexe by eye without
measurement, or improve it still more by using the original outline
as a control with detail added from a 'pace-and-prismatic' traverse.
If the hill-fort were newly discovered, a pace-and-prismatic survey
by itself could give a good indication of shape and entrance
arrangements, but the actual dimensions might be wrong by as
much as 10 per cent, and the area by twice that proportion. If such
a survey is checked by a more accurate control measurement of
overall length, this uncertainty will be greatly reduced.

All these different types of rough plan are useful, but only if
their limitations are known. For example, a detailed statistical
study of hill-fort areas would find the unimproved 1/2,500 plan
reliable, but could be falsified if the uncontrolled paced traverse
were taken as exact; by contrast, the latter might be more helpful in
showing whether the outline is polygonal or curvilinear.

26.2 *'Improving' the Ordnance Survey.* Waste ground is not covered by the 1/2,500 maps, but despite this limitation most of the major field monuments in Britain are represented on this valuable series. On the latest edition the plans prepared under the direction of the staff of the Archaeology Division are likely to be as accurate as anything that can be hoped for, short of a complete new *ad hoc* survey; they are of course copyright (see Para. 25.4). Much of the country, though, is still covered only by older editions, and the representations of earthworks will often need to be 'improved'.

A simple systematic method of doing this was described by one of the pioneers of field archaeology, J. P. Williams-Freeman, in his excellent work *Field Archaeology as Illustrated by Hampshire* (Macmillan, 1915). Details are given in his Appendix I (pp. 329–33), all of which deserves study but which can only be summarised here.

Williams-Freeman's method was to work on a tracing of the 1/2,500 map; a photoprint, not available in his day, would save work, but an enlargement (Para. 26.8) would give more room for annotation. The tracing was fixed on one side of a small drawing-board, and a sheet of paper for note taking on the other. He walked round the earthwork, sketching corrections on the plan and making notes where more detailed explanations were needed. He rightly recommends that *before leaving the site* the fieldworker should 'complete and verify the notes, repair omissions, and write a short description of the camp . . .'

Williams-Freeman also described a step by step method of sketching profiles: a short measuring-rod was held vertically, at the toe of a slope, and the point on the slope and level with the rod's upper end was fixed by eye; the rod was then moved to that point, and the procedure repeated as necessary. By noting the corresponding horizontal distances, the profile could be sketched. Such sketches, especially for multivallate defences, display a lot of information very concisely, but my own view is that having regard to the large inherent inaccuracies they tend to give an unrealistic impression of precision; it seems preferable simply to state that the overall height is 'about' so many metres (but see Para. 26.8).

26.3 *Methods of Measurement.* Williams-Freeman's method requires very little actual measurement, but it is not applicable to a newly discovered site or to one outside the area covered by the 1/2,500 maps. In such circumstances a rough paced survey is always worth while; it may occasionally form the only record of an important earthwork. Rough surveying depends primarily on your pace for long distances and your foot for short ones. In booking, these should be specified as p. and f. (not ft for your foot is not necessarily standard). You should have noted, from previous work, what p. and f. correspond to in metres; if two people are working together, the relevant units should be distinguished by booking them as ps. and pj. say (for Smith and Jones) but it is assumed throughout this chapter that you are working single-handed. Distances measured with your foot, by stepping out heel to toe, are fairly accurate, but unless you have military training your pace will vary considerably according to the nature of the ground and your physical condition; some form of check on a paced survey is always very desirable.

Although a plan can be made with pacing only, a prismatic compass is a great help, and since the need for emergency rough surveying usually arises during a planned campaign of fieldwork you will probably have it available. Similarly a tape or chain is useful. The latter is to be preferred if you have to make a long check measurement, but is otherwise less convenient than a tape. Sometimes you may find it useful to cut a sapling to form a rod '5f.' long, for example if you wish to make fairly accurate measurements on steep slopes or over marshy ground.

Rough surveying falls essentially into three parts: the main outline, detail, and checking. This is illustrated by a genuine example, though it has been simplified for brevity.

26.4 *The Main Outline.* After making a rough sketch for reference (not reproduced), the shape is established by a pace-and-prismatic traverse. The starting-point and most (preferably all) of the other stations should be indicated by some temporary expendable marker, such as a wand or a pile of stones. The more important should be 'named' either with crayon on a stone or with a piece of paper threaded on to the wand; other distinctive marks will suggest themselves. These can be put in while making the traverse, but sometimes it is useful to mark particularly important points during the preliminary examination of the site. This examination can be dispensed with, but if so, very detailed notes will need to be made during the traverse.

In the example (Figure 26.1) the traverse is started at A (the middle of the entrance, which happened to be at the north-east vertex of the enclosure) and proceeds clockwise round the crest of

26.1 Rough Survey: Booking

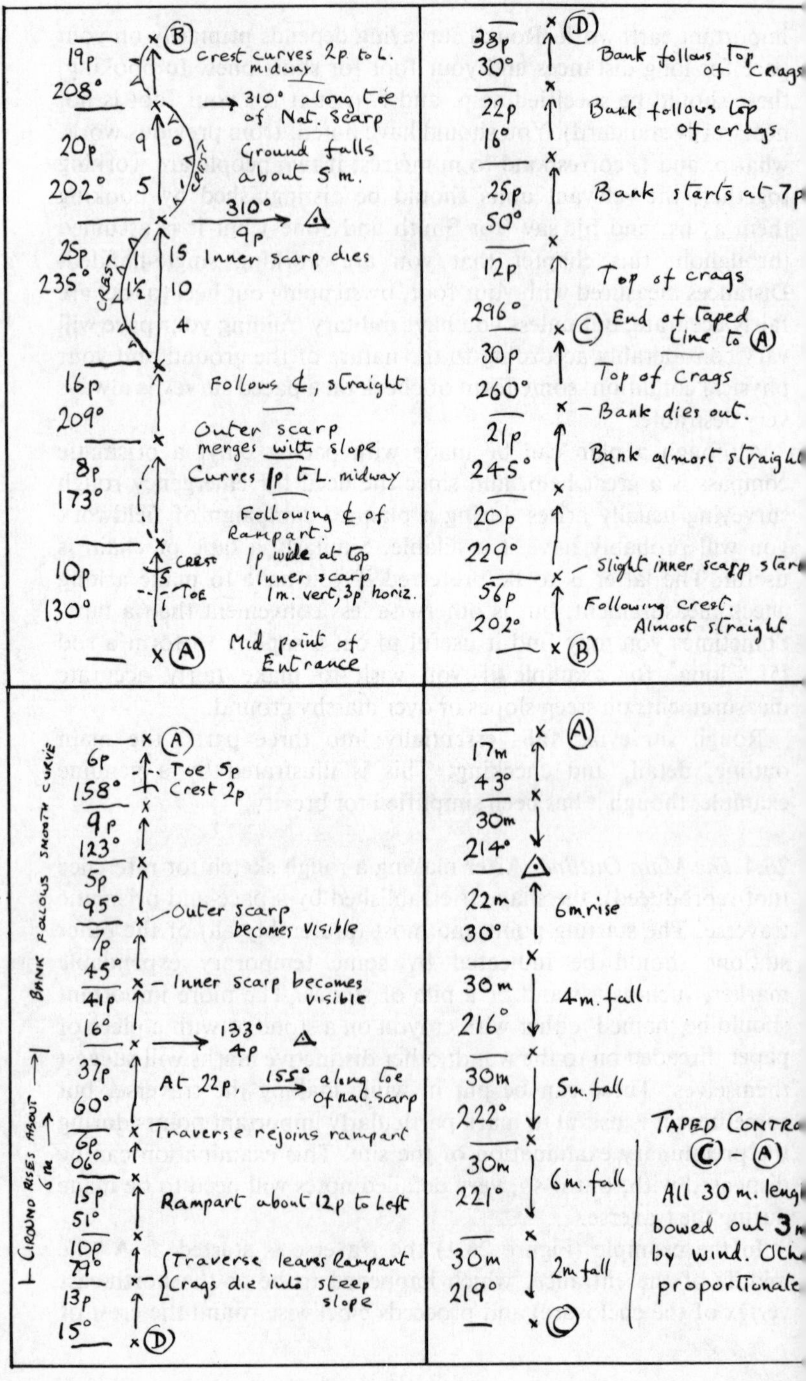

Top-left panel:

(B) ×
19p
208° — crest curves 2p to L. midway
→ 310° along toe of Nat. Scarp
×
9
20p   Ground falls about 5m.
202°   5   1   CREST
310° / 9p △
25p   CREST   15   Inner scarp dies
235°   1½   10
×
16p   Follows ₵, straight
209°
×
Outer scarp merges with slope
8p   Curves 1p to L. midway
173°
Following ₵ of Rampart
×
10p   CREST   5   1p wide at top
130°   TOE   1   Inner scarp
1m. vert, 3p horiz.
Mid point of Entrance
× (A)

Top-right panel:

× (D)
38p   Bank follows Top of Crags
30°
22p   Bank follows top of crags
16°
×
25p   Bank starts at 7p
50°
×
12p   Top of crags
296°   End of taped Line to (A)
×   (C)
30p   Top of Crags
260°
× — Bank dies out.
21p   Bank almost straight
245°
×
20p   Slight inner scarp starts
229°
56p   Following crest. Almost straight
202°
× (B)

Bottom-left panel:

× (A)
BANK FOLLOWS SMOOTH CURVE
6p   Toe 5p
158°   Crest 2p
×
9p
123°
×
5p
95°   Outer scarp becomes visible
×
7p   Inner scarp becomes visible
45°
41p
16°
133° / 4p △
37p   At 22p, 155° along toe of nat. scarp
60°
× Traverse rejoins rampart
6p
06°
GROUND RISES ABOUT 6m
15p   Rampart about 12p to Left
51°
10p   Traverse leaves Rampart
79°   Crags die into steep slope
×
13p
15°   × (D)

Bottom-right panel:

× (A)
17m
43° ×
30m
214° △
22m   6m rise
30°
30m   4m. fall
216°
30m   5m. fall
222°
30m   6m. fall
221°
30m   2m fall
219°
× (C)

TAPED CONTROL
(C) – (A)
All 30m lengths bowed out 3m by wind. Others proportionate

the rampart. Each leg of the traverse is aimed ahead, and the bearing measured *and recorded at once*. Features such as a small bush, or even a conspicuous tuft of grass, will serve to mark the direction. A suitable distance is then paced out, any relevant information being noted on the way, until a change in direction seems desirable, in this case after 10 paces. That distance is noted, and the next leg is then started. No attempt is made to vary the space allotted in the notes according to the length of the leg. The general arrangement will be obvious from the figure. The last station on each page is 'named', to ensure that the record is followed correctly, as also are any stations which may require to be used again. In this case, C is important as it is at the south-western apex of the enclosure and is to be used as one end of a taped measurement (see Para. 26.5); but it is often useful to run a linking traverse to join two opposite points on the main circuit. In this case, such a link is provided by measurements to the OS Trigono-metrical station (indicated by the conventional triangle). The traverse is continued to close on its starting point.

26.5 *Detail*. Features of special importance, as for example entrances, often deserve a more accurate survey than the main outline. Provided a tape is available, that can be weighted down to act as a chain line, and offsets measured 'heel-and-toe'; remember to record in the field book that the offsets are in 'f.' (your feet), while the chainages are in metres. Lacking a tape, wands or even stones can be set at measured intervals in a straight line as a substitute 'chain line', and all measurements made in 'f.'. Any such detailed survey should be tied in to the main outline, and its orientation should be noted.

Where there is a lot of internal detail, such as numerous hut-platforms, the work involved in trying to record it is seldom justified. Usually, all that is needed is to note 'numerous hut-platforms' on the final plan, for a rough survey will not in fact be recording anything more than that; nothing could be deduced from it as to the significance, if any, of their arrangement.

26.6 *Controls*. If a plan is based entirely on pacing, the drawn scale should always be marked as 'Approximate', or more truthfully 'Rough'. With this qualification, such a plan can give a very useful indication of the character of a site. Unfortunately, however careful you yourself may be to specify the inaccuracy of your work, anyone who uses it in a secondary publication is very likely indeed to omit that information. You cannot reasonably be blamed for that, but nevertheless, if you can get the general scale right, one potentially misleading item will be eliminated.

In Britain, most earthworks appear on the 1/2,500 maps (see Para. 25.4 concerning copyright); the Victoria County Histories reproduce nearly all the relevant plans to 1/5,000 in their 'Ancient Earthworks' sections, where these have been published. What is shown on the 1/2,500 maps is almost always accurate; mistakes do occur, but if your plan differs significantly from the Ordnance Survey you are more likely to be wrong, and should check your work. You therefore have a reliable outline plan, and can fit your pace-and-prismatic survey to it, as described in the next section.

Sometimes in Britain, and almost always abroad, no such outline plan is available, so if you wish for a check on the scale you will need to measure one of the major dimensions of the enclosure. Ideally, of course, the distance should be chained, but the assumption here is that you are in a hurry.

In the example given, the OS showed no detail south of the trigonometrical station, so marks were left during the paced traverse at the north-east (A) and south-west (C) ends of the enclosure, and the distance between these was taped; the trigonometrical station lay near the line.

A fairly conspicuous pile of stones was built at C (in other circumstances a wand might be used) and the end of the tape was marked with a piece of white rag, and tied to a moderately heavy rock. Thirty metres length was then measured in roughly the right direction, another pile of stones (the '30 m mark') was built, and the magnetic bearing back to C recorded. Owing to windage, the tape was bowed out an estimated 3 m from the straight line; this was noted, as well as the rough difference in level between C and the 30 m mark (see next section). The tape was then pulled on until the white rag was at the 30 m cairn, the 60 m mark was placed, and a bearing taken on the 30 m mark. The measurement was continued in this way, though at the 120 m mark it was more convenient to take a forward bearing to the trigonometrical station. It was also convenient to take that station as the start of another 30 m length, and again to take a forward bearing from that point to A. When plotting, the measurements must be corrected. Thus the length from the 30 to the 60 m mark is reduced by $6^2/2 \times 30 = 0.6$ m for slope and by 0·8 m to allow for the displacement caused by the wind (see Appendix IV).

The result is of course rough. In the conditions which obtained in this case, the accuracy was probably worse than one part in a hundred, though on level ground and in sheltered conditions one in two hundred or even better might be attained. Nevertheless, it is appreciably better than relying on pacing alone. In a survey of this kind, if time permits, a second taped line running roughly at right angles to the first would ensure a better representation of the shape of the enclosure. In the example, such a line could have been run from B through the '90 m mark' to D.

26.7 *Plotting.* If you have no background control for scale, you must convert all paced distances to metres; the easiest way of doing this is to make a scale of your paces on a piece of thin card, to whatever reduction factor you intend to use for your plan. Such a home-made measuring scale can always be used, but if you have a control, some simple conversion factor which can be applied mentally is almost always adequate. In this example, 10 paces were taken as 9 m, so to correct the distance the whole number of paces is measured on the metre scale and one-tenth of the number counted back.

For most purposes 1/1,250 is a useful scale for plotting, allowing reduction to 1/2,500 for publication; this is probably the most widely used scale for earthworks, where any standard scale is attempted.

The traverse is first plotted to the chosen scale, marking the lines and 'stations' clearly. Again, ordinary ruled paper forms a convenient background, as the rulings can be taken as east-west or north-south and the magnetic bearings drawn with a protractor, without correction. The traverse, and the draft plan, are not intended for publication. In preparing the final tracing (not reproduced) these would be supplemented by notes made during the examination of the site, as for example those relating to the size of the rampart.

For convenience in tracing, the traverse should be plotted in separate parts (Figure 26.2), each part overlapping its neighbour by one leg. Thus in the example, where A and C are control points, one part would run from 6p. before A to 12p. after C, the other from 30p. before C to 10p. after A. If the cross-measurement BD

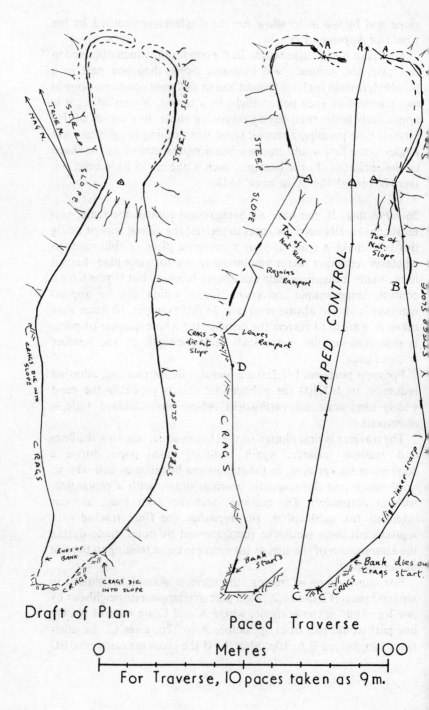

MAG. N.

TRUE N.

STEEP SLOPE

STEEP SLOPE

STEEP SLOPE

SLOPE

STEEP SLOPE

A

A

A

STEEP SLOPE

Toe of Nat Slope

Toe of Nat. Slope

B

Rejoins Rampart

CRAGS die into Slope

Leaves Rampart

D

CRAGS

STEEP SLOPE

TAPED CONTROL

CRAGS DIE INTO SLOPE

CRAGS

Ends of BANK

CRAGS

CRAGS DIE INTO SLOPE

Bank starts

slight inner scarp

Bank dies out Crags start.

C

C

C

CRAGS

Draft of Plan

Paced Traverse

Metres

O   100

For Traverse, 10 paces taken as 9m.

had also been taken, the parts would have run from 6p. before A to 56p. after B, 19p. before B to 12p. after C, and so on. If there is no control, the plots run from vertex to vertex, again with a slight overlap; in this example they would be as before, from near A to near C. If a map is available as control, any two halves are suitable. The reason for drawing the traverse in two parts is to avoid confusion caused by the closing error, and the overlap is to simplify 'smoothing' the detail in the final tracing. Any subsidiary linking traverses are also plotted independently. After this has been done, the detail is added, care being taken not to obscure the actual lines of the traverse.

If a taped control is being used, the control points are plotted and then traced, and the detail from the traverse is copied on to the same tracing, the errors being distributed by eye. In the example, A, C and the trigonometrical station (TS) would be accepted as controls. Starting with A, the detail near A would be traced. Then A and TS on the tracing would be placed roughly equidistant from A and TS on the traverse plot, and detail covering about the middle third of the interval between them copied. Then the tracing would be moved again and detail near TS traced, and so on until the circuit was completed.

With no control, if one point (TS say) is made to coincide, the two halves of the traverse will give different positions for A and for C; the averages of these are then taken as the 'fixed points', and errors distributed as before. If in addition, B and D had been linked by a paced traverse two more 'fixed points' would have been obtained by taking the average positions of the ends of the direct traverse BD (placed as symmetrically as possible relative to the main traverse) and the corresponding points on the main traverse.

If a 1/2,500 map is available, it will need to be enlarged (see next section) and a tracing made of the outline. Detail is then added in essentially the same way as that already described. Recognisable features, such as entrances or angles, are traced first, and then detail from sections midway between them.

On 1/2,500 plans, modern features such as walls or buildings are most accurately shown. Next come the centre-lines of banks or ditches, after those the crests of scarps; in these, minor irregularities, which may none the less be archaeologically important, are sometimes smoothed out. Toes of scarps, however, are often extended further than an archaeologist would accept as justified, so banks may appear wider on the OS map than on your plan.

26.8 *Enlarging a Plan*. This is often necessary. For example, if your 'improved' 1/2,500 plan is to be published at that scale, it will need to be drawn at 1/1,250, and you will need a pencil outline of that scale as basis. The enlargement can be done optically or with a pantograph or similar device, but it can also be done very easily without any such elaboration; an objection to the pantograph is that it also enlarges every slight error in positioning the tracing-point.

The simplest method, and the one which I prefer, is to super-impose a grid of squares on the original, and to transfer the detail to a corresponding grid of larger squares, points which have to be located precisely being fixed by measurement of co-ordinates (Figure 26.3). If the enlargement is to a simple multiple, such as two to one, there is no need to relate the size of square to the scale, but usually it is more convenient to do so. If you are enlarging to a rational scale from a plan published at an awkward one 'to fit the page', the squares superimposed on the original should correspond to some definite dimension in metres (or feet); this can be repro-duced easily on the enlargement. Most of the necessary co-ordinates can be measured and plotted by using scales marked on the corner of a thin card. To avoid defacing the original, a suitable grid can be drawn on transparent material.

The grid can also be subdivided by diagonals (Figure 26.3 bottom). By this means the original large grid can be broken down into smaller sections almost without limit, without the need for further measurement. I find the multitude of small divisions confusing, but the choice of method is a matter of personal preference.

In drawing out the enlargement it is advisable first to complete the circuit of some well-defined outline, such as the crest of a rampart, before adding more detail; this gives a general guide to the shape of the structure, and reduces the risk of plotting a feature in the wrong square.

Although an enlarged drawing is easier to work on, a slight loss in accuracy is unavoidable. Generally, therefore, there is little point in enlarging the original in a ratio exceeding 2:1, and the final plan as published should not be on a larger scale than the original.

26.9 *Profiles with a Clinometer*. For many ramparts, although the profile obtained with a clinometer is not exact, it is perfectly adequate; and the instrument is far more easily portable than a level and staff.

26.3 Methods of Enlarging Plan

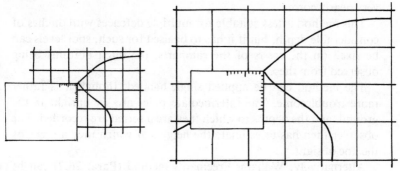

Using cards as movable scales

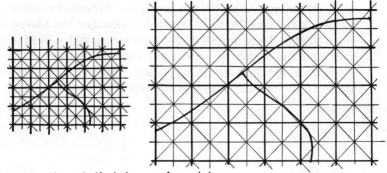

Repeated subdivision of grid

Owing to the inaccuracy of measurement, the instrument should be used sparingly, most levels being fixed by lining in. For a low rampart poles are set up at each end of the profile, and the vertical angle measured from the 1·5 m point on one pole to the same (or if preferred a lower point) on the other; several readings should be taken, and averaged. Levels are then taken by sliding a pencil or chain book up and down a pole held upside-down at an intermediate point until the pencil or edge of the book lines in between the two marks. The height is then noted, as well as the distance (which will usually be horizontal, but can be along the line of sight). The actual heights of the line of sight on the poles at each end must also be recorded; it will be rather less than 1·5 m, as those poles are fixed in the ground. The profile can then be plotted without difficulty. At worst, the only substantial error will be a slight tilt in the assumed 'horizontal'; the relative heights will be very nearly correct.

This method is less suitable for multiple defences with ditches of considerable depth, but if it has to be used for such, spot levels can be fixed on the crests of the ramparts, the ditch bottoms being observed from these.

The method can be applied single-handed, though it is rather more troublesome. The intermediate poles are set upright in the ground, and the depths to which they are inserted are recorded. The observer then has to estimate the heights at which they are cut by the line of sight.

Alternatively, Williams-Freeman's method (Para. 26.2) can be made accurate enough for most purposes if instead of depending on levelling by eye the clinometer is set to zero and is used as a level to fix the point at which the horizontal line through the top of the measuring-rod cuts the slope. Small nontelescopic hand-levels are also available. These are essentially Abney levels with a fixed spirit-level and of course no graduated scale. They are relatively inexpensive, but their possible applications are so limited that they are not really very useful items of equipment.

Part VIII
RECAPITULATION

27 Excavation

27.1 *The Purpose of this Chapter.* Many (too many?) archaeologists
are concerned with surveying only in so far as it applies to
excavation, but to arrange this book with that restricted objective
in mind would have made its use by others too difficult. This
chapter summarises the type of work likely to be needed on a dig,
with references back to the relevant sections. My concern is
exclusively with surveying; I intend no implications of any kind
relative to the merits of different research techniques except to
emphasise that where the need for accurate measurement is not
appreciated the validity of all other information given must be
doubtful. Nevertheless, the recommendations made here are
necessarily generalised, and must be considered in the context of
the site.

  Philip Barker's *Techniques of Archaeological Excavation*
(Batsford, 1977) will be in the hands of all excavators, even though
they may differ from him in detail. His Chapter 8 especially is
essential reading (though his Figure 53b should be amended; see
Figure 7.6d above) and amplifies from the archaeological standpoint much that is said here.

27.2 *The Initial Survey.* On anything other than a 'salvage' dig or a
crop-mark site, an accurate survey of the surface features ought
invariably to precede the actual excavation; it should not, as it too
often does, form a rather reluctant afterthought. On a complex site
it will often indicate problems which require investigation. As
always, chain survey (part II) is the method of choice if the ground
is not difficult. Whether contouring (Paras. 11.4–6; 14.3) is needed
will depend on the nature of the site. For a large area it is very time-
consuming, and profiles and sections can often be arranged to give
an adequate representation of the topography. For a major

excavation, especially under emergency conditions, the advantages of a professional photogrammetric survey deserve to be considered, even though in normal circumstances it might seem unjustified (Para. 22.2).

The pegs defining the grid or other co-ordinate system used in the excavation should always be tied in to the survey stations, not to secondary features such as wall-junctions; the latter method introduces cumulative errors. Similarly, features revealed in excavation, or the outlines of new areas to be examined, should always be measured from the pegs defining the co-ordinate system, never from the sides of excavations, however carefully these may have been cut.

27.3 *Continuity of Record.* Save for a small structure such as a burial-mound, or a site destroyed by quarrying, an excavation is hardly ever 'complete'. Some decades later, further work will be desirable. However careful the earlier records may have been, their value will be greatly reduced if they cannot be linked to the later discoveries. At least some of the stations used, therefore, ought to be made recoverable, especially those near the area excavated. What follows relates to stations used in the plan; levels are considered later.

The ideal permanent station for a long-term excavation is a steel tube, large enough to take the end of a ranging-rod, and set in a block of concrete, the top being at ground level. Expense, and the normal use of the ground, will usually make these impossible. An alternative, nearly as satisfactory, is a substantial steel rod driven into the ground; this was, I believe, first used by Dr Willoughby Gardner at Dinorben, some 60 years ago. Unless the ground is certain to remain undisturbed, the rod should be driven into the bottom of a pit dug to well below plough level; to discourage potential treasure-hunters from digging up 'a Roman Javelin' some old tins might be added before refilling to show that the deposit is modern.

More commonly, especially when a survey is made without a forthcoming excavation in mind, less satisfactory controls have to be accepted. Anything on or near the survey area can be used, provided it is a sharply defined point and likely to survive. Examples are the corner of a building, a stone gate-post, an OS bench mark whether current or disused, or a mark cut on a rock outcrop. These must be tied in as accurately as possible to the main survey, but need not be on it, though it is more convenient if they are.

Details of these permanent points need not be included in the published report, but the fact that they exist should be mentioned, so that any future investigator will be aware that information can be found in the record files relating to the work.

If excavation is expected to take place in a decade or so, wooden pegs may be good enough. In good conditions oak pegs may still be identifiable after 20 years, but soft wood, or pegs cut on site from branches, will probably vanish in less than half that time.

The remarks on recording station-pegs (Para. 7.2) apply particularly to those intended to be permanent. The rediscovery of steel rods is simplified by the use of metal detectors.

27.4 *Excavation Co-ordinates.* Although a co-ordinate system as a basis for records is now used on many excavations, it is not essential, and individual parts of the work can be tied in with reference to separate pairs or groups of pegs incorporated as points in the main survey. Even when co-ordinates are used, it is again not always absolutely essential to set out a complete grid. If relatively few features have to be recorded, the total work involved may well be reduced by measuring from pegs whose co-ordinates are known but random, rather than by setting out the grid on the ground. To determine the co-ordinates of pegs set more or less at random is enormously less laborious than to set out a truly rectangular grid, assuming the same degree of accuracy in each case.

Nevertheless, for some excavations a grid is very desirable indeed (Barker, *Techniques*, pp. 146 ff), sometimes absolutely necessary, as when the position of every stone has to be plotted. The procedure for setting out the main framework has been described in Chapter 15; the high degree of accuracy assumed there can often be reduced (Para. 7.5).

The objective is usually to break down the whole area into squares of one or two metre side. Since setting out pegs with real accuracy is very laborious, a first subdivision can be made with pegs at 10 m intervals. Metre divisions are then marked, usually with large nails, first by measuring along an adjacent pair of lines ten metres apart, and then across between corresponding nails. A string-line is used to get the alignment, and a builder's level (Para. 15.2) is preferable to a plumb-bob. As a check, make sure that the spacing along diagonals is 1·414 m.

If only a few features have to be recorded, 10 m squares can be used, and individual points measured in, either by co-ordinates or by triangulation using at least three of the four corners.

The final breakdown into 10 or 20 cm squares is done by a grid of strings suitably spaced on a frame (Barker, *Techniques*, p. 150). Usually the frame is exactly either 1·0 or 2·0 m square internally, and the corners are placed over the appropriate nails. A preferable arrangement is to make it 1·2 or 2·2 m squares, the 1 (or 2) m square being indicated by strings of different colour or thickness. This makes possible a smoother transition in drawing when a feature crosses from one square to the next. Detail is plotted directly on squared paper.

Provided the surface to be planned is fairly flat, so that the strings (which can be elastic) lie in contact with it, one grid is adequate, but if the surface is irregular the frame should be deep, perhaps five centimetres from top to bottom, with a string grid on each face. Parallax can then almost be eliminated by making sure that the upper square over the area being drawn is symmetrically centred over the lower square.

As excavation proceeds, the pegs and nails will have to be removed and replaced at lower levels. This can be done as described in Para. 15.7, but rather than drive temporary pegs the transfer marks can be made on suitable stone slabs or bricks. Another possibility is to use adjacent nails as transfer marks. In theory, the errors introduced at every transfer should tend to cancel out, but in practice they are more likely to accumulate, so the grid should be checked occasionally.

27.5 *The Site Bench Mark*. The nearest OS bench mark will probably be some distance away, so some reliable site bench mark will need to be established. Anything will do so long as it is not likely to be moved and the staff can be rested on it or against it. Examples are the lower hinge-hanger on a gate-post, a spike driven into a mortared (not dry-built) wall, a doorstep, or a conspicuous boulder. Less obvious, perhaps, is a cut on the trunk of a mature tree; provided this is not near a root the *vertical* movement over years is very small.

Although the level of any point can be defined precisely relative to Ordnance Datum, at least in principle, levels relative to site datum (taken as 100·00 say, to avoid negative levels) are often fully adequate for the excavation report. In that case the unpublished record file should contain full details of the position and nature of the site bench mark, as well as levels on the stations established for permanent reference, such as the tops of the buried steel rods.

In theory, this is not necessary if the site bench mark is tied in to Ordnance Datum, but in practice it remains desirable. Even assuming that your double line of levels (Para. 11.1) connecting with the nearest ordnance bench mark contains neither errors nor mistakes, the possibilities remain that the bench mark may have been moved, or that if you have taken its value from an old map relevelling or a change of datum has altered its nominal level. Your record file should therefore contain a statement such as 'Site BM (on boulder at site co-ordinate 442·2E, 216·4N) 212·23, based on OBM at GR 41452276 on NE corner of Church, taken as 201·45 above OD'. There is no need to publish this; it is only of importance to a possible future excavator. Unless you are working on an aqueduct or something of that kind the immediate value of your report would not be much affected even by a mistake of a metre.

It may well be that no bench mark survives near your work, and that the importance of getting close correlation with OD is not great enough to justify the long runs of levelling which would be needed. An adequate link is often provided by a spot level on a road, or even by the intersection of a contour with a field-boundary (preferably on one of the earlier editions). If these rather rough data are used, they should be mentioned in your report.

Keep in mind that all bench mark levels published on the older maps are in feet above OD so the figures need to be divided by 3·281 to convert to metres.

27.6 *Use of the Level.* In excavations the level is used almost exclusively to establish stratification, usually in drawing sections. Occasional other applications, such as determining the direction of flow in a water-channel, are obvious and need no description.

Sections are usually too complex to be 'booked' for subsequent plotting, and are more conveniently drawn on the site. Strata can be levelled in and plotted directly, but this is very laborious except in unusually simple examples; the normal method is to establish a horizontal string-line (or two or more in deep excavations) and to measure from it. Measurements could, if desired, be made at right angles to, or vertically from, a string-line which followed a defined slope, but it is hard to see any advantage in such an arrangement.

The string-line is stretched between arrows or nails pushed into the face of the section. At least three should be used. They should be spaced at roughly equal intervals of 3 m or less, and not less than three should be used however short the section. This provides an automatic check against mistakes.

The arrows can be located by moving the staff up or down as directed by the man at the level, but to hold a staff upright and at the same time to support it in the air is difficult. A much easier way is to take a level on the bottom of the excavation and then to put the arrow in against the appropriate reading. To draw the profiles of the surface and of the bottom of the excavation independently of the string-line, by levelling, is usually helpful; it provides an outline within which a mistake in plotting detail will become obvious.

Methods of recording stratification in area excavation are fully discussed by Barker (*Techniques*, pp. 78 ff). If they are to be reconstructed from levels on the successively exposed surfaces, time can often be saved by booking the actual staff readings on a drawing of the grid. The profile of each surface can then be drawn without any arithmetic, by measuring down from a line corresponding to the relevant height of instrument above datum. Since the instrument has to be reset, this will differ for every set of levels, so great care must be taken to record it on each sheet; and when plotting successive profiles, rub out one datum line before you draw the next.

28 Part-time Fieldwork

28.1 General Remarks; 28.2 The Nature of Fieldwork;
28.3 Limitations on Research; 28.4 Lines of Research;
28.5 Collecting and Treasure-hunting.

28.1 *General Remarks*. The full-time 'professional' archaeologist seldom has any problem in deciding what work needs to be done; his difficulty is more likely to be how best to do it in the limited time available. Besides the 'professionals' though, there are many 'amateurs' deeply interested in the subject, who would like to make some useful contribution to it in their spare time. This chapter offers some suggestions.

Incidentally, the use of 'amateur' as a derogatory term in contrast to 'professional' seems illogical. Literally, the implication of this would seem to be that the 'professional' only works because he is paid, and does not love the subject (which is untrue). A better distinction would be between 'competent' and 'incompetent', and there is certainly not exact correspondence between that classification and 'professional/amateur' or 'paid/unpaid'.

28.2 *The Nature of Fieldwork*. The amateur is often handicapped not only by insufficient time and funds, but by lack of formal instruction; nevertheless, there is an enormous amount of useful work waiting to be done which requires very little training or equipment, and can be fitted in to week-ends or spare afternoons.

Two books are almost indispensable. One is O. G. S. Crawford's *Archaeology in the Field* (Phoenix House, London, 1953); it is a classic, and conveys better than any other the fascination of the subject and what it is all about. He was one of the founders, perhaps *the* founder, of scientific Field Archaeology in its strict sense as distinct from Excavation. The other is *Field Archaeology in Great Britain* published surprisingly inexpensively by the Ordnance Survey (5th edn, 1973). This describes literally every type of field monument (at least I have found none missing) and it is clear from every page that the anonymous (and possibly composite) official author writes from real personal knowledge. Moreover, unlike many archaeologists, he is aware that there is quite a lot of Britain beyond lowland England; Scotland and Wales get equal treatment. The book includes a very useful section on practical fieldwork, and a full and helpful bibliography.

Even these two excellent works do not provide a complete substitute for personal training, and if at all possible you should try to attend an extramural course, or something similar, on some aspect of local or at least British Archaeology, preferably a course which includes fieldwork. Details are relatively unimportant, for the actual basic techniques of field archaeology are much the same whatever the period being studied. Much of the value of a course comes from the opportunities for discussion and for meeting others with similar interests.

Two warnings may be relevant; if surveying is included in the course, have regard to the comments in Paras. 1.1 and 1.2 above; and despite the great advantage of a colleague when you are engaged in fieldwork, avoid believers in such things as Ley-lines, Zodiacal Landscapes, or Subterranean Currents of Psychic Force.

28.3 *Limitations on Research.* Three considerations will control any research which you may plan. Limiting factors will normally be equipment, helpers, and time.

In developed country, with plenty of landmarks such as field-boundaries, useful reconnaissance is possible with nothing more than a notebook and a 1/25,000 map (Para. 25.3). In open country, a prismatic compass (Para. 25.5) is almost essential, and with it rough surveys become possible (Chapter 26). The addition of a chain, tape, arrows and set of ranging-rods, and preferably a clinometer, will extend your range to accurate plans (without contours) of structures up to about 100 m across (Chapter 8).

All this can be done single-handed, though for any chain surveying a colleague is very helpful. With a colleague, and given enough time, any site can be surveyed with the equipment already listed, though contouring would be very laborious.

Optical surveying instruments are expensive, and worth while only for the most addicted team of 'amateurs'. A level and staff will enable you to draw profiles (Para. 11.2) and sections (Para. 11.3) easily, and to contour simple sites (Paras. 11.4-6), but will hardly justify their purchase unless you are going to help regularly on excavations. A theodolite (Part IV), though less easily portable will fulfil every function of a level and is much more useful; but it is also much more expensive. With it added to the other equipment, and preferably supplemented by a hand calculator, a team of two can make an accurate plan of any terrestrial site.

28.4 *Lines of Research*. No general rules as to suitable lines of research are possible. Apart from the limitations discussed in the last paragraph, much depends on what types of field monument occur in your neighbourhood and what work has been done, or is being done, already. To take an area I know well as an example, it would (I hope) be a waste of time to resurvey structures of which plans are published in the *Glamorgan Inventory*, but such work would be extremely useful in Carmarthenshire or Pembrokeshire. Contact with active investigators can almost always be made through regional museums, county archaeological societies, and the various regional groups of the Council for British Archaeology; but keep in mind that other workers, especially if 'professionals', are usually extremely fully occupied and may be unable to spare time to accompany you into the field.

Ideas for research may be gained from the works listed in the bibliography of the Ordnance Survey's *Field Archaeology*. John Coles, *Field Archaeology in Britain* (Methuen, 1972) is helpful, and is sound on surveying so far as limited space permits, but is largely concerned with excavation. Christopher Taylor, *Fieldwork in Medieval Archaeology* (Batsford, 1974) is valuable for its period in south-east Britain (except on surveying); further books are expected in the series.

One type of investigation, particularly suited to 'amateur' reconnaissance and neglected almost everywhere, is to follow early trackways and to record them in detail. Saxon and other early boundary surveys offer another interesting field for research. Many have been translated and worked out on *maps*, but to follow them step by step *on the ground* can often lead to interesting discoveries. Examples are given by M. Gelling in *Signposts to the Past* (Dent, 1978) especially Chapter 8. All Anglo-Saxon charters and most of the major attempts at tracing the boundaries given in them have been listed by P. H. Sawyer, in *Anglo-Saxon Charters* (Royal Historical Society, 1968). This index is essential for anyone interested; but, unfortunately from the point of view of the fieldworker, it has been arranged primarily with the needs of historians in mind.

Even Roman roads can still repay fieldwork, for I. D. Margary's encyclopedic volume on *Roman Roads in Britain* (London, 1967), though indispensable, is not wholly reliable, and moreover suffers from an extraordinary reluctance to use the national grid.

28.5 *Collecting and Treasure-hunting.* Even to discuss the use of metal detectors is dangerous. To many archaeologists, one of these devices automatically places its owner far below any beast of the field (with the possible exception of the rabbit; but its indiscriminate burrowings have some excuse). Nevertheless, I hope that some suggestions may reduce the archaeological damage liable to be caused.

Anyone who is solely a collector, whether of Old Masters or old bottles, is a menace to the subject in which he pretends an interest. In those particular cases, the damage caused is small, for a masterpiece will ultimately reappear to delight those who appreciate its aesthetic rather than its monetary value, while the disappearance of a nineteenth-century ginger beer bottle is not a great loss to Art or Science. As regards small antiquities such as pottery or metal objects, the position is far more serious, for archaeological knowledge depends to a great extent on these apparently insignificant items and especially on the associations in which they occur. If they are taken from their true contexts into the obscurity of a private hoard much of their archaeological value is lost, even if they escape being discarded as rubbish after the hoarder's death.

A collector of this type is culpable even if he does not use a metal detector, but if he does he will almost certainly cause even more serious damage by burrowing into undisturbed deposits.

Deliberate digging in search of relics, save as part of a properly organised excavation, must be unhesitatingly condemned; but many 'finds' are exposed by ploughing or other accidental disturbance of the surface. The collector who picks up an object exposed in that way may well have saved it from destruction. Archaeologically his sin would consist in his failure to put it on record.

Metal objects are liable to destructive corrosion when exposed, so (subject to the owner's permission, and on scheduled sites to the permission of the Department of the Environment) regular search with a metal detector of a ploughed field or other disturbed *surface* could be valuable, always provided the objects found are recorded. The value of such records is greatly enhanced if, instead of merely recording the field, the actual position is defined. The technique used must depend on the frequency with which objects turn up but in most cases Para. 25.6 would be appropriate.

To emphasise the need for collaboration with an experienced archaeologist, the sad case of a bronze spearhead from Hammersmith deserves mention. It was found complete with a 5 ft wooden shaft, but that was discarded. Since only five other shafts have ever been found, and all have now disintegrated, the destruction must be distressing not only to archaeologists but to the owner who thereby deprived himself of a unique possession and enormously reduced the monetary value of his find. By contrast, collaboration between archaeologists and users of metal detectors on salvage sites, so far mainly in Norfolk, has proved profitable to all concerned, both in additions to knowledge and to collections.

Appendix I: Alternative Units and Conversion Factors

The Metric system for lengths and the Babylonian system for angles are now standard in Britain; but the accuracy of your work depends on you, not on the units used. A metric scale should always be shown on the finished plan, of course.

If you are absolutely certain that you will always be working with the same partner, there is no reason why you should not work in feet, or even in links. Trouble will arise, though, if you have to work with units unfamiliar to you; mistakes are almost certain. So although, in my view, the ideal equipment for this type of work comprises a lightweight 100 foot chain, a theodolite with metric graduation, and a staff showing feet, I do not recommend you to get them. Nevertheless, you may find that nothing else is available, and this appendix will enable you to work with them.

In the 100 foot chain, the links are one foot long, with brass tags every ten feet. The 50 foot tag is round, the others have one, two, three or four points according to their distance from the *nearer* end; the 30-foot tag is sometimes triangular.

In booking feet and inches, the convention is to use a diagonal stroke to separate the units; thus 10/5 indicates ten feet five inches.

'Gunter's Chain' can also be used. This is 66 feet long, divided into 100 links of just under eight inches. It is tagged in the same way as the 100 foot chain. The reason for this odd length was that 66 ft × 660 ft, or 10 square chains, corresponded to 1 acre. By removing some of the small links, evenly distributed over its length, a Gunter's Chain can be converted into a 20 metre (65 ft 7½ ins) chain, but if you should do this be sure to file off the statements of length on both brass handles, and cut M in their place.

Levelling staves graduated in feet are always subdivided decimally, usually with alternate black and white divisions each of 0·01 ft. The system of numbering is standardised: the *top* of each numeral corresponds to the relevant reading. The red figures (feet) are 0·15 ft high, the black (the tenths) 0·10 ft. There is seldom any need to read to a third decimal place. The Scotch staff, of lighter construction, is divided into tenths and twentieths; this is not fine enough for tacheometry.

If working in feet, the ability to convert inches to decimals, and conversely, may be useful. The rule is, take 1/8 inch as 1/100 ft, and count from the nearest of the easily remembered divisions 3 ins = 0·25 ft, 6 ins = 0·5 ft, 9 ins = 0·75 ft. Thus 4¼ ins = 0·25 ft + ten eighths of an inch = 0·35 ft; 0·65 ft = 0·75 − 0·10 = 9 ins − ten eighths = 7¾ ins. This is correct to 0·005 ft.

For plotting to a rational scale, squared paper divided in 0·01 ft is available from specialist stationers, but it is expensive, and probably now obsolescent. Boxwood or plastic scales at 1/2,500 or 1/1,000, in feet, are likely to remain available for some time.

For angular measurements, the grad or grade is often used abroad. For surveying especially it is far preferable to the degree. It is the only metric unit not adopted in Britain, but you may meet with it on some theodolites. It is one-hundredth of a right angle, and is subdivided decimally. The usual notation is (say) 64g·1142, which multiplied by 0·9 gives 57·70278 degrees, or 57° 42' 10''. Confusion is sometimes introduced by calling a hundredth of a grad a (decimal) minute, and a hundredth of that a (decimal) second; the figure above would be written 64g 11' 42''.

Just possibly, you may also meet with the mille (or mil), the angle corresponding to one metre at a thousand metres distance, that is one-thousandth of a radian. It is used on some Artillery Directors, which are essentially crude but robust theodolites, and which may be useful if no better equipment for measuring angles is available.

Finally, an almost forgotten linear measurement deserves mention. Pre-revolutionary French surveyors prepared many plans of castles, other fortifications, towns, and even some hill-forts. Some of the castles are British, and the fortifications in general are of interest to students. The unit of length is commonly the Toise, and it may be useful to record that it was equivalent to 1·949 m (6 ft 4¾ ins), since this information is not readily accessible.

The more usual conversion factors are:
1 metre = 3·2808 feet.
1 foot = 0·3048 metres.
So for rapid visual comparison of drawn scales 100 metres is roughly 10 per cent or 30 ft longer than 300 feet, or 100 ft is 'just a

'little' (half a metre) longer than 30 metres.

For maps, 1 kilometre = 0·6214 miles or 1 mile = 1·609 km.

For rapid visual comparison, 1 km is roughly 5/8ths of a mile.

For areas: 1 hectare (100 × 100 metres) = 2·471 acres.

Appendix II: Equipment

This appendix recapitulates, chapter by chapter, the chief items of equipment needed, and lists some firms from which they can be obtained; the list is not complete, for specialist suppliers exist in most large towns, and some items, such as tapes, are available at many ordinary retailers. The firms are listed alphabetically at the end, and are indicated by numbers in the list of equipment.

The prices stated have been rounded off upwards. They are intended merely to indicate *roughly* the lowest price at which an adequate piece of equipment could be bought new during 1978. The actual prices for closely similar objects may differ by 20 per cent or more, depending on details of their specification, so a full catalogue of what is available cannot be compressed into a brief appendix. It is hoped, nevertheless, that this summary may be useful to anyone considering the purchase of equipment.

The more expensive instruments can often be bought reconditioned, at about half to two-thirds their new price, depending on age and condition. They can also be hired. As an *extremely* rough indication, the cost of hire per month is about 10 per cent of the price new. A week's hire is half that for a month, a day's half that for a week.

Chapter 3

Chain, 20 metre, £25; tape, 30 metre, £10; arrows, set of 10, £3; poles, 2 metre, £5; 1 metre sections, £5 each; carrying case, £10; stand for use on hard surfaces, £8; Abney clinometer, £30. Available from 1, 2, 3, 6; tape and clinometer also from 5.

Chapter 4

Chain book, £2. Available from 1, 3.

Chapter 6

Scales, £2; (it is *essential* that scales are of 'flat', that is, thin trapezoidal, section; those of oval section are completely unsuitable. Preferably also, they should be figured from right to left as well as from left to right); set squares and protractors, up to £6 depending on size; straight-edge, 1 metre, £35; drawing-board, approx. 80 × 60 cm, £27; 110 × 80 cm, £41; T-square, 80 cm, £10; 110 cm, £12; beam compasses, from £25. Available from 1, 2, 3; straight-edge also from 5.

Chapter 9

Level, dumpy or tilting, £200; automatic, £400; these prices do not include tripods, £60 to £90; staff, 4 m, £50; level book, £2. Available from 1, 2, 4, 5, 6; level book and some types of level from 3.

Chapter 12

Theodolite, £600 upwards; vernier reading types are cheaper than direct reading; tripods, extra, £90; self-reducing tacheometer, £2900; extras for theodolite: illuminated cross-hairs, £15; magnetic compass, £120; prismatic eyepiece, £75; angle book, £2. Available from 1, 2, 5, 6; angle book also from 3.

Chapter 14

Tacheometric tables and slide-rules, £3 upwards; Cox's Stadia Computer (a circular slide-rule) is apparently the cheapest, but is fully adequate. Although not catalogued, these should be available through any firm supplying tacheometers.

Chapter 15

Steel band, 50 m, £60; tension handle, £15; clamp handle, £2. Available from 1, 6.

Chapter 16

Chambers' Six-figure Mathematical Tables (with positive characteristics) ed. L. J. Comrie (W. and R. Chambers) £2.50 (in 1978). Available from 3. Electronic calculator, as specified, £25 to £30 in 1978 but now cheaper. New models are frequent, and prices for the same type may differ by 30 per cent depending on the supplier. See advertisement in press.

Chapter 22

Plane table, complete, from £60 upwards. Telescopic or self-reducing alidades cost about the same as a similar theodolite; see Chapter 12. Available from 1, 6.

Chapter 25

Prismatic compass, £35 upwards. Available from 1, 2, 4, 5, 6.

List of firms

1. Chadburn (MDS) Ltd, 24 Trading Estate Road, Park Royal, London NW10 7EG. This firm maintains a stock of reconditioned instruments for sale, as well as for hire.
2. C. Frank, Ltd, 144 Ingram St., Glasgow.
3. W. Heffer and Sons, Ltd, Sidney St., Cambridge. This firm can also supply a very wide range of 'squared paper' with many different spacings, as well as other types of specialist 'graph paper'.
4. W. F. Stanley and Co., Ltd, Avery Hill Road, London SE9.
5. J. H. Steward, Ltd, Enbeeco House, Carlton Park, Saxmundham, Suffolk IP17 2NL.
6. Survey and General Instrument Company, Fircroft Way, Edenbridge, Kent. This firm maintains a stock of reconditioned instruments for sale, as well as for hire.

Appendix III: Data Used in Numerical Examples

It is interesting to have some idea of the results given by various methods of balancing 'errors'. Most of the examples in the text have therefore been based on a network with thirteen nodes or 'stations' with specified co-ordinates. From these the true lengths and angles have been calculated, and the 'measured' figures have been derived from these by adding 'errors', which were chosen randomly to give an approximately normal distribution. The results were then rounded off. For lengths, the imposed errors range from 0·5 % to −0·5 % in steps of 0·1 %, the standard deviation being about 0·16 %; for angles similarly, from 0·05° to −0·05°, in steps of 0·01°, s.d. about 0·016°.

STATIONS

	Coordinates E	N			Coordinates E	N
A	169·10	779·25		H	136·75	332·35
B	441·20	801·10		J	470·00	455·00
C	635·80	820·55		K	684·80	494·50
D	781·10	557·75		L	807·25	422·70
E	580·30	659·90		M	711·75	330·60
F	247·70	639·75		N	480·00	235·55
G	114·75	622·75				

LINES

Line	True Bearing Degrees and decimals	Lengths True	Measured	Line	True Bearing Degrees and decimals	Lengths True	Measur
AB	085·4089	272·976	273·00	EK	147·7152	195·646	195·4
AF	150·6013	160·119	159·65	FG	262·7133	134·032	134·0
AG	199·1513	165·669	165·65	FH	199·8461	326·810	327·1
BC	084·2923	195·570	195·75	FJ	129·7294	289·050	288·7
BE	135·4293	198·208	197·80	GH	175·6667	291·232	290·9
BF	230·1769	251·945	252·20	HJ	069·7943	355·104	355·4
BJ	175·2432	347·296	348·70	HN	105·7490	356·638	357·3
CD	151·0621	300·293	300·90	JK	079·5802	218·402	218·4
CE	199·0586	169·967	170·15	JM	117·2295	271·879	271·9
DE	296·9631	225·289	225·05	JN	177·3909	219·678	219·9
DK	236·7030	115·214	115·20	KL	120·3857	141·948	142·1
DL	169·0413	137·558	137·00	KM	170·6624	166·101	166·6
EF	266·5331	333·210	334·20	LM	226·0383	132·675	132·7
EJ	208·2941	232·702	233·15	MN	247·6995	250·485	250·7

306

The co-ordinates assigned to the stations, the corresponding true lengths and bearings of the lines, and the 'measured' lengths, are tabulated below. The shape of the network is given in Figure 27.1, and the 'measured' angles are all set out in table 20.4, so they are not repeated here. The true angles can easily be found from the bearings. Further, by using these data, it is easy to devise problems with known solutions, in order to gain experience in applying the numerical methods described in the text.

Appendix IV: Corrections to Linear Measurements

The corrections should always be deducted from the Measured Length to give the correct Horizontal distance. The effects of Slope and Sag can be added to give the total correction.

The following data are adequate for ordinary chain surveys:

For gentle slopes, of less than 4° (about 1 in 15), or more than 20 paces to eye level, the correction may be neglected.

For steep slopes, over 15° (about 1 in 4), or less than 8 paces to eye level, measurements should be made in steps.

For intermediate slopes these tables can be used; the corrections are for a 20 metre chain, and can be increased proportionally for greater lengths.

(a) Angle of Slope measured.

Angle (degrees)	4	5	6	7	8	9	10	11	12	13	14	15	16
Correction	0·05	0·08	0·11	0·15	0·19	0·25	0·30	0·37	0·44	0·51	0·59	0·68	0·77

(b) Rough correction.

Paces to eye level.	6	7	8	9	10	11	12	13	14	15	20	25
Correction	1·03	0·75	0·57	0·45	0·36	0·30	0·25	0·21	0·18	0·16	0·09	0·05

Correction for sag is not often needed during a chain survey, but may be useful when measuring across a depression or when a tape is used on a windy site. In the former case the sag will be small, but in the latter it can be considerable. The table gives the corrections for various measured lengths, for sags up to one-twentieth of the measurement, for a catenary.

Normally the sag will be estimated by eye, and the table will be adequate, but if the sag is measured a more accurate correction can easily be worked out. It varies directly as the square of the sag, and inversely as the measured length. Thus for a sag of 4·2 m in a measured length of 28 m the correction would be:

$$\frac{4\cdot2^2}{4\cdot5^2} \times \frac{25}{28} \times 2\cdot22 = 1\cdot73$$

The correct figure is 1·71.

Sag	Measured Length			
	20	25	30	50
0·5	0·03	0·03	0·02	0·01
1·0	0·13	0·11	0·09	0·05
1·5	0·30	0·24	0·20	0·12
2·0	0·54	0·43	0·36	0·21
2·5	0·84	0·67	0·56	0·33
3·0	1·22	0·97	0·81	0·48
3·5	1·68	1·33	1·10	0·66
4·0	2·21	1·74	1·44	0·86
4·5	--	2·22	1·83	1·09
5·0	--	2·76	2·27	1·34
5·5	--	--	2·77	1·63
6·0	--	--	3·31	1·94
6·5	--	--	--	2·29
7·0	--	--	--	2·66
7·5	--	--	--	3·06
8·0	--	--	--	3·49
8·5	--	--	--	3·95
9·0	--	--	--	4·44
9·5	--	--	--	4·96
10·0	--	--	--	5·52

Formulae. For accurate work, as when setting out a grid, the corrected lengths should be calculated using the following formulae; interpolation from tables is seldom accurate enough. The symbols used are:

L = Horizontal Distance
M = Measured Distance
C = M − L = Correction
S = Sag
h = Difference in Level of ends of measurement
a = Angle of Slope (so tan a = h/L)
w = Weight of tape in kilograms per metre.
P = Average of tensions at ends of tape, in kilograms.

Provided that S and h are small relative to M, as almost always when measurements are being made to set out a grid:

C for Slope $= M (1 - \cos a)$
$= M - \sqrt{M^2 - h^2}$
$= h^2/2M$ very nearly
C for Sag $= w^2M^3/24P^2$
$= 8S^2/3M$
and Sag $= wM^2/8P$

Very rarely indeed, a measurement may have to be taken in catenary with a large sag. The accurate formulae are:

$$L = \frac{\sqrt{M^2 - h^2}}{M} \times \frac{M^2 - 4S^2}{4S} \times \log_e \frac{M + 2S}{M - 2S}$$

In this case S is the average sag to the mid point (*not* to the lowest point). That is, if the levels of the ends of the chain or tape are h_1 and h_2 and the level of the chain halfway between the ends is h_m,

then $S = \dfrac{h_1 + h_2}{2} - h_m$

Alternatively, if the chain is supported by a known tension P applied at the upper end,

$$L = \frac{\sqrt{M^2 - h^2}}{2} \times \sqrt{v^2 - 1} \times \log_e \frac{v^2 + 1}{v^2 - 1}$$

where $v = \dfrac{2P - hw}{Mw}$

Index

Abney clinometer 23
accuracy: reasons for 1, 5; various
  methods compared 13-14
adhesive lettering 54
adjustments: for level 95; for
  theodolite 113-14
aerial photographs, oblique, plotting:
  direct comparison of distances 233;
  lines of constant scale 233-41;
  methods compared 242; Möbius
  network 226; necessary conditions 225; network method 226;
  Palmer's method 228; paper strip
  method 228; theory 230-3; vanishing
  line 230, 233-5
algebraic notation 142
alidade 252
Allan, A. L. 143
anchoring tape or chain 67, 258
angle-book 115
angles: booking 115-18; drawing 159;
  observation to displaced pole 118
Anglo-Saxon Charters (Sawyer) 297
Archaeology in the Field
  (Crawford) 295
areas, calculation of 181
arrangement of book 8-10
arrows 21
astronomical observations,
  limitations on 6, 181

backsight, defined 99
balancing errors 51 *see also* networks,
  traverses
Barker, Philip 289, 291-2, 294
base-lines, detached 135-6
basic principles 13-17
bearing: defined 144; from National
  Grid 180; of line, given co-ordinates
  of ends 148-50; reduced 144

bench-marks: on excavations 292-3;
  on OS maps 267; Ordnance 102;
  site, establishing 102-3, 292-3
booking: angles 115-18; basic
  principles 16; for chain survey:
  linear features 69, mistakes 68, use
  of squared paper 69; levels 98
boundary surveys (early) 297
bricklayer's or builder's level 131, 291
buildings, surveying 73-4

calculations in field, increased risk of
  mistakes 17
calculators: arrangement of keys 142;
  electronic 142; hand 142;
  programmable 144; programme
  cards for (Allan) 143
cartridge paper 55
chain 21, 30; anchoring 67, 258
chain: broken, treatment in field 68;
  care and use 24-6; 30 metre,
  disadvantages 21
chain book 34
chaining 29-31; across low obstacle 65;
  correction for sag 32, 308-10;
  correction for slope 31-2, 308-9;
  correction for stretch 25
chain-lines, corrected lengths 49
chain surveying: antiquity of 8; basic
  equipment 17; basic principles 21;
  booking 32, 34, 38-42; booking,
  legibility 38; chain book 34;
  conditions assumed 35; conventions
  for booking 34; conventions for
  stating measurements 34; detail 32;
  measuring 38; network, choice of 35;
  single-handed 81-3
change-point, 99-100
chaotic terrain, sites on 79-80
checking in field 16

311